SOVIET AIRLAND BATTLE TACTICS

SOVIET AIRLAND BATTLE TACTICS

William Baxter
Lt Col USA (Ret.)

PRESIDIO

Library of Congress Cataloging-in-Publication Data

Baxter, William P., 1933-
  Soviet airland battle tactics.

  Includes bibliographies and index.
  1. Soviet Union. Armiia. 2. Military art and
science – Soviet Union. 3. Tactics. I. Title.
UA772.B35 1985   335'.0094   85-19236
ISBN 0-89141-160-7

Printed in the United States of America

Contents

Introduction

Oh wad some power the giftie gie us
To see oursels as others see us!
It wad frae monie a blunder free us,
    An' foolish notion.

Robert Burns

The Scottish bard reminds us that people perceive themselves rather differently from the way in which they are perceived by others. His poem, "To a Louse," from which this verse is drawn, also reminds us that behavior is more rooted in self-perception than in how others perceive us, so that behavior that is incomprehensible, foolish, or just plain wrong from a viewer's standpoint is usually perfectly reasonable and logical to the actor.

This microcosm of the individual remains true when translated to the larger scale of societal groups, and it specifically applies to the subject of this book, the Armed Forces of the USSR. That which seems to us in the West as enigmatic, irrational, or wrong in the Soviet military profession is eminently logical, reasonable, and correct from the Soviet viewpoint. Even when we discover practices with which we can agree, we often find that the motivation seems wrong, that they do the right things but for the wrong reasons.

The purpose of this book is to describe how the Soviet Army thinks about itself, and how it intends to perform on the battlefield. The motivation is to make Soviet tactics comprehensible from a Soviet point of view. The goal is to explain to those concerned with the art of war as a vocation or an avocation how the Soviet Army intends to fight on a modern battlefield, and why it chooses to fight in that way. It is naive to think that a book can teach anyone to think like a Russian. It is my hope, however, that this effort will impart an understanding of the Soviet military mind, of how it thinks about

1

modern battlefield tactics, and an appreciation of why it thinks that way.

To achieve this stated purpose and goal, this book has been written from the Soviet point of view. It relies heavily upon original Soviet sources, and uses Western sources only for clarification or to fill gaps. The book is footnoted so that readers can discern sources of information from which to judge the accuracy of the work, or pursue their own investigations. Transliterated titles indicate works consulted in the original Russian, and the author takes full responsibility for the accuracy of the translations. Titles only in English were consulted in translation. In keeping with the purpose of the book, military terminology is used as it is understood in the Soviet military profession. As these meanings often differ in some degree from accepted Western usage, there are occasional digressions into etymology to clarify meanings in Soviet military jargon.

While closely hewing to my intention to write from the Soviet point of view, I must admit to some occasional lapses, intentional or otherwise. At the outset, the title, *Soviet AirLand Battle Tactics* is an admitted misnomer. Purists will note that there is no such thing as a Soviet version of Airland Battle, this being a purely U.S. concept. The proper Soviet term is Combined Arms. I chose my title, however, to convey to readers not all that familiar with Soviet terminology the essence of the book, that this is about the Soviet concept opposing Airland Battle. I hope that by the time they have read to the end of the book, this anomaly will have corrected itself.

This is a book that tells a story, with an introduction to characters, location, and plot, followed by an elaboration, and ending with a climax. For this reason, it is not really a reference where one goes to find facts or data, although it is possible to use it that way. To gain the story, one must begin at the first page, and sequentially work through to the end, since there is a sort of building block logic in the order of presentation.

Chapter 1 develops the intellectual model that describes the architecture of Soviet military theory and describes the pattern for what might be called the Soviet military mind. Chapter 2 describes the stuff from which the Soviet Army is made, its officers and men, and how they are welded together into a military organization. Chapter 3 addresses the system for exercising authority in the Soviet Army, the rank structure that makes it operate. Taken together, these first three chapters picture the Soviet military mind, body, and spirit. If my depiction seems a bit too positive, it is because it is how the Soviet Army sees itself, and not so much how others see it.

Chapters 4 through 8 describe how the Soviet Army sees itself operating on the battlefield. In many ways, Soviet tactics are very similar to those of other armies, but there are some uniquely Russian aspects that are determined by the material with which it must work, the Soviet military mind, body and spirit, and the uniquely Russian environment within which the Soviet Army functions. These chapters present a condensed and integrated presentation of Soviet how-to-fight manuals.

The final chapter draws together the common threads that run through the rest of the book, and underlines the main points that the reader should acquire. It looks to the future by suggesting the general course of development of Soviet battlefield tactics. While this is a book on how the Soviet Army plans to fight and win the next war and not about how to fight the Soviet Army, the process of summarizing and projecting does expose possible weaknesses and flaws in Soviet battlefield tactics, and these are pointed out for the reader.

I hope that a thoughtful and careful reading of this book will dispel some of the mystery that has gone towards creating the Soviet enigma, and that the reader will come to see that there is a very logical and reasoned structure to Soviet battlefield tactics. At the same time, I hope to dispel some of the mythology, prejudice, and stereotypical imagery of the Soviet Army that has bedeviled Western military thinking since 1945. Hopefully, the reader of this book will not be impressed by such ponderous slogans as—"Russians lack initiative," nor will he fall for such preposterous judgments as "Soviet tactics are terrain independent," and he will cease searching for non-existent templates of Soviet tactics.

The result of this study should be an appreciation of the Soviet Army as a formidable and very professional fighting machine. It is neither omnipotent, as some would have us believe, nor is it impotent as others would like to believe. Like any other good military organization, the Soviet Army does many things very well, but some things not so well. History has proved that it can be defeated by a tough, smart opponent. No book can make a soldier tougher than he is, but it is hoped that this effort will make him smarter.

CHAPTER 1

Problem Solving in
Military Affairs
The Theoretical Base

> Marxist-Leninist theory of war and the
> Army . . . serves as the ideological, the-
> oretical, and methodological foundation of
> Soviet military science and doctrine, and
> all our military development.
>
> The Soviet *Officer's Handbook*

Military tactics exists at the point where military capabilities, i.e., forces, equipment, and weapons, and military theory, or the intellectual constructs as to how to employ capabilities, collide with the reality of the battlefield. Tactics exists at the cutting edge of war. In the Soviet view, tactics is an integral part of military theory and practice influenced by, and in turn influencing, all other components. The first step to understanding Soviet tactics is, therefore, to appreciate its relationship to Soviet military theory. At the tactical level, U.S. Army Field Manual 100-5, *Operations,* states that the U.S. Army's mission to fight and win the first battle of the next war against numerically superior forces requires commanders to understand the enemy's capabilities and intentions.[1]

Both formulations pose essentially the same question, but at different levels: What is the Soviet military leadership thinking? But to understand what it is thinking presupposes a grasp of a more basic problem: How does it think? Traditionally, Western observers have viewed Soviet thought processes in the Churchillian perception of "a riddle wrapped in an enigma inside of a conundrum," asserting that Soviet logic is too obtuse for Western understanding. Rather than seeking to sift through the admittedly turgid verbiage of Marxist-Leninist rhetoric, the tendency has been to force Soviet thought processes into a traditional Western mold, assuming that the Soviet armed forces, since they perform the same functions as our forces, must in reality think and act as we do.

This model ignores the very elemental differences in cultural, philosophical, and historical experiences that shape the values and beliefs central to both societies. Overly simplistic behavior models, however comfortable they might be, are an unaffordable luxury in the deadly serious business of survival in a nuclear world.

Although it is generally not well understood in the United States, the present leadership of the USSR has created a highly sophisticated and well-organized intellectual structure to support the decision-making process in military affairs. Far from being enigmatic, this structure is extremely logical, precise, and systematic.

The purpose of this discussion is to explain how this structure evolved into its present form, to define its components and their interrelationships, and to outline the general content of Soviet military theory. To avoid molding the Soviet Union into their own image, readers are urged to view the structure as a complete system rather than in segments, and to defer seeking similarities or dissimilarities with their own thought processes until they understand the Soviet structure as a whole. This will create a better appreciation of how the Soviet military profession perceives and resolves problems.

The Theoretical Base

Seminal to the structure of Soviet military theory is the Marxist perception that the historical process is governed by discoverable laws in much the same way that natural processes are governed by laws of nature. According to this perception, laws are defined as ". . . the essential, stable, or repetitious interrelationships according to which the seeming chaos of observable historical phenomena or facts interact."[2] Although observed facts and phenomena have a number of interrelationships, not all are essential or repetitious. Thus, relationships that are unique to a specific event, even if they were critical to that event, do not qualify as laws and are therefore scientifically unimportant.

In the Soviet view, laws have a character of *necessity;* they determine a certain order, structure, and relationship of phenomena and events. As written or stated, they express the degree of man's cognition of the essence of the world process.[3] Since an observed phenomenon may comprise a number of facts, some essential and some not, the process of recognizing the essential and discarding the nonessential is a continuous one that, as understanding increases, leads to better definition of laws. Further, new facts can enter into a phenomenon and revise relationships. For example, the development of air power and nuclear weapons are new facts in this century that have revised relationships in war. Similarly, certain essential relationships can lose their significance in the process of history. For instance, the value of a charge by massed cavalry mounted on horses died before the machine guns and barbed wire of World War I. Thus, laws are not fixed; they can—and do—change gradually in response to reality.

Modern Soviet military philosophy operates on the supposition that war is a social phenomenon and, like other social phenomena, is governed by laws expressing its unique nature.[4] Its nature is a function of three parameters: technology, history, and ideology. Technology is a physical parameter, ideology (Marxism-Leninism) is the moral parameter, and history proves the necessary or essential character of the relationships.[5] Military success comes from proper application of the laws, and violation of the laws will result in failure and disaster. The laws of war, simply stated, determine the course and outcome of a war.[6]

Interestingly, the investigation of the laws of war is, in the Soviet perception, the domain of the physical and social sciences. Because they encompass all of society, the laws of war are neither purely nor even primarily a military concern.[7] Indeed, the highest military educational institution of the USSR, the Academy of the General Staff, does not include the laws of war in the discussion of its functions.[8] Investigation of the laws of war is a function of the various institutes of the Academy of Sciences of the USSR.[9] The laws of war, in the Soviet view, are a province of the political leadership, not the military leadership.

The Laws of War

Historically, the laws of war are an outcome of the reexamination of military affairs after the death of Stalin. Until his death in 1953, the point of departure for Soviet military thought was the thesis of

Stalin's five permanently operating factors, generally advertised as his greatest discovery in the field of military science and his unchallengeable perception of the political course of the CPSU in military affairs.[10] These factors are as follows:

- The strength of the rear
- The moral spirit of the army
- The quantity and quality of the divisions
- The arms of the army
- The organizational capabilities of the military command authority[11]

During the period of doctrinal change in the post-Stalin era, the role of the military in the political sphere was apparently under debate. In the foreword to the second (1963) edition of Sokolovskiy's *Soviet Military Strategy,* the author notes that he "did not find it possible to agree with the recommendations of some reviewers to exclude from the scope of military strategy the problems of directing the preparation of the country for war. Such a recommendation was motivated by the idea . . . that the military preparation of the country is, as they say, a political matter."[12]

The third edition, published in Russian in 1968, also included discussions of "political matters," indicating that the problem had not yet been resolved. However, a decision had apparently been made to exclude military participation in political decision making by 1971, when the following passage defining the Communist party's leadership role in the armed forces appeared in the *Officer's Handbook:* "All questions relating to the defense of the Socialist fatherland, military development, theory, and practice are, as they were in the past, resolved in strict accordance with Party ideology and policy. . . ."[13] More to the point, the Soviet book *Basic Principles of Operational Art and Tactics,* edited by V. Savkin and published the next year, contained the following passage, probably directed at the authors of *Soviet Military Strategy:* "We believe it necessary to stress that military science does not investigate the laws of war in general, but strictly the laws of armed conflict guided by Marxist-Leninist theory. A more expansive interpretation of the laws of military science proposed by the authors of some theoretical works may lead to an underestimation of the specific nature of war which is included in armed conflict."[14]

Apparently the content of the laws of war was still under study

in 1972, when Savkin published his book, as the following four laws
were only "suggested," and not presented as definitive.

- Course and outcome of war waged with unlimited employment
  of all means of conflict depend primarily on the correlation of
  available strictly military forces of the combatants at the beginning of the war, especially in nuclear weapons and means
  of delivery.
- Course and outcome of war depend on the correlation of the
  military potentials of the combatants.
- Course and outcome of war depend on its political content.
- Course and outcome of war depend on the correlation of moral-
  political and psychological capabilities of the people and armies
  of the combatants.[15]

It is apparent why the political leadership might wish to reserve
to itself the discussion of the content of the laws of war. Taken as a
whole, they address subjects that are extremely sensitive for political
leaders: the economic, political, and social factors that they believe
will govern the course and outcome of future wars.

Comparison of Savkin's four proposed laws with Stalin's five permanently operating factors provides an interesting insight into trends
in the development of the military thinking of the Soviet leadership
over the post-Stalin period. Under Stalin, the outcome of war was a
product of primarily military factors: the skill of commanders, the
quantity and quality of arms and troops, and the capability to logistically support operations. Further, these factors were based on conventional, primarily ground, forces.

By 1972 when Savkin published his perceptions of the laws of
war, a significant change in thinking had occurred. First, a political
content had been introduced. Not only morale of the army, but also
morale of the civilian population was a critical factor. The political
causes of war were seen as critical to its outcome, a point that Stalin
largely ignored. While Stalin's concern with existing military forces
was still accepted, Savkin also recognized that the military potential
behind the standing forces also influences the course and outcome of
war. Also by 1972 the emphasis had shifted from conventional ground
forces to nuclear forces, and especially the missile forces.

Still, it is apparent that Savkin's proposed laws of war evolved
from Stalin's five permanently operating factors. For example, Sta-

lin's first, third, and fourth factors concerning the strength of the rear, the quality and quantity of divisions, and the arms of the army roughly correspond to Savkin's first law of war. Stalin's second factor, the moral spirit of the army, was absorbed in Savkin's fourth law. Stalin's fifth factor concerning command authority was subsumed in Savkin's second law.

An interesting point is that, in spite of destalinization, the Soviet Union did not "throw the baby out with the bath water." Soviet military theoreticians revised, updated, and expanded upon earlier work; they did not discard it. This is a practical example of the process of change in the laws of war in response to reality.

By 1977 the military thinking of Soviet leadership had further evolved, and six laws of war were officially stated in *Sovetskaia Voennaia Entsiklopediia,* the *Soviet Military Encyclopedia.* These laws and their general meaning are as follows:

1. *The dependence of war on its political goals.* War is a social function whose essence is determined by the political character of the involved states and social classes. Their policies define its goals, its forms, and its means, and thus guide the armed forces and the nation in the prosecution of the war. Political goals are a cause of war.

2. *The dependence of the course and outcome of war on the correlation of economic strengths of the warring states (coalitions).* In the final instance, the relative military power of the warring sides is a function of their relative ability to use their economic power for the mass production of war material.

3. *The dependence of the course and outcome of war on the correlation of the scientific potentials of the warring sides.* The scientific-technical development and the scale and degree of its application in the armed forces has a significant impact on the military power of a state or coalition of states.

4. *The dependence of the course and outcome of war on the correlation of moral-political strengths and capabilities of the warring states (coalitions).* The character of the ideologies of the warring sides and the degree of psychological preparation of their armed forces and population for war have a major impact on relative military power.

5. *Dependence of the course and outcome of war on the corre-*

lation of military forces (potentials) of the warring sides. Victory and defeat in war and its length and final results are defined by the relative military power of the armed forces and the mobilization potential of the warring sides.

6. *Historically, the side wins that offers and uses the resulting capabilities of a new and more progressive social and economic order.* History demonstrates that, in the end, the new, progressive social and economic structure will defeat the older, reactionary structure.[16]

There are several interesting differences between these laws and Savkin's four laws proposed in 1972. Savkin's first law of war is now the fifth law of war and was expanded to include not only available forces but also the military potentials of the warring sides. Apparently, the CPSU now feels that standing forces are no longer the primary determining factor.

Political considerations apparently are now given more weight than in 1972, as dependence of war on political goals moved from third to first place, and the emphasis is upon political goals causing wars, while political causes predict their outcome. Actually, Savkin's third law was split in 1977. The sixth law of war, addressing progressive social and economic orders, is actually a restatement of the influence of political content on the outcome of war. Savkin's fourth law, addressing moral-political and psychological capabilities, is generally embodied in the fourth law of war.

The present laws of war have added economics and science to those factors that determine the course and outcome of wars, factors not included by Savkin. Also, greater weight is ascribed to military potential, and less value is attached to standing forces. Additionally, economic and scientific potentials are now specifically recognized as being critical to the course and outcome of war.

Another new factor in the 1977 laws that was not apparent in previous renditions is an emerging concern for coalitions of forces. It is no longer sufficient to compare the relative capabilities of the leading antagonists; the aggregate capabilities of all participants on both sides of a conflict must be measured.

As in the case of changes between Stalin and Savkin, changes between Savkin and the current laws of war clearly show an evolutionary change to a more sophisticated and broader perception of the historical processes governing the phenomenon of war.

The content of the laws of war indicates their application. Taken as a body, the laws of war are statements of the factors that the CPSU believes will determine the course and outcome of future wars. In fact, four of the six laws begin with the phrase "the course and outcome of war depend on." Defining these statements as laws effectively removes them from the sphere of private views and evaluations; they become guides for actions and decisions in the realm of national defense. In fact, Soviet writings state this to be the case. General of the Army I. E. Shavrov asserts that "the impact of the laws of war is concentrated upon Soviet military doctrine which guides the development of strategy, operational art, and tactics."[17] In this sense, the laws of war express the political philosophy of the CPSU in the military sphere.

In a second sense, the laws of war serve as a blueprint for evaluating relative world power in conflict situations. When Soviet leaders assert that the "world correlation of forces" is shifting in their favor, the quantitative and qualitative factors used to calculate relative strengths are outlined in the laws of war.[18] In fact, four of the six laws of war include the term "correlation." In a third sense, the laws of war are predictions of the future. They neither explain the outcome of past wars nor justify the present. They define the factors that will determine the outcome of future wars. In these senses, they meet the two tests of law, necessity and essentiality. Or, in reverse logic, if they did not predict the future, they could not be laws.

Military Doctrine

It is obvious that the laws of war, while providing a theoretical framework for developing military policy, need much elaboration and definition to govern practical activity. The elaboration of the laws of war into a definite state view on military questions is the province of military doctrine, which is defined as "A nation's officially accepted system of scientifically founded views on the nature of modern wars and the use of armed forces in them and also on the requirement arising from these views regarding the country and its armed forces being made ready for war."[19] Soviet military doctrine is the political policy of the party and the government in the military field. Its directives have legal force; they govern all the actions of the military and unify the views of military personnel in the solution of present day military tasks.[20]

Elaboration of military doctrine is the responsibility of the Communist party. Military personnel study doctrine and are guided by its principles.[21] Military doctrine is a unified system of views and a guide to action that is not open to controversy.[22] In simple terms, military doctrine is the party line on military affairs, and internal party discipline demands unquestioning acceptance of party decisions, regardless of service or post.[23]

Having established that Soviet military doctrine is the unquestionable party line on military affairs, it is well to see what it in fact proposes. Essentially, Soviet military doctrine answers the following five basic questions:

- What kind of enemy will the USSR have to deal with in a probable war?
- What is the character of the war in which the USSR will take part, and what will be its aims and tasks?
- What forces will be necessary to fulfill the tasks, and what direction will military development follow?
- How should preparation for war be carried out?
- What will the means of warfare be?[24]

Obviously, these questions address complex matters that do not lend themselves to simple or fixed answers. For this reason, military doctrine is not fixed; it is constantly under review and revision to meet changing political and military conditions.[25] Unfortunately there is no single source that treats the detailed content of Soviet military doctrine, and a precise analysis of so complex and extensive a subject is beyond the scope of this discussion. It is possible however, to look at the general outline of the answers to the five basic questions addressed by military doctrine.

Soviet military doctrine proceeds from the standpoint that if another world war is unleashed, it may begin with a surprise nuclear attack by the imperialist powers against the socialist nations, or it may escalate from a local conflict.[26] According to this view, the United States and NATO may deliberately decide to start a war, or a local conflict may expand into a world war by accident rather than by design. This view sets the stage for answering the five basic questions of Soviet military doctrine.

- What kind of enemy will the USSR have to deal with in a probable war?

Soviet military writings stress that the enemies of the Soviets are the capitalist states, imperialism, and aggressive military-political blocs.[27] War involving the USSR will be a war between opposing social systems (capitalism and socialism) or between classes (the proletariat and the bourgeoisie).[28] According to this view, the warring sides will break down in one of two ways: with the United States and NATO on one side and the USSR and the Warsaw Pact on the other, or along class lines with the capitalist states and the conservative, or reactionary, states on one side and the socialist and radical states on the other. The former case apparently supports the concept of surprise attack by the West, and the latter case most likely refers to escalation of a local conflict into a world war. The Soviet Union–People's Republic of China conflict is treated within these parameters by the often stated assertion that China is aiming at fomenting a war between the United States and the USSR or at becoming a member of the Western alliance.[29]

- What is the character of the war in which the USSR will take part, and what will be its aims and tasks?

The Soviet Union believes that, as has been indicated, a future war will be a coalition war with a sharply defined class character and resolute political and military objectives.[30] Resolute, in this instance, carries the connotation of decisive, meaning that the conflict between the warring sides will be definitely decided in favor of one side or the other; socialism will either destroy capitalism or it will be destroyed by capitalism. Since a future war is essentially a war of survival, it sets forth, by definition, twin tasks of defending socialism and destroying capitalism. It is not enough for the USSR to be able to defend itself, it must be able to destroy its enemy.[31]

- What forces will be necessary to fulfill the tasks, and what direction will military development follow?

The decisive means of war, in the Soviet view, are missiles with nuclear warheads.[32] It is, therefore, basic to Soviet military doctrine that its strategic rocket forces (SRF) be capable of surviving an enemy attack and of delivering a decisive blow to the enemy. START and disarmament notwithstanding, Soviet survival requires that the SRF have sufficient quantities and quality of missiles to accomplish the defeat of the United States and NATO under any circumstances.

Although nuclear missiles are decisive, conventional forces are also important. While a world war will be a nuclear war, under certain circumstances combat operations at division level and below may involve only conventional forces.[33] Under any circumstances, conventional forces are necessary nuclear strikes on a theater level. It is therefore necessary to maintain a balance between conventional forces and nuclear forces.

For both conventional and nuclear forces, rapid technological progress demands rapid improvement of weapons systems to assure modernization of the armed forces.[34] Therefore, the defense industry will continue to hold a top priority in Soviet economic planning.

• How should preparations for war be carried out?

Answers to the previous questions to a great extent define the answer to this question. Basic to the capability for fighting a coalition war is the strengthening of the alliance of socialist states, not only in the military but in all spheres.[35] The class content of war demands that ties with progressive noncommunist parties, as well as with communist parties, be extended.[36]

Since the enemy in a future war will be the technologically developed capitalist states, it is necessary to be fully prepared for war at its beginning. Kozlov quotes Lenin as saying, "It is a crime to undertake war with a better prepared opponent."[37] Soviet military doctrine requires that Soviet armed forces be equipped with the newest weapons and technology so that they are prepared to destroy any aggressor threatening the USSR and the socialist states.[38] Since a future world war will be a coalition war, it is imperative to maintain close cooperation with the armies of the other socialist states.[39]

Soviet military doctrine stresses that the armed forces must be capable of winning a war from its outset, under conditions of surprise or unexpected escalation. It does not accept the concept of a transition from peace to war that allows for extended mobilization.

• What will the means of warfare be?

Soviet military doctrine preaches that the offense is the decisive means of military activity.[40] Obviously, the principal means of warfare are those that favor the offense. Of course, nuclear-capable missiles are basic to this concept, as are mechanized ground forces. An offensive doctrine also provides a justification for the rapid development of Soviet naval forces as a modern means of attack from the oceans.[41]

Both the offense and the defense will require highly maneuverable forces that can move both laterally and in depth.[42] The outcome of battles and of the war as a whole will not be determined by position warfare or battles of attrition, but will result from a series of battles fought on a battlefield of great size and lacking defined front lines. In this type of combat, large standing forces are needed to fight and win the first battles. While doctrine no longer asserts that only standing forces will count in deciding the outcome of the war, they are clearly critical to ultimate victory.[43]

Formulation of Military Doctrine

While military doctrine is elaborated by the CPSU, there are several inputs to its formulation, including scientific, technical, and political. Through its investigations of the laws of war, the several institutes of the Academy of Sciences of the USSR provide both physical and social sciences inputs. The Central Committee of the CPSU, of course, provides the political input. Technology and industrial capabilities are introduced through the government, probably by way of the Defense Council. This process melds theoretical research, practical economic and technical capabilities, and political goals into a logical and coherent doctrine.

One must remember, however, that theory and practice seldom coincide. While the structure and functioning of the CPSU and the Soviet government are beyond the scope of this discussion, some salient factors must be kept in mind. To begin with, the Academy of Sciences of the USSR is a government-owned and -operated institution. Its deliberations are free and independent only insofar as they respond to the needs and beliefs of the government leadership. Likewise, the government and the CPSU are well integrated at the top. Ministers in the government are generally members or *kandidat* members of the Central Committee of the CPSU.

There are, of course, other connections, but this short discussion makes the point that inputs to the process of formulating Soviet military doctrine are quite uniform and very conservative. It is therefore unreasonable to look for sudden and extreme changes in Soviet military doctrine.

It has been pointed out that the professional Soviet military establishment, or *kadre,* has no authority to formulate military doctrine. In fact, the dismissal of Marshal of the Soviet Union (MSU) Ogarkov from his post as Chief of the General Staff of the Soviet Armed Forces on September 6, 1984, is at least partly related to the fact that he took public issue with approved Soviet military doctrine. In a May 9, 1984, article in *Red Star,* the official organ of the Ministry of Defense, MSU Ogarkov challenged the basic tenet of Soviet military doctrine concerning the decisiveness of nuclear missiles, arguing instead that a nuclear stalemate exists that shifts the decisive role in war to conventional forces equipped with the latest technology.[44] Although MSU Ogarkov was a Soviet officer of the highest rank with close ties to the then minister of defense, MSU Ustinov, he was not a member, or even a *kandidat* (nonvoting) member of the Politburo, and was not therefore a policymaker. When he attempted to insert himself into that sphere, he lost out.

The *kadre* does, however, have means of influencing the formulation and development of military doctrine. One conduit is through the office of minister of defense, who is traditionally a member or *kandidat* (nonvoting) member of the Politburo. In this light, it is interesting that MSU Sokolov, who replaced MSU Ustinov, has been given *kandidat* membership in that body, as this will indicate the degree to which the Soviet military will continue to influence policy. There are other less obvious conduits for the military to influence national policy. For example, many professional officers with advanced academic degrees sit in the various institutes of the Academy of Sciences of the USSR, and many officers hold seats in the Central Committee of the CPSU, and in the Supreme Soviet.[45] Of course, the minister of defense is a member of the ruling body in the Soviet government by definition, regardless of his party rank.

The fact remains, however, that the formulation of Soviet military doctrine remains an application of Lenin's concept of democratic centralism: information and recommendations may flow upward, but decisions are made at the top, and orders flow downward, to be obeyed without question. Military doctrine is the means by which the CPSU creates and controls Soviet military power.

The content of Soviet military doctrine, as outlined above, suggests some interesting propositions concerning the motivations behind recent Soviet activities worldwide. If the third world war will be a coalition war, current Soviet emphasis on "proletarian internationalism" is more than communist rhetoric.[46] It is a drive to tighten the bonds of its own alliances in order to improve its war-making potential. This perception also provides a specific justification for Soviet policies in Afghanistan, in the Third World, and in relations with most other noncommunist states. By loosening bonds between Western states and breaking ties between the West and the Third World, the coalition of states that the USSR may have to fight is being weakened. Thus, Soviet goals do not simply require establishment of pro-Soviet regimes; they will be equally well served by progressively reducing the number of pro-Western states in the rest of the world. This theme, in fact, appears not only in Soviet military doctrine, it also is stressed in Soviet foreign policy, wherein former Chairman Brezhnev stated: "The Soviet Union offered and shall continue to offer help to peoples struggling for their independence. In this, the USSR does not seek any advantage for itself in the developing countries, no concessions, no political control, no military bases."[47]

Soviet belief that a future world war will be a war of survival fought with nuclear weapons as well as conventional weapons finds expression in several practical ways. It explains Soviet preoccupation with civil defense, which many in the United States view as illogical. As long as it holds this belief, the USSR will continue to seek means of reducing the relative degree of destruction that it may suffer.

The USSR's belief that the only good defense is an offense explains why it has created conventional combat capabilities in excess of what most Western observers consider necessary for simple defense of Eastern Europe and the USSR. In event of war, the Warsaw Pact intends to defend Eastern Europe in Western Europe.

Further, since the USSR perceives a future world war as resulting either from a surprise attack or the unexpected escalation of a local conflict, it is not comfortable with any scenario that requires extensive mobilization time. Basically, a war will be fought with the munitions and materiel available on day one, and therefore it is believed that it is critical to manufacture and stockpile war needs in peacetime. Until this view changes, it is unrealistic for Western strategies to expect any significant reduction in Soviet defense expenditures.

Soviet military doctrine sets the realistic parameters for any arms reduction talks. The USSR will not accept any formula that does not leave it with a clear-cut offensive capability. Likewise, the USSR will not accept any START agreement that might leave it with a less than clearly defined capability to destroy the war-fighting and industrial/ economic capabilities of the United States and Western Europe. It will at the same time continue to seek means of reducing the U.S. threat to its own survival.

There is a tendency among some Western observers to deride Soviet doctrine and theory on the basis that Soviet leaders, as pragmatic politicians, will do as they please. This view misses the point. Soviet military doctrine *is* the definitive statement of what pleases the leaders of the USSR in the sphere of military affairs. As Stephen P. Gibert noted, many Americans have created a false dichotomy between Marxist-Leninist ideology and national interest when in fact, ideology is a statement of national interest.[48] Since military doctrine is ideology translated to the military sphere, any changes in the thinking of Soviet leaders concerning military affairs will soon became apparent in military doctrine.

At this juncture, it seems that Soviet military philosophy is the property of the CPSU. Insofar as the laws of war and military doctrine are concerned, influence of the professional military establishment is marginal and indirect. The decisions and judgments as to who the enemy will be, what means will be used to fight, when and where the military forces will be used, and why the military will fight are reserved for the national political leadership. That leaves just one question, albeit an important one, to be resolved by the professional military establishment, and that is how to fight. The investigation of this problem is the province of military science.

Military Science

Although etymology is beyond the scope of this book, Soviet (and Russian) logic can only be understood if key terms are viewed in their basic Russian meaning, rather than assuming—erroneously—that they have identical meanings in English. A case in point involves the Russian perception of science (*nauka*). Since at least the eighteenth century, the Russian term has expressed the concept of "skilled technique."[49] Lenin carried this traditional Russian perception into modern Soviet political thought when he stated that "science is applied logic," a view that is fully accepted in the Soviet military profession today.[50] The Soviet perception of science is obviously narrower and more pragmatic than the more general Western perception of science as "theoretical knowledge."[51] Without becoming too deeply involved in theory, the Russian view of science stresses the application of knowledge, while the Western view of science stresses the discovery of knowledge.

Having this basic view of science in mind, it is instructive to look at the field of Soviet military science. Generally, the term means the study and analysis of the diverse material and psychological phenomena of armed combat for the purpose of developing practical recommendations for the achievement of victory in war.[52] Officially, Soviet military science is defined as "a system of knowledge concerning the nature, essence, and content of armed conflict, and concerning the manpower, facilities and methods for conducting combat operations by means of armed forces, and their comprehensive support."[53]

Since it addresses the specifics of armed combat, military science comes within the authority of the professional military establishment. By virtue of its content, it is the field of investigation of the highest level of the military profession, the Ministry of Defense (MOD). Unlike doctrine, military science is characterized by controversy. The *Officer's Handbook* states that "in . . . military science there may be several different points of view, diverse scientific concepts, original hypotheses which are not selected as doctrine . . . and thus do not acquire the character of official state views on military questions."[54] This point is critical to understanding contemporary Soviet military thought. It is designed to accommodate controversy within defined limits. Further, since military science is the concern of the MOD, controversy can—and does—appear within the senior leadership of the Soviet armed forces. The previous discussion of the laws of war describes the controversy in their formulation. Once selected, however, they were removed from the realm of controversy. It is therefore incorrect to attribute controversy to political factionalism or splits within the leadership of the Soviet Union; it indicates an absence of an official state view, not necessarily disagreement.

Military science covers a much wider and more complex range

of questions than does military doctrine, and is divided into the six parts shown in Figure 1.

The general theory of military science covers the laws governing the application of violent means (the armed forces) to achieve political objectives.[55] These laws, titled "the laws of armed conflict," state the deep internal, essential, necessary, stable, repetitious ties and relationships among the phenomena manifested on battlefields in the course of armed conflict.[56] In treating the laws of armed conflict, the general theory of military science unifies military science into a single discipline by establishing the interrelationships between the six principal parts of military science. (Figure 1.1.)[57] Each of the parts of military science is a discipline in itself that is subject to its own rigorous examination and application. The fields of knowledge included in each of these parts are described below.

Military Organization

Military organization studies and proposes optimal methods for the organization and administration of the armed forces as a whole and of their component parts.[58] The subjects of mobilization, demobilization, and military government of occupied territory are included in military organization.

Military Training*

Military training is that part of military science concerned with developing the methodology and format of training soldiers, officers,

MILITARY SCIENCE

General theory of military science comprising

Military organization	Military training	Military art	Military history	Military geography	Military technology

Figure 1.1. The structure of Soviet military science

Source: S. N. Kozlov, ed., *Officer's Handbook*, Moscow: Voenizdat, 1972. Published under the auspices of the U.S. Air Force, p. 50.

small and large units, and senior officers and staffs.[59] It is concerned with training both for the regular establishment and the reserves. Military training is not only concerned with purely professional or technical military skills, it also addresses questions of general education and political indoctrination within the armed forces.[60]

Military History

Since armed combat is by nature chaotic and antagonistic, its laws are deeply concealed and difficult to understand. The investigation of the laws of armed conflict is further hindered because peacetime exercises can only approximate the conditions of battle. Therefore, the study of military history has an important role in the process of current decision making because it offers a means of introducing the conditions of actual combat into evaluation of peacetime exercises.[61] In the same vein, the study of military history investigates the conditions and possible results of the introduction of various new capabilities and forms of battle into combat.[62] The study of military history is not limited to strictly military affairs. It is used to investigate the interaction between military activity and the social, economic, and political activities in society, not the least of which is the role of the CPSU in military affairs.[63]

The USSR views military history as a genuinely scientific interpretation of the development of military science.[64] It is officially defined as "a branch of historical science, and at the same time a branch of military science, because a research topic in military history is a generalization of the military experience of the past, serving as one of the sources of development for modern military science. In studying the objective laws that govern war, Soviet military science uses the basic tenets of Marxist-Leninist philosophy. The main scientific disciplines of military history include the history of wars, history of military art, and the history of the services."[65]

Historical determinism is certainly not a new or unique theme in Russian history or in Marxism-Leninism. However, its particular importance in Soviet military affairs was indicated in 1973, when the CPSU gave the Academy of the General Staff a special mission to prepare a qualified cadre of military historians to teach military history in military academies and schools and to perform scientific investigative work.[66]

Military Geography

Military geography comprises two disciplines: area studies and the description of theaters of war. It includes investigation of natural, political, economic, and military characteristics of regions and countries.[67]

Military Technology

Military technology is a heading that groups together the military applications of various technologies and physical sciences. It includes scientific investigation and the production of equipment.[68] On the theoretical side, military technology provides a vehicle for the introduction of the contributions of modern science into the investigations of military science, thus modernizing the impact of military history.[69]

Military Art

As the most important field of military science, military art (not to be confused with operational art) addresses the actual forms and methods of armed combat, and its principles are the basic ideas for the organization and conduct of battles, operations, and wars as a whole.[70] Military art includes the three disciplines concerned with the theoretical and practical aspects of armed conflict: strategy, operational art, and tactics.[71] It is officially defined as "the theory and practice of engaging in combat operations and armed conflict as a whole, with the use of all the resources of the service branches and services of the armed forces, and also support of combat activities in every regard. Military art, as a scientific theory, is the main field of military science, and includes tactics, operational art, and strategy, which constitute an organic unity and are interdependent."[72]

As in the case of the laws of war and military doctrine, military art has gone through an extensive period of investigation and change. As of 1972, Savkin stated, "There is still no uniformity in our military press with regard to a classification of principles."[73] By 1978, however, a consensus had apparently been reached; volume six of the *Soviet Military Encyclopedia*, which appeared that year, included what it defines as the most important principles of military art in modern times.[74] These eleven principles are listed and described below. Emphasis, where it appears, is from the original source.

1. *High **military preparedness for fulfilling of missions** under any conditions for starting or conduct of war.* The emphasis on preparedness is yet another iteration of a theme that runs through the laws of war and military doctrine. It is a logical result of Russian historical experience with countless invasions and defeats at the hands of stronger hostile neighbors. In the Soviet perception of the term, preparedness is measured through two parameters. First, there is a need for strong military forces in being—a large, well-equipped, professional military establishment. Second, very little can be left to chance. There must be well-developed plans, procedures, and dispositions to meet foreseeable contingencies. Spur of the moment operations conducted on a shoestring are not in keeping with the Soviet character.

2. ***Surprise,** decisiveness, aggressiveness of military activity, continuous striving to achieve and retain the **initiative.*** This principle is complementary to Soviet doctrinal emphasis on the offense. The active and passive measures necessary to achieve surprise again imply the need for careful and detailed planning before executing an operation.

3. *Full use of the various means and capabilities of battle to achieve victory.* This principle simply argues for the efficient use of all assets to their maximum capability. It implies the coordination between various services and branches of the services in well-planned operations. This is the opposite of graduated response or economy of force.

4. *Coordinated application of and close **cooperation** between major units of all the armed forces and branches of service.* This principle argues two points: that which we call unity of command, and joint operations. There must be a single commander for any operation, and the activities of all services and branches of service in that operation will be under his control. It is his function to integrate their separate functions into a unified plan.

5. *Decisive concentration of the essential force at the needed moment and in the most important directions and for the decision of the main mission.* This is a restatement of the old principle of mass. However, the problem of massing sufficient forces and means is compounded by the addition of the

time factor, obviously included to avoid presenting too lucrative a target for weapons of mass destruction. The time factor presupposes a high degree of mobility and makes significant demands on command and control facilities.

6. *The simultaneous destruction of the enemy to the entire depth of his deployment, the timely accumulation of forces, the clever maneuver of forces and means for the development of military action at a rapid tempo, and the destruction of the enemy in a short period.* Battle will be characterized by rapid maneuver, violent execution, and intensive combat on a deep battlefield that lacks clearly defined front lines. The employment of nuclear missiles also will extend the depth of the battlefield and will increase the tempo of battle.

   Operations extending over long periods of time or along fixed fronts are not in the Soviets' concept of combat. Apparently they see a series of short operations, each aimed at precisely defined goals, the sum of which will achieve the final objective.

7. *Calculation and full exploitation of the moral-political factor.* Soviet operational planning will include extensive use of propaganda to motivate troops and psychological warfare to demoralize enemies.

8. *Strict and uninterrupted leadership.* Mission-type orders that allow subordinate commanders wide latitude in conduct of operations are not compatible with Soviet combat operations. Soviet commanders are expected to exercise detailed supervision over subordinates to ensure that plans are properly executed in a timely manner.

9. *Steadfastness and decisiveness in fulfilling assigned missions.* This principle is the corollary of the previous principle. It tells subordinate commanders to carry out the spirit and letter of the plan. To the Soviets, *initiative* means finding ways to execute the plan as written in spite of difficulties. It does not include the concept of revising intermediate steps to meet changed circumstances. This principle is a very strict interpretation of the superior-subordinate relationship.

10. **Comprehensive security of combat activity.** Traditional Russian concern with secrecy is reaffirmed in this principle, which complements the principle of surprise. Security will be an

integral part of Soviet operational planning, both in its active
and in its passive aspects.

11. *Timely restoration of reserves and combat capability of forces.*
Soviet concepts of intensive combat will rapidly deplete supplies and forces. Therefore, resupply and reconstitution of
forces will be a major concern of Soviet commanders, and
combat plans will reflect steps to achieve these requirements.
The Soviet concept of echelons is a means of addressing this
requirement.

The significance of these eleven principles to Soviet military
thinking should not be underestimated. Individually or collectively,
they do not represent any startling military insight or radical ideas.
What they do is define the principles that Soviet military leaders consider to be the most important in the conduct of armed conflict. They
represent the parameters within which Soviet commanders will plan,
direct, and fight future battles. To underline their significance, the
official review of the sixth volume of the *Soviet Military Encyclopedia,* written by Marshal of Armored Forces O. Losik, specifically
referred to this entry by praising its *partinost* and stating that it is
"characterized by the application of the theoretical position of Marxism-Leninism on the analysis and forecasting of military phenomena
in the visible future."[75]

The content and emphasis of the principles of military art suggest
that Soviet combat operations will have certain unique characteristics,
unique in the sense that they will exhibit certain characteristics more
strongly than others. Basically, these characteristics are compatible
not only with the military but also the political, social, and economic
aspects of Soviet society. They include an emphasis on careful and
deliberate planning and preparation, a conservative attitude toward
risk taking, concentration of efforts and assets on specific and well-
defined objectives, strong centralized control and strict discipline, an
emphasis on propaganda, and a devotion to secrecy and security.

The Soviet ideas of aggressiveness and initiative would appear to
us to be determination and perseverance. The real measure of success
in Soviet military operations, as in other aspects of Soviet life, is in
fulfilling the plan, and this is measured by achieving indicators (*pok-
azateli*).

Through secrecy and maneuver, Soviet commanders will seek to achieve preponderant combat superiority both in force ratios and fire-power along the main axes of attack, and they will force the tempo of the battle to rapidly achieve objectives, using reserves and fresh units to replace units rendered ineffective.

In summary, the principles of military art guide Soviet military commanders in planning, preparing, and waging war and its campaigns. They are the link between military science and military strategy.[76]

Military Strategy

The highest level of military art is military strategy, which deals with the use of all of a country's forces and resources in war.[77] Specifically, military strategy is concerned with preparations for war and the planning and conduct of military operations in the theaters of military operations.[78] Military strategy is officially defined as

the highest level in the field of military art, constituting a system of scientific knowledge concerning the phenomena and laws of armed conflict.[79]

By definition, military strategy is wholly concerned with the problems that armed conflict presents to a nation as a whole. Soviet military strategy is the province of the supreme high command and the General Staff.[80] In its training function, military strategy is concerned with the armed forces as a whole and with the individual services; that is, with operational training as opposed to the technical training of individuals and small units, which is under military training. This means that joint exercises involving major elements of more than one force, large-scale land, air, and sea exercises, and combined exercises involving major elements of non-Soviet Warsaw Pact forces come under the authority of Soviet military strategy.

The investigation and elaboration of military strategy examines these eight problems:

- Structure and organization of the armed forces
- Preparation of the nation and the armed forces for war
- The planning of armed combat
- Strategic use of the armed forces as a whole and of the various branches in war

- The forms and methods of conducting strategic operations
- The principles of strategic leadership over the armed forces
- Questions of the overall support of the actions of the armed forces
- The general principles of civil defense[81]

These problems can be generally grouped under the three tasks of military strategy postulated by Sokolovskiy as follows:

- Developing a strategic concept and plans dealing with the preparation of the country for war
- Practical guidance for the preparation of the armed services for war
- The leadership of the armed forces during war[82]

The essence of Soviet military strategy is that it is a function of command. It requires a concept, guidance for subordinate elements, and leadership during execution, the traditional roles of commanders. The supreme military command is the leadership of the members of the CPSU in their military roles.[83] The senior command authority is the Defense Council, chaired by Mr. Gorbachev.[84] Therefore, military strategy is the vehicle by which the leadership of the Soviet Union exercises direct command over the activities of the Soviet armed forces and those of its Warsaw Pact allies. Since military doctrine, the official policy of the state in military affairs, is decided by generally the same individuals as are in the Defense Council, military strategy serves as an additional conduit for assuring the reliability of the Soviet military establishment. It is the means by which the leadership of the USSR governs the conduct of war.[85]

Operational Art

The second discipline of military art is operational art, the connecting link between strategy and tactics. Operational art is officially defined as

a component part of military art, dealing with the theory and practice of preparing for and conducting combined and independent operations by major field forces or major formations of Services. Operational art is the connecting link between strategy and tactics. Stemming from strategic requirements, operational art determines methods of preparing for and conducting operations to achieve strategic goals, and it gives the initial data for tactics which organizes the preparation for and waging of combat in accordance with the goals and missions of operations. Besides the general theory of operational art, which investigates the general principles of conducting operations, each Service has its own operational art.[86]

Like strategy, operational art is essentially a function of command since it deals with the planning, preparation, and conduct of military operations. Operational art, however, applies to the middle of the military structure: the arms of service, theaters of military operations, fronts, and field armies. The theoretical base of operational art is the study and application of the principles of operational art. Basically, these are identical with the principles of strategy in their statement, although their scope varies according to the level of application.[87]

Tactics

The third, and lowest ranking, discipline of military art is tactics, that part of military art directly concerned with preparing for and conducting combat at division level and below in all branches of the armed services.[88] Each of the armed services and each branch of the armed services has its own tactics that governs the preparation for fighting and supporting different types of military actions.[89]

Military tactics is officially defined as

a special field in the theory and practice of military art which studies the objective laws of combat and develops methods of preparing for combat and conducting it, on land, at sea, and in the air. Military tactics occupies a subordinate position with respect to operational art and strategy, acting in their interests, and serving to achieve the goals set for it by the operational art. Each Service and branch, by virtue of its intrinsic peculiarities, has its own theory and practice for the organization and conduct of combat and, consequently, its own tactics too, which are called Service tactics or branch (arms) tactics.[90]

Service tactics, a subordinate branch of military tactics, is defined as the branch of military art appropriate to a particular Service, encompassing problems pertaining to the theory and practice of preparing for, and waging, combat in which use is made of the various service branches (branches of aviation, arms of the navy) of the given Service. Service tactics determine the role and place of each of the branches (or their naval or air force equivalents), and the procedure for their coordinated action in combat, and also establish the methods for using them in the various types of battle, and under various conditions of the combat situation.[91]

Interestingly enough, tactics for ground forces is referred to as general tactics, a term that probably reflects the traditional Soviet (and Russian) emphasis on ground forces. General tactics is defined as a scientific discipline dealing with questions related to preparation for, and conduct of, combined arms combat by units and formations of ground troops, with the participation of the other services.[92]

In the USSR, tactics is studied and taught in the various military schools that train officer candidates for the individual branches of the armed services.[93] Tactics is governed by the princi;·.es of tactics, which are derived from the principles of operational art by modifying them to apply to this more basic level of military activity. At the present time, Soviet military theory recognizes eight main principles of tactics.[94]

1. *Continuous high combat readiness of all units, organizations, and commands*. This principle is a restatement of the military tradition of maintaining combat readiness through training, maintenance, and discipline. It encompasses the traditional Russian military maxim, generally attributed to Marshal Suvorov, the hero of the battle of Borodino who defeated Napoleon, to the effect that "The harder the training, the easier the battle." Modern Soviet usage has added the obligation for political training and indoctrination to the application of this principle.

2. *High activity, decisiveness, and continuity in the conduct of battle*. This principle teaches that battle is dynamic, rather than static, activity. Activity (*aktiv'nost* in Russian) includes the concepts of aggressiveness, tenacity, resoluteness, and cour-

age in the face of difficulty and danger. Decisiveness requires destruction of the enemy's capability and will to carry on the battle. Continuity means maintaining the level of violence at a level that deprives the enemy of any respite.

3. *Surprise in actions.* Surprise means to gain the advantage by doing the unexpected, and by subjecting the enemy to an unbearable level and duration of violence. Surprise is best achieved through speed, mobility, and violence guided by a precise understanding of the enemy.

4. *Coordinated employment of all branches of the armed services in battle, and their uninterrupted combined action.* This principle states the essence of the Soviet concept of combined arms battle. It means unity of purpose, action, and command for all forces committed to an operation. Soviet military theory holds that the application of this principle is an absolute prerequisite for victory in battle. It is an elaboration upon the familiar Western military principle of unity of command.

5. *Decisive concentration of combat power in the main effort at the necessary time.* This is a restatement of the universally recognized principle of mass. In the Soviet application, this principle includes the parameters of quantity, mass, quality, firepower and mobility, and time, all focused upon a single location. The calculation of the correlation of forces is crucial to the application of this principle, and it guides the Soviet approach to the automation of command and control.

6. *Maneuver of nuclear and conventional fires, and of forces.* In the Soviet view, maneuver is the key to flexibility in combat. It is supported primarily by technology that allows greater mobility on the battlefield, increased range and lethality for weapons, and improved systems for command and control. Maneuver is the method for concentrating combat power and seizing and retaining the initiative.

7. *Comprehensive security in battle.* This principle encompasses the active and passive measures taken to secure their own operations from hostile interference. Air and ground reconnaisance and radio-electronic warfare to disorganize enemy communications and electronic intelligence collection are active measures. Rear area security and *maskirovka*—camouflage, cover, and concealment—are passive measures.

8. *Support, and timely reconstitution of combat forces.* The Soviet Army appreciates the fact that its modern, mechanized forces cannot fight or survive without an effective logistics base to feed, fuel, and maintain its engines of war and the men who operate them. This principle also requires Soviet tactical commanders to plan for the heavy casualties and damage that they expect to suffer from their enemy's nuclear and modern conventional weapons.

As in the case of the laws and principles for the higher levels of military activity, these eight principles of tactics are not fixed. As recently as 1981, Gen. Maj. I. Vorobev described in *Soviet Military Review* the four principles of tactics as being: combat activity, concentrate the main effort, coordination, and surprise. Of course, these four principles can be related to the present eight principles, but the change describes the increasing sophistication in Soviet tactics.

One noteworthy change is the increased attention to the problems of logistics. Logistics is an inherent part of Soviet battlefield tactics, and the supply and maintenance problems of the modern Soviet Army are causing changes in tactics.

Another change is an increasing role for tactical commanders in the nuclear fire-planning process. Heretofore, this was a province of little concern to commanders at levels below division.

A third change is increased attention to what the Soviet Army refers to as the radio-electronic struggle, the sum of efforts to secure one's own use of the electronic spectrum while denying or at least curtailing its exploitation by the enemy. While the Soviet armed forces have long been proficient practitioners of this art, it has traditionally been a responsibility of echelons above division.

These changes do not suggest any sudden awakening of the Soviet military to the problems of logistics, nuclear warfare, or REW. It has had well documented capabilities in all of these fields for decades. What is of interest is that they are becoming subjects of greater priority at the lowest echelons of the Soviet military establishment. These changes reflect a growing sophistication in Soviet tactics, and imply increased authority and responsibility for junior Soviet commanders.

Since this book is about tactics, the elaboration of these generalities is the subject of subsequent chapters.

Summary

In its totality, Soviet military theory is a highly structured, vertically organized system that assures detailed and systematic evaluation of problems, careful coordination of actions, and strongly centralized enforcement of decisions at all levels. It is characterized by centralization of authority, conservatism, deliberate and detailed planning, and determined pursuit of goals. Change, although expected and accepted, is slow, deliberate, and incremental.

The conservative nature of Soviet military thought subjects proposed revisions to extended periods of examination and discussion prior to adoption. Single issues that have been debated for a period of time and then faded from view normally have failed the test. Those issues that expand and suffer elaboration over time are more likely to be adopted. Future changes in Soviet military thought are indicated therefore, not simply by the degree of attention devoted to them, but by the maturation of the discussion as it expands and elaborates upon the various aspects of the subject, while at the same time displaying an increasing consensus among the sources addressing the subject. Examples of this process of change will appear in the ensuing chapters.

The Soviet structure for decision making in military affairs is the application of Marxism-Leninism, as defined by the current national leadership, to military affairs. It is based upon Marxist historical determinism, the belief that war, like other social phenomena, is governed by certain necessary, repetitious, and stable relationships between events. These relationships, called the laws of war, define the economic, political, and social factors that govern the course and outcome of war. Since they predict the future, the laws of war express the factors that determine the world correlations of forces and they form a general statement of the philosophy of the Soviet leadership in the military sphere.

Military doctrine is the practical application of the laws of war to current military affairs. It is official Soviet policy through which the national leadership extends its actions to create military power into the social sphere upon which power depends, and into the armed forces where it is realized.

By content and purpose, the elaboration of the laws of war and military doctrine are the province of the national leadership of the USSR. They are legally binding upon the Soviet defense establishment and are not open to controversy or debate.

Military science is formulated on the basis of military doctrine through the study and analysis of the material and psychological phenomena of armed combat. Military science, being limited to the specifics of armed combat, lies within the province of the military profession. Unlike the laws of war and military doctrine, military science is not authoritative and is often characterized by controversy and debate.

Of the several branches of military science, the most important, military art, is concerned with the organization and conduct of combat operations. Its concepts are elaborated in the principles of military art, fundamental ideas that guide military activity. Military art comprises three levels: strategy, operational art, and tactics. Strategy, the highest level of military art, addresses the use of the country's resources in war. It is the province of the supreme high command, the national leadership of the USSR in their military roles. Operational art is the connecting link between strategy and tactics. It addresses the planning and conduct of military operations by the arms of service, in the theaters of military activity, and by *fronts*. Tactics is the level of operational art directly concerned with battle. It applies at army and division levels and below.

The structure of Soviet military thought can be shown graphically, as in Figure 1.2. There is a hierarchy of theory beginning at the top with the laws of war and progressing through the principles of tactics. There is a corresponding hierarchy of institutions charged with examining theory, which consists of the Academy of Sciences of the USSR, the several military academies, and a large number of military schools. The output of the institutional theory is expressed in the hierarchy of military doctrine, science, strategy, operational art, and tactics, which in turn are applied by the corresponding levels of the Soviet military structure.

Some in the West consider such carefully constructed frameworks unnecessarily restrictive and stultifying and, in fact, unnecessary.

Theory	Development	Expression	Application

Laws of war → Academy of Sciences → Doctrine ⟶ CPSU

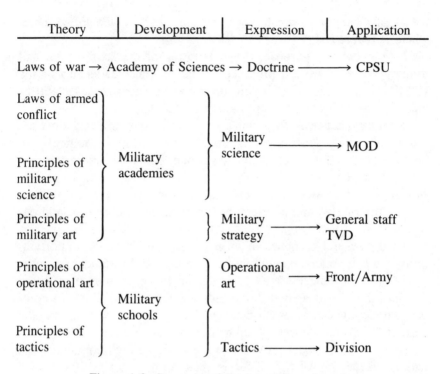

Figure 1.2. Structure of Soviet military thought

Whether this is true is debatable. It is true that Soviet military thought is bounded by certain parameters, but this bounding serves to focus analysis on critical questions rather than to stultify thinking. Its directive nature forces the rethinking of traditional beliefs, and its hierarchical structure ensures that changes are integrated throughout the structure. From the Soviet point of view, the structure of Soviet military thought, rather than being restrictive, forces the careful analysis and implementation of new ideas, and defines controversial and significant problems. The Soviets believe that the complexity, danger, and expense of modern warfare are too great to be left to ad hoc decision making based upon incomplete and unscientific analysis.

Far from being enigmatic, Soviet military thought is logically structured, precise, and well defined. There is no justification for failing to understand how the Soviet military leadership thinks. As Peter Vigor noted, it is necessary for the CPSU, in combating heresy and dissent, to define the correct party attitude toward everything, to publish those definitions, and to make them readily available.[95] The structure of Soviet military thought as outlined herein provides for careful examination of national defense problems to develop the correct party attitude, disseminate decisions, and enforce their implementation.

Notes

1. FM 100-5, *Operations,* Washington, D.C.: HQ Dept. of the Army, 1 July 1976, pp. 1-1, 2-22.
2. V. Ye Savkin, ed., *The Basic Principles of Operational Art and Tactics,* Moscow: Voenizdat, 1972. Translated and published under the auspices of the U.S. Air Force, p. 52.
3. V. I. Lenin, *Polnoe Sobranie Sochinenii,* 55 vols., Moscow: Political Literature Publishing House, 1970, vol. 29, p. 135.
4. Savkin, op. cit., p. 56.
5. *Sovetskaia Voennaia Entsiklopediia,* 8 vols., Moscow: Voenizdat, 1976–1980, vol. 3, p. 493.
6. Ibid., vol. 3, p. 375.
7. Savkin, op. cit., p. 56.
8. Gen. of the Army V. G. Kulikov, ed., *Akademiia General'nogo Shtaba,* Moscow: Voenizdat, 1976, p. 5.
9. Savkin, op. cit., p. 56.
10. Roy A. Medvedev, *Let History Judge,* New York: Alfred A. Knopf, 1972, p. 512.
11. Sidorov and Lialikov, eds., *O Sovetskoi Vonnoi Nauke,* Moscow: Voenizdat, 1954, p. 54.
12. V. D. Sokolovskiy, *Soviet Military Strategy,* ed. Harriet F. Scott, New York: Crane Russak & Co., 1975, p. xvii.
13. Gen. Maj. S. N. Kozlov, ed., *Officer's Handbook,* Moscow: 1971. Published under auspices of the U.S. Air Force, p. 15.
14. Savkin, op. cit., p. 56.
15. Ibid., pp. 89–92.
16. *Sovetskaia Voennaia Entsiklopediia,* op. cit., vol. 3, pp. 375–78.
17. Gen. of the Army Shavrov and Col. Galkin, eds., *Metodologiia Voenno-Nauchnogo Poznaniia,* Moscow: Voenizdat, 1977, p. 59.
18. A. A. Grechko, *The Armed Forces of the Soviet Union,* Moscow: Progress Publishers, 1977, p. 339.
19. *Dictionary of Basic Military Terms,* Moscow: Voenizdat, 1965. Published under the auspices of the U.S. Air Force. Translated by the DGIS multilingual section, Translation Bureau, Secretary of State Dept. Ottawa, Canada, p. 37.
20. *Officer's Handbook,* op. cit., pp. 63, 66.
21. Ibid., p. 62.
22. Ibid., p. 65.
23. *Praktika Partiinoi Raboty V. Armii i Flote,* Moscow: Voenizdat, 1977, p. 112.

24. Grechko, op. cit., p. 270.

25. Ibid., p. 273.

26. V. G. Kozlov and Gen. Maj. V. V. Milovidov, eds., *Problems of Contemporary War,* Moscow: Voenizdat, 1972. Translated and published under the auspices of the U.S. Air Force, p. 100.

27. *Sovetskaia Voennaia Entsiklopediia,* op. cit., vol. 3, p. 229. See also Sokolovskiy, op. cit., p. 185.

28. *Marxism-Leninism on War and the Army,* Moscow: Progress Publishers, 1972. Published under the auspices of the U.S. Air Force, pp. 72, 78.

29. M. Dalnev, "Maoist Falsifiers Rewrite History," *Far Eastern Affairs* 1 (January 1979): 38, 39.

30. Kozlov and Milovidov, op. cit., p. 100.

31. Ibid., pp. 101–2.

32. Ibid., p. 101.

33. Ibid.

34. Grechko, op. cit., p. 157.

35. Ibid., p. 317. See also F. Konstantinov, *Socialist Internationalism,* Moscow: Progress Publishers, 1978, p. 205.

36. *Documents and Resolutions, XXVth Congress of the CPSU,* Moscow: Novosti, 1976, p. 38.

37. Kozlov and Milovidov, op. cit., p. 102.

38. *Sovetskaia Voennaia Entsiklopediia,* op. cit., vol. 3, p. 229.

39. Ibid.

40. Ibid.

41. Adm. of the Fleet of the Soviet Union S. G. Gorshkov, *Morskaia Moshch' Gosudarstva,* second Russian ed., Moscow: Military Publishers, 1979, pp. 305–6.

42. Sokolovskiy, op. cit., p. 203.

43. Ibid., p. 204.

44. Bernard Gwertzman, "Soviet Dismissal Now Being Laid to a Policy Split," *New York Times,* 13 September 1984, p. 1.

45. Harvey, Goure, and Prokofieff, *Science and Technology as an Instrument of Soviet Policy,* Miami: University of Miami Press, 1972, p. 2.

46. Konstantinov, op. cit., p. 85.

47. Prof. H. I. Lebedev and Prof. N. M. Nikol'sky, eds., *Vneshniaia Politika Sovetskogo Souza,* Moscow: International Affairs Publishing House, 1976, p. 97.

48. Stephen P. Gibert, *Soviet Images of America,* New York: Crane Russak & Co., 1977, p. 19.

49. James H. Billington, *The Ikon and the Axe,* New York: Alfred A. Knopf, 1966, p. 182.

50. Kozlov and Milovidov, op. cit., p. 95.
51. Billington, op. cit. See also *Webster's New Twentieth Century Dictionary*.
52. *Officer's Handbook*, op. cit., p. 48.
53. *Dictionary of Basic Military Terms*, op. cit., p. 38.
54. *Officer's Handbook*, op. cit., p. 65.
55. Kozlov and Milovidov, op. cit., p. 98.
56. Savkin, op. cit., p. 56.
57. *Officer's Handbook*, op. cit., p. 51.
58. Ibid., p. 60, see also *Dictionary of Basic Military Terms*, op. cit., pp. 36–37.
59. *Dictionary of Basic Military Terms*, op. cit., p. 38.
60. A. M. Danchenko and I. F. Vydrin, eds., *Military Pedagogy*, Moscow: Voenizdat, 1973. Translated and published under the auspices of the U.S. Air Force, p. 7.
61. Savkin, op. cit., p. 65.
62. *Sovetskaia Voennaia Entsiklopediia*, op. cit., vol. 3, p. 629.
63. Ibid.
64. *Officer's Handbook*, op. cit., p. 59.
65. *Dictionary of Basic Military Terms*, op. cit., p. 37.
66. Kulikov, op. cit., p. 183.
67. *Officer's Handbook*, op. cit., p. 60. See also *Dictionary of Basic Military Terms*, op. cit., p. 37.
68. *Officer's Handbook*, op. cit., p. 60.
69. Col. Gen. N. A. Lomov, ed., *Scientific Technical Progress and the Revolution in Military Affairs*, Moscow: Voenizdat, 1973. Translated and published under the auspices of the U.S. Air Force, p. 238.
70. Savkin, op. cit., p. 1. See also p. 154.
71. *Officer's Handbook*, op. cit., p. 57.
72. *Dictionary of Basic Military Terms*, op. cit., p. 39.
73. Savkin, op. cit., p. 153.
74. *Sovetskaia Voennaia Entsiklopediia*, op. cit., vol. 6, pp. 542–43.
75. Professor Marshal of Armored Forces O. Losik, "K Vykhodu 6ogo Toma Sovetskoi Voennoi Entsiklopedii" ("On the Release of the 6th Volume of the *Soviet Military Encyclopedia*") *Voenno-Istoricheskii Zhurnal*, No. 2, February 1979, pp. 78–79. *Partinost'* is a Soviet term that roughly means displaying proper spirit, philosophy, activity, and attitude for a member of the CPSU.
76. *Officer's Handbook*, op. cit., p. 54.
77. Sokolovskiy, op. cit., p. 7.
78. Lomov, op. cit., p. 134.
79. *Dictionary of Basic Military Terms*, op. cit., p. 215.

80. Lomov, op. cit., p. 134.

81. Ibid.

82. Sokolovskiy, op. cit., p. 11.

83. *Sovetskaia Voennaia Entsiklopediia,* op. cit., vol. 2, p. 510. See also p. 113.

84. *USSR: Organization of the Ministry of Defense,* Washington, D.C.: Central Intelligence Agency, CR-78-15357, December 1978.

85. *Officer's Handbook,* op. cit., p. 65.

86. *Dictionary of Basic Military Terms,* op. cit., p. 143.

87. Savkin, op. cit., p. 154.

88. *Officer's Handbook,* op. cit., p. 58.

89. Ibid., p. 59.

90. *Dictionary of Basic Military Terms,* op. cit., p. 218.

91. Ibid.

92. Ibid., p. 137.

93. *Officer's Handbook,* op. cit., p. 104. See also A. A. Grechko, op. cit., pp. 192–200.

94. *Taktika (Tactics),* Gen. Lt. V. G. Reznichenko, ed., Moscow: Voen-izdat, 1984, pp. 51–68.

95. Peter H. Vigor, *The Soviet View of War, Peace, and Neutrality,* London: Routledge and Kegan Paul, 1977, p. 3.

*Also referred to as military pedagogy.

CHAPTER 2

The Soldier and the State

Samuel P. Huntington observed in the introduction to his book, from which the title of this chapter is borrowed, that the military institutions of any society are shaped by the threats to the society's security and the social forces, ideologies, and institutions dominant within the society.[1] Huntington reminds us that the armed forces of a state reflect national concerns and values.

Since 1918 when the Russian Army "voted with its feet," in Lenin's words, for an end to participation in World War I, the government of the Soviet Union and the CPSU have taken great care to ensure that the Soviet Army is closely identified with Soviet concerns and values. The purpose of this discussion is to outline how these concerns and values are related to the stuff from which the Soviet Army is made—the peoples of the Soviet Union.

Some methods used to enforce this identification have been extensively reported upon in the West. Included in this category are the various organs for political control of the armed forces and, in particular, the use of political deputies or *zampolits* in the Soviet chain of command. Other methods include military training and discipline, which are traditional in all armed forces. Less well understood in the West but equally important are the unique Russian organizational and structural traditions that bind the military services and society together. It is on this last subject that initial attention should focus, because it sets the stage for all that follows.

Armed Forces and Society

At the outset it is important to recognize that the strict separation of military and civilian authority that is such a fundamental and unquestioned part of Western political thought simply does not apply in the USSR, where civilian and military authority and functions are so intermingled that it is often impossible to separate one from the other.

One reason for this has to do with the history of the Soviet Army. Organized in January of 1918 as the Workers' and Peasants' Red Army, it was a conscript force used to fight the Civil War and to enforce the authority of the fledgling Soviet state.[2] Thus, Lenin intertwined military and political authority at the very birth of the Soviet state, and this interrelationship continues today. In its most visible forms, we have seen Brezhnev appearing in the uniform of a marshal of the Soviet Union, and Ustinov and his predecessor as Minister of Defense, Grechko, were uniformed military officers who held portfolios in the government and occupied seats on the Politburo of the CPSU. M.S.V. Sokolov, Ustinov's successor, is a government minister but is only a *kandidat* member of the Politburo.

Civil-military integration is not limited to the top of the Soviet power structure. The Supreme Soviet, the senior legislative body of the Soviet government, includes fifty-seven active duty military members of all ranks. More than one hundred and fifty military personnel are currently serving as deputies in the Supreme Soviets of the various republics of the USSR, thirty-seven are deputies in the Supreme Soviets of the autonomous republics, and thirteen thousand servicemen are deputies in local Soviets.[3]

The point is that active duty military personnel occupy positions of responsibility within the civilian government at national, regional, and local levels. In fact, military representation bears a relationship to the relative size of local military population, and certain national, regional, and local political offices are designated for military personnel in specified command and staff positions.[4]

Integration is not limited to governmental functions. Aeroflot, the Soviet civil air transport organization, is a branch of the Ministry of Aviation, which is headed by an active duty Air Force officer.[5] The Soviet merchant marine and fishing fleets are considered major components of Soviet naval forces and support the Soviet Navy in the same manner as Aeroflot supports the Soviet Air Force.[6]

Traditionally, the Soviet Armed Forces is actively engaged in the economic life of the country. Every fall, military units participate in the harvest in the USSR and in the non-Soviet Warsaw Pact countries where Soviet forces are stationed. Military construction units have played a major role in the extension of the Trans-Siberian Railroad from Lake Baikal to the Amur River, the BAM.[7] Conversely, traditionally Soviet mobilization practices such as the *avtokollona* allow the Soviet Army to draw upon civilian assets for military purposes. In these ways, the Soviet Army is integrated into the political and economic life of the USSR to a degree that is unprecedented in traditional Western experience.

Since the USSR does not disaggregate this civil-military integration, Western analysis of Soviet tactics and military capabilities often proves misleading. A case in point is the argument of a few years ago concerning relative U.S. and Soviet "tooth-to-tail" ratios, wherein critics of the size of the U.S. logistics system failed to appreciate the degree to which Soviet logistics depends upon the local economy.

Obligations of the Law

In addition to special relationships between the armed forces of the Soviet Union and Soviet society as a whole, there are specific responsibilities and relationships for individual citizens. These obligations are defined in Soviet law.

The essential nature of the military obligations of Soviet citizens was defined in the early days of the Soviet republic by Lenin. Basically, Lenin abandoned the concept of voluntary military services in favor of obligatory military service by the entire male population of the country and universal military training for the whole populace.[8] Since 1918, these obligations have been an integral part of the lives of Soviet citizens.

The current basis of the legal obligation of Soviet citizens for military service is set forth in the 1977 (Brezhnev) Constitution of the USSR. Article 62 states in part that "defense of the Socialist Motherland is the sacred duty of every citizen of the USSR," and Article 63 states that "Military Service in the ranks of the Armed Forces of the USSR is an honorable duty of Soviet citizens."[9]

These constitutional obligations are defined by the Law of the USSR on Universal Military Duty.[10] Article 3 of this law states that "all male citizens of the USSR . . . shall serve their term of service in the ranks of the Armed Forces of the USSR." According to this law, all physically, mentally, and morally fit males begin active service at the age of eighteen. The term of service is two years in the Soviet Army, three years in the Soviet Navy, and one year for those with a higher education degree.[11]

Under limited circumstances, deferments may be granted to finish education or in cases of extreme hardship, but these conditions are relatively rare. As a general statement, every qualified Soviet male can expect to serve in the Soviet Armed Forces within two years of reaching his eighteenth birthday. After completing active service, he retains an obligation for military service in event of mobilization until the age of fifty. Those on active duty are called servicemen (voennosluzhii); reservists are called military obligated (voennoobiazannyi).[12]

Those wishing to become officers may enroll in military schools at the age of seventeen or upon finishing their secondary education. Upon completing the course of instruction, generally two years, graduates are commissioned in one of the branches of the Soviet Armed Forces.[13]

Soviet women, although they have the same legal obligation for defense of the homeland as men, are not subject to the draft, and they may not serve in combat units. At present, there are only about ten thousand women in uniform, mostly in the enlisted ranks serving in medical, administrative, communications, and other support areas.[14] Women are not subject to the same rigid discipline and austere living conditions as are male conscripts, although they receive the same pay.[15] Their small numbers and restrictions on assignments severely curtail promotion potential. Upon discharge, women are transferred to the reserve and maintain a military obligation until the age of forty.[16]

Induction into the armed services is carried out twice each year, once in the spring and once in the fall, upon the orders of the minister of defense. At the same time, he orders the release of those who have completed their obligated service.[17] Selection and notification of individuals is by local draft commissions (prizivnaia kommissia) composed of veterans and party officials. Since virtually all males are expected to serve if fit, the function of the draft commission is that of ruling on applications for deferment, assignment to the various branches, and publishing the list of those selected for service. Individuals desiring to enlist do so by notifying their draft commission that they wish to be selected in the next call.

Simple arithmetic tells us that the Soviet Army has a turnover of 25 percent of its enlisted strength every six months. Since nearly 77 percent of its personnel are conscripts (1.4 million out of a total of 1.83 million), this semiannual change has a rather prominent cyclical impact on Soviet combat capabilities and training.[18] For example, the traditional large-scale spring and fall maneuvers mark the end of the training cycle. Shortly after these maneuvers, troops completing their obligated service are demobilized and replaced by recruits, and the training cycle starts again with basic individual training. Commanders of squads, tanks, and gun crews are selected from those who have completed two or three cycles.

While in uniform, servicemen assume the additional obligation of Soviet military law, which provides a large part of the authority for enforcing military order and discipline. While juridical philosophy is far beyond the scope of this discussion, it is important to understand that law in the Soviet view is primarily an instructional tool rather than a means of regulating society. Thus, punishment under Soviet military justice serves to teach the individual his responsibilities and to provide an example to others.[19] For this reason, there need not be any direct proportionality between the seriousness of the offense and the degree of punishment, and the accused has very few rights.

Military law divides offenses into three categories which are taught to soldiers as responsibilities.[20] The first category is disciplinary responsibility, the duty to obey all military regulations. The second category, material responsibility, is the duty to safeguard military and government property. The last category, criminal responsibility, refers to acts against the person, well-being, or property of the state, the society, or other individuals.

The *Distsiplinarnyi Ustav Vooruzhennykh Sil Souza SSR* (*Disciplinary Regulations of the Armed Forces of the USSR*) obligate every serviceman to "strictly observe the laws and exactly fulfill the demands of the military oath, military regulations, orders and commands of superiors."[21] The basis of the regulations is strict obedience and precise execution of orders. Initiative, in the Western sense of imaginative problem solving, is not a part of the curriculum. Nor, as in the United States, is the word *lawful* included in the obligation.

Servicemen are not expected to judge the lawfulness of orders, they must assume that all orders are lawful.

The obligation of the serviceman to obey is mirrored in the disciplinary responsibilities of commanders to enforce obedience. The responsibility of superiors is stated as follows: "The interests of defense of the Homeland obligate the superior to decisively and strictly demand observance of military discipline and order and not to permit a single misdemeanor of a subordinate to go unpunished."[22] Here again, the emphasis is on obedience. A commander who looks the other way in cases of minor infractions is, himself, in violation of disciplinary regulations.

Interestingly, Soviet regulations do not prescribe specific punishments for violations of disciplinary responsibility, other than stating that punishment must be administered within ten days of a superior becoming aware of the offense. There are limits on the severity of punishment that superiors at various levels may impose, but there are no relationships of these punishments to specific infractions. Severity may range from summary execution, as has reportedly happened in Afghanistan, to a reprimand.

In the case of use of force, disciplinary regulations state: "In event of open insubordination or opposition of a subordinate, a superior is obligated for the maintenance of order to take all necessary measures to place the guilty party under arrest and to place him in legal restraint. In so doing weapons may only be used in combat situations or, in peacetime, only in exceptional circumstances not permitting any delay, when the subordinate's actions are patently traitorous to the Homeland or constitute an actual threat to the life of the superior, other servicemen, or civilians."[23] In other words, a senior may, in a combat zone, shoot a subordinate to enforce his authority. In peacetime, the use of weapons is restricted to self-defense or to such crises as preventing defection or putting down a mutiny.

For the more routine administration of disciplinary responsibility, penalties are those traditional in most armies. At the low end of the scale is a rebuke, an informal "chewing out," or a formal oral or written reprimand which may be administered in public and include a requirement for self-criticism. The middle level of penalties include restriction, extra duty, and confinement in the guardhouse. More serious punishment includes revocation of awards and reduction in rank.

An interesting aspect of Soviet disciplinary regulations is that all ranks, including officers, may be punished by confinement in the guard-house for a period of up to fifteen days, and that confinement does not require reduction in rank. Table 2.1 summarizes the types of punishment and the authority necessary to impose them upon servicemen.

Soviet disciplinary regulations are not limited to negative incentives; they include positive incentives for exceptional performance.[24] These generally consist of oral or written pronouncements of appreciation that may be announced in formation or posted on unit bulletin boards. Superiors may also commute punishment that they previously adjudged. In an army where there are no passes or leaves for servicemen, the most impressive incentives are probably a forty-eight-hour pass from garrison or, in rare cases, ten days leave. Leave is

Table 2.1

Types of Punishment and Authority to Impose Them Under Soviet
Disciplinary Regulations

	Rebuke	Repri- mand	Restric- tion[1]	Extra Duty[2]	Confine- ment[1]	Revoke Award[3]	Reduc- tion
Squad commander	yes	yes	7	1			
Assistant platoon commander			14	2			
Company senior sergeant			21	3			
Platoon commander			21	4			
Company commander			30	5	3		
Battalion commander					5		
Regiment commander					10	yes	yes
Division commander					15		

[1]Days in restriction to the unit area or confinement in the guardhouse
[2]Turns on the extra-duty roster out-of-order (except for guard duty or charge of quarters)
[3]Revocation of previous award of Outstanding Badge for exceptional performance

Source: *Distsiplinarnyi Ustav Vooruzhennykh Sil Souza SSR (Disciplinary Regulations of the Armed Forces of the USSR)*, Moscow: Voenizdat, 1971, arts. 36–46.

authorized only at the serviceman's home and the ten days is in addition to travel time. Superior performances may also be recognized by award of a certificate, a valued gift, such as a watch, or a cash award. An even more tangible recognition is award of the *Otlichnyi Znak* (Outstanding Badge). This award is important not only because it gives the serviceman a medal to wear, but because it is entered into his personal work record and can help him get a better job after leaving the service. The most prestigious recognition is to record the name of the serviceman in the permanent unit history. Among other things, this means that his exploit will be read to subsequent bevies of recruits in that unit, and, more to the point, his place of civilian work will be notified so that he will almost certainly receive a better job and recognition upon return to civilian life.

Material responsibility is based upon a decree of the Supreme Soviet passed on 23 May 1966. Under this decree, individuals can be required to reimburse the state for property loss or damage. Even given the paltry pay of a Soviet private, this does not appear at first glance to be a terrible punishment, until one remembers that this responsibility is based upon state law and the obligation can follow the individual into civilian life.

In the Soviet Armed Forces, criminal reponsibility covers a wide spectrum of acts that includes the traditional criminal offenses such as murder, robbery, and treason as well as some uniquely Soviet crimes.[25] However, even traditional criminal offenses are treated in a uniquely Soviet way. For instance, punishment for individual criminal acts is generally less severe than that for crimes committed in concert with others. For example, insubordination by an individual is punishable by one to five years imprisonment, whereas group insubordination is punishable by three to ten years' imprisonment. In the Soviet Army, there is no safety in numbers, and mass punishment gives commanders a useful tool for winnowing out the guilty party or parties.

Among the unique Soviet crimes is one called *guliganstvo* (literally, hooliganism). This undefined transgression, punishable by one to five years' imprisonment, is often invoked to cover any activity that displeases authorities but is not otherwise defined as a violation of criminal, material, or disciplinary responsibility. It is often applied to acts of individual or group political protest or to certain "antisocialist" acts such as holding unauthorized religious services.

Criminal responsibility is the most serious of the three categories of law and carries the heaviest penalties. The single basis for punishment is guilt in committing the crime; there are no mitigating circumstances. Punishment is generally incarceration in the Soviet criminal penal system, since the Soviet Armed Forces do not operate any penitentiaries. Punishment for some of the crimes listed in Soviet military justice manuals is shown in Table 2.2

Finally, there are certain extralegal punishments such as the use of mental hospitals, drugs, and administrative procedures to enforce conformity. While we hear of many famous Russian dissidents suffering this sort of treatment, it is also used against the members of the armed forces. The most well-documented military case is that of Gen. Maj. Viktor Grigorenko who, as a result of criticizing a local party organization, was branded as anti-Soviet, forced to retire, reduced in rank to private, and subjected to a continuing cycle of incarcerations in "terrifying mental institutions."[26] This punishment was for an officer twice wounded in combat and five times decorated for bravery in combat, and a graduate cyberneticist of the General Staff who authored seventy-six professional papers published in important journals.[27]

This short discussion has shown that the Soviet Army has powerful legal and administrative tools for enforcing discipline and that the state has ample legal authority for imposing military obligations upon the citizens of the USSR. One should not, however, conclude that Soviet citizens serve in the army only or even primarily because of fear or coercion. Soviet soldiers serve and fight for far more complex reasons. Their attitudes toward military service result from a mixture of positive as well as negative forces.

Attitudes Toward Military Service

By and large, Soviet youth do not wish to serve in the armed forces. Military service in the USSR is unpopular for many of the same reasons it is unpopular in the United States and in Western Europe. To begin with, the draft interrupts education and career and personal plans. Then too, there are the psychological problems associated with leaving home and family for the first time for a difficult and perhaps dangerous life in an alien place.

Very few Soviet draftees elect to remain in the service. Life is

Table 2.2
Representative Punishments Under Criminal Responsibility

Crime	Punishment
Crimes against the state (espionage, treason, helping foreign powers, fleeing)	10–15 years or death and confiscation of property.
Crimes against life or health	10 years or death
Threatening or killing a superior	5–15 years or death
Theft or misappropriation of	
Government property	6–15 years, depending on value
Military property	1–3 years in peace, 2–7 in war
Weapons	1–15 years
Desertion or malingering	3–7 years in peace, 5–10 years or death in war
Misuse of equipment or vehicles resulting in injury	2–10 years
Misuse of firearms	3–7 years
Failure to safeguard state and military secrets	1–5 years
Allowing state and military secrets to fall into foreign hands	5–10 years

	Committed by	
	Individuals	Groups
Hooliganism	1–5 years	3–7 years
Insubordination	1–5 years	3–10 years
Disobedience of orders (resisting a superior)	1–5 years	3–10 years

Source: S. S. Maksimov, *Vysokii Dolg, Pochotnaia Obliazannost (High Duty, Honorable Obligation)*, Moscow: Juridical Literature Publishers, 1978, pp. 107–22.

hard, discipline is strict and unrelenting, and pay is meager. With a guaranteed semiannual resupply of new recruits, the Soviet Army is not greatly motivated to make service in the enlisted ranks attractive. Training is relentless and repetitive and is based upon the ancient Russian Army tradition of "The harder the training, the easier the battle."[28]

There are, however, indications that the Soviet Army is beginning to be concerned about the life of its enlisted troops. In 1977 an all-Army conference in Moscow was dedicated to discussing improvements to the living conditions in the service.[29] As a direct result of this conference, commanders are now required by regulations to assure troops in garrison eight hours sleep and one hour personal time daily.[30] A typical soldier's daily schedule is shown in Figure 2.1.

Another indication is the adoption of a standard for barracks that provides each soldier with space for a bed, a night stand, and a foot locker. In this case, the standard applies to new construction; it does not offer much to troops living in established barracks, who presumably have considerably less. The living conditions of soldiers is now a matter of official party concern, which means that party organs within units will "assist" commanders in finding ways to improve the physical living conditions of servicemen.[31]

A similar degree of concern is being shown for the quality and quantity of troop rations.[32] The quality of rations is to be improved by serving fresh meat and vegetables from unit gardens. The serving style is being bettered by such improvements as tablecloths and ceramic teacups.

In the Soviet Army, however, progress does not come without its drawbacks. One unit commander found that when he poured tea at the required 90° Celsius temperature into his newly issued teacups, the bottom broke out of almost every cup. Soviet industry can provide excellent tanks for the Soviet Army, but the teacup problem has yet to be solved.

While it is undeniably true that military service is unpopular among the masses of Soviet youth, it would be dangerously wrong to equate unpopularity of military service with unwillingness to serve or to project an unwillingness to fight. Such evidence as is available, while it is spotty and admittedly subjective, strongly suggests otherwise.

To begin with, there is the strong and unreserved emotional love of country that is basic to the Russian psyche. As Hedrick Smith observed, "In an age grown skeptical of undiluted patriotism, Russians are perhaps the world's most passionate patriots. Without question a deep and tenacious love of country is the most powerful unifying force . . . the most vital element in the amalgam of loyalties that cements Soviet society."[33] This strong, passionate patriotism transcends communism or any form of social structure. It involves an emotional attachment to land and clan that gives the "homeland" a pull on the

FIGURE 2-1
DAILY SCHEDULE OF A SOVIET SOLDIER

TIME	ACTIVITY
0550	First Call for reveille
0600	Reveille Formation
0610–0700	Daily Physical Training
0700–0710	Make Beds
0710–0720	Morning Inspection
0720–0730	Hear The Orders of the Day
0730–0750	Political Lecture
0750–0800	Wash Hands
0800–0820	Breakfast
0820–0830	Wash Utensils
0830–0900	Preparation for Duty
	Training Day
0900–0950	Period 1
1000–1050	Period 2
1100–1150	Period 3
1200–1250	Period 4
1300–1350	Period 5
1400–1450	Period 6
1450–1500	Prepare for Dinner
1500–1530	Dinner
1500–1540	Prepare the Tea Pot
1540–1610	Personal Time
1610–1650	Care of weapons and equipment
1650–1840	Sanitation Requirements (Police barracks and area)
1840–1920	Political Work
1920–1930	Wash Hands
1930–1950	Supper
1950–2000	Prepare the Tea Pot
2000–2035	Watch the Evening News on TV
2035–2135	Personal Time
2135–2145	Evening Formation
2145–2155	Evening Inspection
2200	Retreat

SOURCE: A Soviet Soldier's notebook captured in Afghanistan in 1984.
(Compliments of Mr. David C. Isby)

heart of any Russian that is beyond the understanding of the citizens of the mobile, commercial, sophisticated Western or American societies.[34] Smith summed up the effects of this patriotism as producing a clannish defensiveness toward outsiders and an intolerance of nonconformists within society, a nineteenth century–style pride in national power and worldwide influence, a blinding ethnocentrism, and a conviction of moral, if not material, superiority.[35]

Other Westerners who have had intimate contact with Russians have generally experienced similar revelations. Andrea Lee, in her book *Russian Journal*, pointed out that Russian dissidents she met while a graduate student in Moscow in 1978 still claimed to be first and foremost Russian and Soviet citizens and that they felt that the United States was decadent and spiritually bankrupt.[36] They felt, as do most Russians, that there will be war and that they will win because of their superior moral strength, the willingness to sacrifice and to work together for Russia.

The point to be learned is that, while Soviet youth by and large do not desire to serve in the Soviet Army, patriotism motivates them to do so. Although Russian youth are not militarized in the sense of eighteenth-century Prussia or ancient Sparta, they will fight bravely and well for Russia and against foreigners under the most trying battlefield conditions. The Soviet Army, therefore, does not need to build patriotism and discipline among its soldiers; it must merely exploit and nurture what is already there for its own purposes. It does so under the banner of proletarian nationalism and internationalism.

Proletarian Nationalism and Internationalism

Although it is a powerful force for building the Soviet Army, Russian nationalism has certain negative features. One theoretical problem is that ethnic nationalism is non-Marxist. Marxism-Leninism has always sought to inculcate class (proletarian) loyalties as superseding or overlying national or ethnic loyalties. On a more practical level, appeals to Russian nationalism are not always attractive to ethnic minorities that have been incorporated into the Soviet empire. The Moslems of central Asia and the Catholics of Baltic states, for example, have a long history of resisting domination by Russians, be they from the czarist or Soviet mold.

Under the Czars, the minority problem was addressed within the armed forces by creating national or ethnic units such as the Cossack Guards. The Soviet approach has been the opposite. In the Soviet Army, an attempt has been made to create a "new" morale in the soldier based upon Soviet patriotism (as opposed to national patriotism) and on class identity (as opposed to national identity).[37] This does not imply that national patriotism and national identity are wrong, but it does mean that they are subordinate to Soviet patriotism and proletarian internationalism.[38]

The goal is for the Soviet Army to train a soldier who hates the enemy and is loyal to his Soviet homeland, whose motto is "For the homeland, for the Party, and for Communism."[39] Through the inculcation of these values, the Soviet Army fulfills its role as a school for socialism.

A School for Socialism

The Soviet Army is an integral part of the Soviet state, and military training is an inseparable part of the total process of molding the new man of socialist society.[40] Thus, military training serves two purposes in the USSR: the obvious one of producing a disciplined soldier proficient in his military specialty, and the equally important one of turning out masses of loyal Soviet citizens. The first purpose serves obvious military requirements. The second purpose serves an immediate military need but is also aimed at the larger target of attitudes after completion of military service.[41]

This second purpose in part explains the seemingly (to Western observers) excessive emphasis in Soviet Army training on political subjects and the large number of assets in the form of political officers and agitators in Soviet units. They are a basic part of a process of socialization and Sovietization as well as a means of ensuring the loyalty of the troops.

This process is not limited to lecturing on political subjects or urging better performance of duty. The Main Political Directorate of the Soviet Army and Navy, the GPU, directs the political staffs to assume such responsibilities as teaching Russian-language skills to soldiers from non-Russian nationalities.[42] Other functions include planning and arranging cultural and social activities and sports to inculcate the values of socialist internationalism.[43]

This is not to be taken as an implication that political training is not important. Training schedules specifically reserve at least one hour per week for political lectures, and the soldiers selected to present each lecture are permitted four hours time for preparation of the lesson.[44] Unit newspapers, wall newspapers, and posters on bulletin boards and mounted in "Lenin Rooms" (similar to unit day rooms) espouse official party political themes. These methods serve to mold the political qualities of the troops.

A part of the process of forming the "new Soviet man" is to indoctrinate him with a proper attitude toward work and his duties. Within the Soviet Army, the political organs also assume a major role in this effort. This influence is generally exerted through the *kollektiv*, a form of social organization that is totally unknown in the West. Virtually every Soviet citizen belongs to a small social group organized around his or her place of work and/or residence. Members of a *kollektiv* both watch and support one another, and *kollektivs* form the basis for "voluntary" labor projects and "spontaneous" demonstrations. Within the army, *kollektivs* generally correspond to squad level organizations. Leaders of *kollektivs* are usually elected, are connected with the GPU, and are seldom the military squad leaders. They serve two purposes: they motivate by drumming up enthusiasm for the military task at hand, and they provide a means for checking performance outside of the regular chain of command. Through his *kollektiv*, the Soviet soldier finds that he is under observation and control even during what little free time that is available to him.

The *kollektiv* provides social pressures to conform to military discipline that complement formal obligations under military law that were described earlier. It is that part of the entire apparatus created by the Soviet elite to ensure the reliability of the Soviet Army that touches every soldier every day.[45]

The *kollektiv* is the fundamental means used to indoctrinate servicemen with basic military virtues. Every serviceman takes the military oath (*voennaia prisiaga*) individually by reciting it in a solemn ceremony in front of his *kollektiv*. The oath is translated in Figure 2.2. First term soldiers must take the oath within one and a half months of joining their units, after proving that they understand its meaning and the obligations entailed and having been indoctrinated into the traditions of their unit and military discipline. Military obligated personnel without prior service assigned military mobilization duties (e.g., in *avtokollonas*) must take the oath within five days of mobilization. Those who have previously served and are being recalled need not retake the oath.[46]

This use of the military oath is consistent with the fundamental difference between Western and Soviet attitudes toward law. In West-

Figure 2.2

The Soviet Military Oath

I _____, a citizen of the Union of Soviet Socialist Republics entering into the ranks of the Armed Forces, take an oath and do solemnly swear to be an honorable, brave, disciplined, vigilant warrior, strictly safeguarding military and state secrets, unswervingly fulfilling all military regulations and orders of commanders and chiefs.

I conscientiously swear to master military affairs to protect fully military and national property and, to my last breath, to be loyal to my nation, to my Soviet homeland, and to the Soviet government.

I am always prepared, upon orders of the Soviet government to go to the defense of my homeland—the Union of Soviet Socialist Republics and, as a warrior in the Soviet Armed Forces, I swear to defend her manfully, skillfully, with dignity and honor, not sparing my own blood and life itself for the achievement of total victory over the enemy.

If I should ever violate this, my solemn oath, then let the severe punishment of Soviet law, and the universal hatred of the working masses, fall upon me.

Source: Ustav Vnutrennei Sluzhby, Vooruzhennykh Sil SSSR (Internal Service Regulations of the Soviet Armed Forces), Moscow: Military Publishers, 1977, p. 4.

ern armed forces, taking the military oath is the legal step by which individuals accept military authority. In the USSR, military authority is a condition of citizenship imposed upon all citizens in the constitution. Taking the military oath is an individual rite of passage into the warrior caste. Rather than a legally binding statement, it is an emotionally and morally binding sacrament carefully designed to influence the attitude of each young man toward his military service. Rather than stating a legal obligation it appeals to the individual's patriotism and sense of honor and acceptance of social and legal pressures to conform.

The Soviet Army serves the Soviet national leadership in two important ways: by providing the military component of national power, and by indoctrinating the young men of the USSR to be good Soviet citizens. While military service is not popular, and the cost is high in the general sense of impact on the standard of living and on the personal level of time in service, the Soviet people seem to accept it. One reason is that military service seems to be rather like a ritual passage into manhood where fathers and sons have a shared experience.[47] Another reason is that by and large, Soviet citizens view the Soviet Army as a defender of the homeland, the Reliable Shield of Socialism.

Defender of the Soviet Homeland

Citizens of Western democracies tend to view arms expenditures in peacetime as unjustified and even dangerous. Defense budgets detract from programs that seem more acceptable socially or politically. There is a sometimes latent but nonetheless powerful antiwar sentiment that turned against U.S. involvement in Vietnam and is now fostering antinuclear demonstrations of unprecedented size in Western Europe.

We tend to assume that these sentiments are so right and just that they have universal application and that they therefore apply to the Soviet Union as well. These assumptions appear in statements of national leaders expressing their wonderment as to why the USSR maintains a military establishment that is far larger than what (we think) they really need for national defense. They also give rise to a naive faith that economic problems within the USSR and increasing desires for consumer goods among the Soviet public will somehow push the leadership into reducing its level of military expenditures.[48]

Regrettably, the facts do not warrant such optimism. The entire spectrum of Russian twentieth-century experience has been one of the costs of military unpreparedness. World War I, the revolution, intervention, the Civil War and, above all, World War II were a series of brutal lessons on the relationship of military strength to national and even individual security.

Considering World War II alone, it is generally accepted that 20 million Russians were killed in the war and that perhaps 80 percent of the man-made structures in the USSR were damaged or destroyed.[49] Stalin is purported to have said that the death of a man is a tragedy; the death of a million is a statistic. To understand the meaning of this statistic, one must consider that the figure of 20 million refers to deaths attributable to the war *in addition to* those that would have normally occurred. One should also take into account that for every combat death, there were at least three wounded, if traditional ratios applied.[50] Thus, the USSR can be estimated as having suffered perhaps 80 million killed and wounded men, women, and children between 1941 and 1945. Since the total population of the USSR was estimated as approaching 195 million in 1940, one could conclude that between one of every two and one of every three Soviet citizens was a war casualty.[51]

These statistics are not in themselves important. They do, however, underline the fact that virtually every Soviet citizen old enough to remember the wartime period learned the lesson of unpreparedness in a vivid way. This certainly includes every generation born prior to 1936. This memory appears in curious ways. For example, the air of reverence around war memorials in the USSR always impresses Western tourists. In a casual conversation, a Soviet tourist in East Germany in 1975 looked about and burst out bitterly, "We will *never, ever* forget!" A Russian-born instructor in Soviet literature who lived through the German occupation of Kiev as a young girl of eight or nine, lapsed into uncontrolled weeping during a class discussion of Yevtushenko's poem *Babuy Yar*.[52]

Without belaboring the point, the simple fact of the matter is that the average Soviet citizen feels a need for security that powerful armed forces seem to offer. Were they permitted to choose between military security and an improved standard of living, the great mass of Soviet citizens would opt for military security because it fits their patriotism, their nationalism, and their historical experience.

This is not to say that Russian people are warlike, indeed they are not. Nor does it mean that they have no interest in improved economic conditions, which they certainly do want. It does mean that as long as the Soviet government can convince the people that there is a military threat, the people will make the sacrifices necessary to support the Soviet Army. The Russian people form a vibrant and viable constituency for military preparedness.

This constituency shows itself in a number of ways. Andrea Lee was surprised by the sight of co-eds at Moscow State University practicing throwing hand grenades and participating in marksmanship classes.[53] Younger children in secondary schools practice a form of basic training as a part of their educational curriculum, and preteenagers participate in organized military maneuvers called *zarnitsa* (lighting) on weekends and holidays.[54] In classrooms, a part of the curriculum is devoted to such subjects as assembly and disassembly of weapons and gas mask drills.[55] These exercises, although military in nature, are apparently funded through the education budget rather than the defense budget.[56]

There are other military training exercises within the *kollektiv* outside of the classroom. For instance, in the Young Pioneers, a Soviet equivalent of Scouting, there are exercises in guerrilla warfare and solemn military style ceremonies.[57] For children over the age of fourteen, the DOSAAF (an acronym for All Union Voluntary Society for Cooperation with the Army, Navy, and Air Force) provides instruction in basic military skills.[58]

This rather extensive system of premilitary training serves two important purposes. The first is the obvious one of teaching basic military skills. The second purpose, however, is possibly more important than the first—the training serves as ideological education.[59] Through military indoctrination, the generations of Soviet citizens born after World War II are recruited into the Soviet national constituency for military preparedness. They learn the sacrifices and costs of "the Great Patriotic War" and are brought to accept the validity of the need for national defense.[60]

Like their parents and their grandparents, each new generation of Soviet youth is being indoctrinated to feel the need for the Soviet Army as a shield against a hostile world. It is, of course, impossible to find hard data as to the effectiveness of the indoctrination program. However, empirical evidence from those who have had a chance to meet and get to know average Russians in the USSR suggests that the effort is generally successful. As Hedrick Smith observed, "In the years since the war, the hold of patriotism has grown as Communist fervor has waned so that today nationalism has more magnetism and meaning for the overwhelming majority of Soviet people than does Marxist-Leninist ideology."[61] The Soviet government has been successful in ensuring, in Huntington's words, that the Soviet Army reflects the concerns and values of the citizenry. The stuff from which the Soviet Army is made, the peoples of the Soviet Union, identify with the Soviet Army. They can be relied upon to fight, perhaps not for the party or for communism, but certainly for the homeland.

Notes

1. Samuel P. Huntington, *The Soldier and The State*, Cambridge, Mass.: Harvard University Press, 1957, p. 2.
2. A. A. Grechko, *The Armed Forces of the Soviet State*, Moscow: Ministry of Defense Publishers, 1975. Translated and published under the auspices of the U.S. Air Force, p. 16.
3. V. Ryabov, *The Soviet Armed Forces Yesterday and Today*, Moscow: Progress Publishers, 1976, p. 156. See also M. G. Sobolev *Sviaschennyi Dolg (Sacred Duty)*, Moscow: DOSAAF, 1980, p. 68.
4. For a detailed discussion of the civil-military interrelationship, see Jerry Nolan, "USSR: The Unity and Integration of Soviet Political, Military, and Defense Industry Leadership" DIA, DDI-2250-17-77, 1977.
5. Harriet F. and William F. Scott, *The Armed Forces of the USSR*, Boulder, Colo.: Westview Press, 1979, p. 159.
6. Ibid., p. 166.
7. See, e.g., *Znamenosets*, no. 8, 1981, p. 13. See also Sobolev, op. cit., p. 64.
8. Grechko, op. cit., p. 11.
9. *Constitution of the Union of Soviet Socialist Republics*, Moscow: Novosti, 1980.
10. Ryabov, op. cit., p. 156.
11. Ibid., p. 152.
12. S. S. Maksimov, *Vysokii Dolg Pochotnaia Ob'iazannost (High Duty, Honorable Obligation)*, Moscow: Juridical Literature Publishers, 1978, p. 27.
13. For a detailed description of officers' training, see Scott, op. cit., pp. 341–74.
14. Mitzi Leibst, "Women in the Soviet Armed Forces," DIA, DDI-1100-109-76, February 1976, p. iv.
15. Ibid, p. 7.
16. Ibid.
17. Ryabov, op. cit., p. 152.
18. Figures from *The Military Balance 1981–1982*, London: International Institute for Strategic Studies, p. 11.
19. Maksimov, op. cit., p. 105.
20. Ibid., p. 102.
21. *Distsiplinarnyi Ustav Vooruzhennykh Sil Souza SSR (Disciplinary Regulations of the Armed Forces of the USSR)*, Moscow: Voenizdat, 1971, art. 3.
22. Ibid., art. 6.
23. Ibid., art. 7.

24. Ibid., art. 17.

25. For a full description, see Maksimov, op. cit.

26. D. Pospielovsky, "General Gregorenko and the Mental Institutions," Radio Liberty Dispatch, 10 March 1970.

27. Ibid.

28. M. Ruban, *The Soviet School of Courage and Warcraft*, Moscow: Progress Publishers, 1976, p. 26. (This dictum is generally credited to Marshal Kutuzov, who commanded the Russian Army against Napoleon in the War of 1812.)

29. Sobolev, op. cit., p. 72.

30. Ibid.

31. Col. G. Skvortsov, *"Partiinaia Zabota O Voinskom Byte"* ("Party Concern Over Soldiers' Living Conditions"), *Tyl i Snabzhenie*, no. 9, September 1981, pp. 43–45.

32. For example, see *"K Soldatskomu Stolu"* ("For the Soldier's Table"), *Znamenosets*, no. 8, 1981, p. 20.

33. Hedrick Smith, *The Russians*, New York: Quadrangle Books, 1976, p. 303.

34. Ibid., p. 307. See also Donald Mackenzie Wallace, *Russia on the Eve of War and Revolution*, New York: Vintage Books, 1961. Wallace, an English diplomat who traveled extensively in Russia in the nineteenth century, described the same characteristics as does Robert K. Massie in *Peter the Great, His Life and World*, New York: Alfred A. Knopf, 1980. Massie's description of seventeenth-century Russian chauvinism and suspicion of foreigners is based upon scholarly research into contemporary Russian and European documents. His descriptions differ little from those of Wallace, Smith, or Lee.

35. Smith, op. cit.

36. Andrea Lee, *Russian Journal*, New York: Random House, 1979, pp. 62, 164.

37. *Marxism-Leninism on War and the Army*, Moscow: Progress Publishers, 1972. Published under the auspices of U.S. Air Force, pp. 337, 338. See also p. 359.

38. Gen. of the Army A. A. Epishe, *"Monolitnoe Edinstvo"* ("Monolithic Unity"), *Agitator Armii i Flota*, no. 3, February 1979, pp. 1–7. See also F. Konstantinov, *Socialist Internationalism*, Moscow: Progress Publishers, 1978, p. 125.

39. *Agitator Armii i Flota*, no. 3, February 1980, p. 1. See also *Marxism-Leninism on War and the Army*, op. cit., p. 353.

40. Ruban, op. cit., p. 11.

41. K. A. Vorob'ev, *Vooruzhennye Sily Razvitogo Sotsialistichecheskogo Obshchestva*, (*Armed Forces of a Developing Socialist Society*) Moscow: Voenizdat, 1980, pp. 48–49.

42. *"Povyshat' Effektivnost' Politicheskikh Zaniatii"* ("To Improve the Effectiveness of Political Activity"), *Agitator Armii i Flota*, no. 9, May 1980, p. 2.
43. Ruban, op. cit., p. 129.
44. Ibid., p. 148.
45. For a detailed discussion of political control of the Soviet Armed Forces, see Eugene D. Betit, "Political Control of the Soviet Armed Forces: The Committee of People's Control," DIA, DB-2600-1279-78, April 1978.
46. *Sovetskaia Voennaia Entsiklopediia*, 8 vols. 1976–1980, Moscow: Voenizdat, vol. 6, p. 547.
47. See, e.g., Konorov Uy, *"Spasibo Armii Za Syna"* ("Thanks to the Army for My Son"), *Znamenosets*, no. 8, 1981, pp. 14–15.
48. See, e.g., 96th Congress, 1st Session, Joint Economic Committee Report, "Soviet Economy in a Time of Change," 10 October 1979, vol. 2, p. 15.
49. The scale of destruction was so great that records do not exist. A good Soviet study of this problem was published by the Soviet demographer B. Urlanis in *Wars and Population*, Moscow: Progress Publishers, 1971.
50. Ibid., p. 50.
51. *Narodnoe Khozaisttvo SSSR v 1977 g (Economy of the USSR in 1977)*, Moscow: Statistika, 1978, p. 10.
52. Urii Yevtushenko, *Babuy Yar*, a heartrending account of the mass extermination of the Jewish population of Kiev by Nazi occupation forces during World War II.
53. Lee, op. cit., p. 11.
54. Smith, op. cit., pp. 320–21.
55. See, e.g., *Voennye Znaniia*, no. 9, 1981, p. 19.
56. Smith, op. cit.
57. See, e.g., cover of *Voennye Znaiia*, no. 5, 1981.
58. For a detailed discussion of the DOSAAF, see Scott, op. cit., pp. 307–11.
59. See, e.g., L. I. Brezhnev, *Voprosy Razvitiia Politicheskoi Sistemy Sovetskogo Obshchestva, (Questions on the Development of the Soviet Political System)* Moscow: Political Literature, p. 384.
60. D. N. Shcherbakov, ed., *Patrioticheskoe i Internatsional'noe Vospitanie Sovetskoe Molodezhi v Usloviiakh Razvitogo Solsializma, (The Patriotic and International Education of Soviet Youth Under the Conditions of Developing Socialism)*, Kiev: Vishchi'a Schola Publishers, 1980, pp. 44–45.
61. Smith, op. cit., p. 304.

CHAPTER 3

Command and Staff

The Soviet system for exercising military authority evolved from the unique Russian historical social experience. While it is quite correct to point out that Soviet commanders must resolve the same battlefield problems as commanders in any army, it is incorrect to assume that they must solve those problems in the same way. Indeed, the Soviet Army has evolved its own unique way of planning, directing, and fighting the battle.

This chapter explains how military authority is exercised in the Soviet Army by examining the structure of rank and grades through which authority is bestowed and distributed, the commander in whom authority resides, the staff through which he exercises his authority, and the communications system for transmitting decisions. The sum of these components defines how Soviet commanders influence the battle and explains the character of Soviet battlefield operations.

The system through which military authority is exercised is generally referred to as command, control, and communications, or C^3. Authority, the power to make decisions, is a complex thing, involving a number of related functions through which commanders plan, direct, and fight the battle. These include the process of making decisions, transmitting them to subordinates, enforcing obedience, and many other related functions. The traditional approach to understanding Soviet C^3 has been to stress the technical aspects of communications hardware and software. This chapter is titled "Command and Staff" because it approaches the problem from a primarily operational viewpoint of social and human, rather than technical, considerations.

Kto Kogo

This Russian phrase, roughly translated as "who does it to whom," encapsulates the Soviet attitude toward rank, grade, and authority. The key, of course, is authority, which often, but not always, is equivalent to rank (A KGB colonel is more "equal" than a colonel of militia, for example). Authority, since it is bestowed from above, tends to encourage servility toward superiors and, at the same time, condescension toward subordinates, and the Soviet Army's stress on loyalty to the party or the state and not to individuals reinforces this indifference toward individuals.

Other examples of the Soviet Army's attitude toward authority are included in regulations. Positions of authority are defined by the title *komandir* (commander) or *nachal'nik* (chief). The term "leader" (*vozhd*) is never used. Manuals stress strict enforcement of regulations as the best way to exercise command, and precise and timely execution of orders as the ideal for subordinates. In the Soviet Army, the proper affirmative response to a superior is *tak tochno* (exactly so), and the accepted negative response is *nikak net* (in no way). A simple yes (*da*) and no (*net*) will not do.

This downward flow of authority is normal in most armies, but it has an extraordinary ferocity in the Soviet Army that even extends to families. For instance, when rations are delivered to family quarters, the commander's wife draws her share first, and so it goes down to the *kadre serzhant*'s wife. By quantity, each receives what the size of their family permits. By quality, however, the last in line literally get the scraps, and if there is a shortage, it is they who do without. This concern with rank is a significant contradiction to the communist ideal of a classless society, although Soviet citizens justify it as being based upon *what you are* as opposed to *who you are*, therefore implying no social class.

Regardless of ideology, the Soviet Armed Forces has a well-defined structure of rank, defined in Table 3.1. There are fourteen officer grades divided into three components, Highest Officers, Senior Officers, and Junior Officers. The highest rank is Generalissimo of the Soviet Union, a position held only by Stalin, but still recognized in regulations. Immediately below that are three grades of marshal and four general grades. The lowest marshal grade and the highest general grade have equal authority. The Senior Officer component

Table 3.1

Military Rank in the Soviet Armed Forces
Higher Command Personnel

Army	Air Force	Navy
Generalissimo of the Soviet Union		
Marshal of the Soviet Union		
Chief Marshal of Artillery	Chief Marshal of the Air Force	Admiral of the Soviet Union
General: Marshal of Engineers, Artillery, or Communications	Marshal of the Air Force	Admiral of the Fleet
General-Colonel	General-Colonel	Admiral
General-Lieutenant	General-Lieutenant	Vice Admiral
General-Major	General-Major	Rear Admiral
	Senior Officer Personnel	
Colonel	Colonel	Captain 1st Rank
Lieutenant Colonel	Lieutenant Colonel	Captain 2nd Rank
Major	Major	Captain 3rd Rank
	Junior Officer Personnel	
Captain	Captain	Captain Lieutenant
Senior Lieutenant	Senior Lieutenant	Senior Lieutenant
Lieutenant	Lieutenant	Lieutenant
Junior Lieutenant	Junior Lieutenant	Junior Lieutenant
	Warrants	
Praporshchik	Michman	
	Sergeants	
Starshina	Principle Shipboard Starshina	
Senior Sergeant	Principle Starshina	
Sergeant	Starshina First Step	
Junior Sergeant	Starshina Second Step	
	Soldiers and Sailors	
Corporal	Senior Sailor	
Private	Sailor	

Ranks for KGB officers and other arms of service are the same as those for the Army, except that the highest grade is Colonel General.

Source: *Vedemosti Verkhovnogo Soveta SSSR No. 18,* 26 April 1984.

comprises three grades roughly comparable to what the U.S. Army calls field grades. The Junior Officer component includes four grades that correspond roughly to company grades in the U.S. Army.

The changes in the current (1984) table of ranks over the previous (1971) table involve changes in the higher command personnel only. Specifically, the rank of Marshal of Tank Troops is eliminated, and the subordinate status of all branches of service to the Army is codified. In furtherance of the combined arms concept, only combat support functions maintain a marshal of branch of service. The rank of Chief Marshal of Artillery is probably reserved for the commander of Strategic Rocket Forces.

In November of 1971 a new rank, that of warrant, or *praporshchik* was added between the enlisted ranks and officer grades. This rank was created for technical or administrative specialists who possess specific skills needed in the armed forces. It awards them authority over enlisted men, while separating them from officer components.

The enlisted ranks comprise four sergeant ranks and two soldier ranks. There is no difference in rank between first term and extended service enlisted men.

The personnel structure of the Soviet Army is approximately 20 percent *kadre* and 80 percent inductees. The *kadre* is almost entirely composed of officers, with a few career NCOs and warrant officers. The concept of a professional NCO corps is not part of the Soviet military tradition. Enlisted men of all ranks do exactly as they are told, on time, and without question. Officers are the thinkers and decision makers. A result of this strict division is that every minor detail in the Soviet Army is supervised by an officer, and without an officer in charge, things tend not to get done. Soviet commanders apparently like things this way, because it gives them tighter control.

Title and Addresses

Rank or grade is always used in official addresses, and is always preceded by the traditional communist *tovarishch* (comrade). In addition, certain individual academic achievements are added to the form of address. For instance, an officer earning an engineer *diplom* or license, is referred to as captain (or lieutenant, etc.) engineer. The title "engineer" after rank does not indicate branch of service, it shows educational achievement. Officers who carry their education to the middle level have the title *tekhnicheskoi sluzhboi* (technical service) added to the form of address. Again, the title refers to level of academic achievement rather than branch of service.

Officers' Training and Education

Continuing education is vital to the career of a Soviet officer. Babenko reports that one of every two Soviet officers has completed a middle level education and has earned the title "engineer" or "technical service." In addition, one of every four has completed higher level education and earned the degree of *kandidat* or *doktor*, roughly equivalent to a master's degree or Ph.D.

While it is difficult to compare U.S. and Soviet educational levels because of differences in the systems, one could equate the two-year officers schools that lead to a commission in the Soviet Army to junior colleges. Middle level education is attained after one or two more years in school, and is roughly equivalent to a bachelor's degree. Higher level education requires two years and a major research project for a *kandidat* degree, and three years with major research resulting in a published book for a *doktor* degree.

Soviet officers are, therefore, well educated as a group. Indeed, when compared to Soviet society as a whole, they form an educated elite. Education alone, however, does not make a good commander. As the French military philosopher Ardant Du Picq said, "If you make an officer a schoolboy all his life he will send his profession to the devil, if he can. And those who are able to do so, will in general be those who have received the best education."[1] The Soviet Army avoids this problem by providing commanders with extensive experience at a young age. Most Soviet commanders get their command experience quite early, and they have a lot of it. Even though the official grade for company commanders is captain, most companies are commanded by lieutenants or senior lieutenants. Battalion commanders are majors and captains, even though the authorized rank is lieutenant colonel. Regiments are normally commanded by majors and lieutenant colonels, and colonels often command divisions. In the peacetime Soviet Army, tactical command is generally exercised by officers one to two grades below that which is authorized.

The standard tour of service for Soviet officers is five years, and it is not unusual for an officer to spend all or most of that tour in the same assignment. At first glance, this may seem to imply that the Soviet Army has relatively few highly experienced commanders, that it lacks depth in command experience in event of mobilization. The Soviet ground forces, however, comprise 119 motorized rifle divisions, 46 tank divisions, 8 airborne divisions, 14 artillery divisions, and a host of smaller units. That adds up to a lot of commanders who have been raised in the system. Further, since most commanders received their assignments one or two grades below the authorized grade, there are many experienced commanders available in event of mobilization. It is also well to remember that principal Soviet staff officers are also commanders and are, therefore, experienced and qualified to assume principal command positions.

The Commander

Abraham Lincoln once observed that he would rather have one mediocre general than two good ones, by which he meant that some one identifiable person must be in charge in any military operation. In the Soviet Army, the *komandir* is the responsible person (*otvetsvennyi chelovek*). In a nation of faceless bureaucrats, the army has used this title both to bestow recognition and to define individuals who must answer if things go wrong. So, while the authoritarian character of Soviet society as a whole closely relates to the authoritarian nature of the Soviet Army, the military has found a way to at least partly avoid the deadening effects of the mindless bureaucratism that characterizes Soviet society as a whole.

Edinonachalie

The military term used to describe the authority and responsibility of Soviet military commanders is *edinonachalie*. This essentially untranslatable Russian word is generally rendered into English as "one-man command" or "unity of command." Actually, no English term fully explains the concept of *edinonachalie* or imparts the significance behind it. *Edinonachalie* is defined in the *Soviet Military Encyclopedia* as the most important obligatory requirement from which the structure of the armed forces of the Soviet Union is created.[2] It is the fundamental concept of command in the Soviet Armed Forces.

Reduced to its essence, *edinonachalie* makes the Soviet *komandir* personally responsible to the Communist party of the Soviet Union and to the Soviet government for the morale, discipline, military and political training, combat readiness, and combat activity of his command.[3]

To a degree, most professional soldiers can identify with the concept of *edinonachalie* by way of the tradition that a commander is responsible for everything his unit does—or fails to do. While this perception is correct insofar as it goes, the Soviet concept is much broader.

Philosophically, *edinonachalie* fixes responsibility on an individual. This is generally a difficult task in any large bureaucracy, where anonymity and numbers mask and blur the audit trail for wrong decisions. Hedrick Smith describes the typical attitude toward authority in the Soviet Union as "narrow and finicky adherence to the technicalities and a bull headed stubbornness not to venture an inch beyond the rules, for fear that any initiative will be chastized."[4] *Edinonachalie* holds Soviet commanders individually responsible for results and does not permit them to hide in collective anonymity or to take refuge in the mindless observance of regulations.

Politically, *edinonachalie* marks a maturing of the Soviet state. From the time of the revolution well into the first stage of World War II, the Soviet state maintained a healthy distrust of its military leaders. In the purges of 1937–38 so many officers were eliminated that the Soviet Army was nearly crippled.[5] In fact, until Marshal Zhukov succeeded in curbing the power of the political commissars in the latter half of World War II, the Red Army actually practiced what might be called *dvoenachalie*—two man command—in that no order was official until countersigned by the unit political commissar. In the political sense, *edinonachalie* demonstrates the confidence of the CPSU and the Soviet government in the political reliability, as well as the military competence, of the officer *kadre*.

Militarily, *edinonachalie* means that command authority is centralized and vertically organized. In practical terms, it appears in the concept of an *edinonachalnik*, or unified commander, being appointed for every military administrative, training, or combat operation. The commanders of all elements involved in the particular operation are subordinate to the *edinonachalnik* regardless of their rank or service.

Obshchevoiskovoi Komandir

In operations involving forces from more than one combat arm (such as tank, motorized infantry, frontal aviation, naval, artillery, etc.) the *edinonachalnik* may be designated an *obshchevoiskovoi komandir* (combined arms commander). Normally, the commander of the principal maneuver force in the operation is named the *obshchevoiskovoi komandir*. In some independent operations by large units (army or *front*), a staff officer may be named *obshchevoiskovoi komandir* of the task force, and he may be provided with a staff, or he may create one out of the assets of his subordinate units.

However selected, the *obshchevoiskovoi komandir* has full command authority over all combat, combat support, and combat service support forces assigned to the operation for which he was appointed, regardless of the service affiliation of units or the ranks of the other commanders. In a sense, *obshchevoiskovoi komandir* is an application of the generally accepted military principle of unity of command. It is much stricter and a lot less flexible, however, than other systems such as the U.S. concept of "support" to indicate priority of effort for combat support units or "operational control" to differentiate between command authority and operational authority. The Soviet system does not allow for shadings. Soviet commanders either have full authority and responsibility, or none.

The concept of combined arms operations under a designated combined arms commander is not really new to the Soviet Army. It was often employed in World War II, and in the postwar years it was commonly seen at army level and above (e.g., the designation "combined arms army"). In recent years, however, the practice of using combined arms is becoming increasingly prevalent at lower levels of command, at regiment, battalion, and occasionally even at company level. This will be discussed in detail later.

The Exercise of Command

Someone defined the difference between a celebrity and a VIP by pointing out that the former is important for *who* he or she is, while the latter is important for *what* he or she is. In the Soviet Union, celebrity status, except for a few artists or sports figures, is to be avoided because it implies egoism, personality cults, and other antisocialist values. All Russians, however, want VIP status because it shows recognition for achievement within the *kollektiv*. This recognition is expressed by rank, titles, medals, and badges.

There is in the Soviet exercise of command a sharp distinction between individual responsibility and individualism. Soviet leadership manuals never speak of loyalty between a commander and his subordinates. Loyalty belongs only to the CPSU and the government, and all other personal loyalties interfere with and threaten that structure. Soviet commanders therefore neither expect nor desire loyalty from their subordinates; they do demand strict subordination and exact obedience.

Another example of the distrust of individualism is apparent in the Soviet stress upon collectivism. Commanders, although they have personal responsibility for making command decisions, are expected to consider collective wisdom in reaching their decisions. Soviet military writings describe the official position in these words: "The collective always possesses more experience, wisdom, and insight than any commander. It can do what one man is powerless to do."[6]

The Soviet preference for collectivism in decision making also appears in the Soviet "scientific" perception of combat. The reverence for rules, norms, and regulations in part stems from a perception that these represent a distillation of collective wisdom and are presumably arrived at as a result of careful study. In Soviet terms, they incorporate and generalize a wealth of experience accumulated in armed struggle against the enemy.[7]

A more modern example of the same phenomenon is the growing Soviet interest in the automation of troop control through the use of computers. Automation is seen as a way of reducing the contradiction between the requirement on a fluid battlefield for strict centralized control and the need for more initiative by subordinates.[8] It is also a means of assuring that military decision making in combat is "objective" (i.e., is not based upon individual opinions).[9] A noted Soviet officer explains the Soviet interest in automating troop leading in the following words:

The training of commanders is enhanced by the modeling of battles and mathematical methods in planning the fighting of units. When a commander correctly constructs a battle model, foresees in detail the way in which a battle is to be prepared and conducted with due regard for his own and the enemy's forces, the terrain and all the other factors that influence the outcome, it means that he selects the optimal decision. But this requires the efficient employment of the technical control devices, computers and other instruments, i.e., it requires the automation of troop control.[10]

Modeling is another means of applying collective wisdom to the solution of battlefield problems. In this instance, rather than being expressed in rules and norms, the collective wisdom is applied in building the algorithms and mathematical equations used in the models.

In sum, the Soviet perception of command is that it is not an art, but a science. Soviet officers would be mystified by the old British dictum that "the best tactics are those of the senior officer present." Likewise, any Soviet officer who acts on the American premise that "regulations are but a guide . . . " will probably have a very short, undistinguished military career. The Soviet system tends to produce commanders who are technically qualified and professionally competent. It eliminates the extremes of very poor commanders and inspired and innovative leaders.

The Staff

The staff is a Soviet commander's principal assistant. It extends his presence and carries out the details of planning and executing his mission. While the mission of a Soviet staff is similar to that of other armies, its organization and function are uniquely Russian. For this reason, it is best looked at in its own right and should not be compared with traditional Western models.

All Soviet commanders at battalion level and above have a staff to assist in exercising command. Regiment is the lowest level having a staff performing all the basic staff functions, and for this reason it is a good model for describing the organization and function of a Soviet staff. A Soviet regimental staff is a layered organization under the commander comprising five deputy commanders, eleven chiefs, and two specialists, organized as shown in Figure 3.1. This basic structure is augmented or modified to meet the specific requirements of the various types of units, or it may be tailored to the needs of special missions.

The deputy regimental commander, properly speaking, is not a

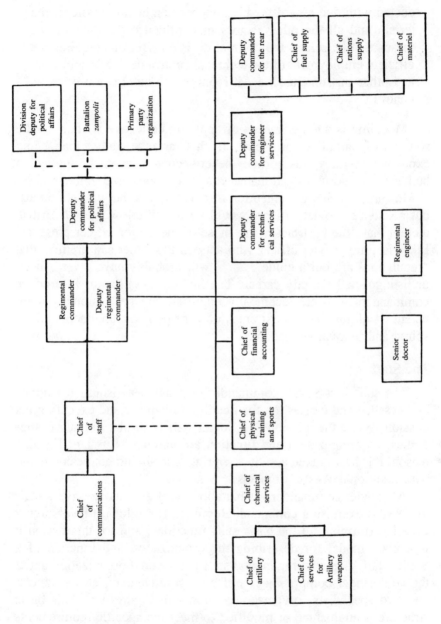

Figure 3.1.   Organization of the Soviet staff

Source: *Ustav Vnutrennei Sluzhby Vooruzhennykh Sil Souza SSR (Internal Service Regulations of the Armed Forces of the USSR)*, Moscow: Voenizdat, 1971, pp. 31–60.

staff officer. He exercises command authority in his own right over all personnel and units attached or organic to the regiment and is specifically responsible for organization, combat readiness, and internal order and discipline in the regiment.

The deputy commander for political affairs, or *zampolit* as he is referred to in Russian, is a uniquely Soviet creation that has long fascinated Western military observers. Historically, this office came into being in the revolutionary period when the fledgling Red Army had to rely upon the military skills of ex-czarist officers whose political loyalty to the new regime was suspect. Stalin perpetuated the concept to split command authority and thereby ensure that the armed forces remained politically subordinate to the party by instituting what was, in essence, a two-man rule: any order had to be signed by both the commander and the *zampolit* to be official. Marshal Zhukov ended this cumbersome arrangement in World War II by subordinating the *zampolit* to the commander in purely military affairs.

This staff position survives today and has become an organic and important part of the Soviet staff system. The *zampolit* is a GPU (Main Political Directorate) officer with a separate chain of communications and command to division and to battalion. In accordance with the principle of *edinonachalie*, however, he is operationally subordinate to the regimental commander. He is specifically answerable to the regimental commander for the organization and condition of party-political work in the regiment.

In a perverse sort of way, the *zampolit* assists the regimental commander by using his separate chain of communications to battalion as a check on the status of subordinate units. This chain extends through the *zampolit* at battalion to the primary party organs at company and platoon levels. The *zampolit* system provides an alternative source of checking and reporting on the situation and conditions within the regiment that is independent of the chain of command.

The *zampolit* also uses his system to promote the success of the regiment. He organizes "voluntary" off-duty activities in support of the objectives of the regimental commander and encourages socialist competition between units for superior military performance. The *zampolit* is, in fact, a key member of the staff who has important combat functions and makes significant contributions to the combat readiness of his unit. At the same time, he adds a degree of tension to the unit because the regimental commander knows that the *zampolit* is reporting to division on activities and on the situation within the regiment. This serves to keep the regimental commander honest.

The **chief of staff,** like the **deputy regimental commander,** exercises command authority in his own name. He is responsible for the overall supervision of the work of the staff in planning and directing combat, combat support, and combat service support in the regiment. By regulations, only one staff officer, the **chief of communications,** is directly subordinate to the chief of staff. The **chief of communications** develops the communications plan for the regiment and supervises the training and operation of communications elements.

The largest staff section is the rear services under the **deputy commander for the rear,** who answers to the **regimental commander** for the organization and security of the regimental rear and directs supply functions related to fuel, rations, and quartermaster. The **deputy commander for the rear,** by regulations, directs the operations of the **chief of fuel supply,** who manages POL (petroleum, oil, and lubricants) resupply in the regiment; the **chief of rations supply,** who procures, stores, and distributes rations; and the **chief of materiel**, who supervises the procurement, maintenance, distribution, and repair of clothing and shelter materiel and equipment. The **deputy commander for technical services** commands all transport units in the regiment and answers to the regimental commander for motor maintenance and repair of wheeled and tracked vehicles. He is a combination transportation officer and motor maintenance officer. By regulations, he is directly subordinate to the regimental commander, but in practice he normally responds to the **chief** of **staff.**

The **deputy commander for engineer services** is responsible for repair, maintenance, and supply of weapons and instruments. His is a technical and logistical function; he is not a sapper or combat engineer. By regulations, he is directly subordinate to the regimental commander, but in practice he normally responds to the **chief of staff.**

The **chief of artillery** answers to the regimental commander for the training of artillery and mortar crews and directs artillery maintenance, resupply of ammunition, and distribution of artillery equipment. He is not a fire support planner, this function being reserved for the artillery battalion commander, as explained in more detail in Chapter 7. In his supply function, the **chief of artillery** is assisted by the **chief of services for artillery weapons,** who is an ordnance specialist. In the field, the **chief of artillery** normally responds to the **chief of staff.**

Sapper and engineer support is planned, coordinated, and supervised by the **regimental engineer,** who also directs the maintenance and resupply of engineering equipment and materiel. He is one of the two specialists on the staff and is directly subordinate to the **regimental commander,** although in the field he normally responds to the **chief of staff.**

The **chief of chemical services** directs chemical, biological, and radiological (CBR) defense measures and training. He also supervises procurement, maintenance, and distribution of CBR equipment and materiel. By regulation, **the chief of chemical services** is directly subordinate to the **regimental commander,** although in the field he normally responds to the **chief of staff.**

The **chief of physical training and sports,** as the title implies, plans and directs physical training, sports, and recreational activities. By regulations, he is directly subordinate to the **regimental commander,** but normally operates under the supervision of the **chief of staff.**

The **chief of financial accounting** maintains the regimental money records and accounts. This is a tedious but important duty, as the Soviet regiment operates on cash for purchase of some rations and supplies and uses cash awards as incentives. The **chief of financial accounting** by regulations reports to the **regimental commander.** While the **chief of staff** normally supervises his daily operations, the wise **regimental commander** takes a personal interest in this function.

The other specialist on the regimental staff is the **senior doctor.** He tracks health problems, directs health and medical services, and supervises medical training, maintenance of medical equipment, and the distribution of medical supplies. The **senior doctor** by regulations reports directly to the **regimental commander,** but normally functions under the supervision of the chief of staff.

At a glance, it appears that the **regimental commander** has a rather wide span of control, extending to thirteen staff officers as well as his subordinate commanders. In actual practice, the system is much more streamlined. In the field, the regimental commander normally operates from a forward command observation post with the **deputy regimental commander** and the *zampolit,* along with combat support and intelligence unit commanders. The operations and intelligence functions are performed by this group at the regimental command observation post. The **chief of staff** normally directs the operations of the regiment's main command post and supervises the operations of the remaining staff.

An interesting aspect of the Soviet staff system is that two of the most important functions in the U.S. staff system, operations and intelligence, are apparently left out. This is because the Soviet system is designed to incorporate these in one tactical function and place it firmly in the personal hands of the commander. Soviet commanders, especially at division and below, are expected to concentrate their attention on fighting their units and to use their staffs to attend to the other functions. The **chief of staff** gathers and maintains pertinent data on the enemy, terrain, weather, and friendly forces to keep the regimental commander informed on the current situation. He is assisted in this intelligence function by the commander of the reconnaissance company, who also acts as the **chief of reconnaissance** and coordinates all of the regiment's intelligence gathering and reporting. It is important to understand that in the Soviet staff system, the commander personally performs intelligence analysis and makes the tactical decisions. The chief of staff maintains the situation and supplies data.

The functional chiefs in the Soviet staff system are responsible for three functions: training, planning, and logistics. In their training and planning functions, regimental staff officers actively involve themselves in battalion operations and training in their particular specialty. The same is true in logistics where functions are separated by arm of service rather than centralized. This structure involves higher headquarters staff officers in the day-to-day business of subordinate units to a far greater extent than is acceptable in Western military tradition.

The battalion staff is a much simplified version of a regimental staff. The battalion commander is supported by a **deputy battalion commander,** a *zampolit,* a **chief of staff,** and a **deputy commander for technical services,** who is primarily a motor maintenance officer. Medical service is directed by a **senior aidman,** and there is a CBR NCO. Obviously, a battalion is not organized to operate for any extended period of time without logistical and administrative support from regiment, and the involvement of regimental staff officers in battalion functions is, to a degree, necessary.

A Soviet tactical unit normally operates two command installations in the field: a **command observation post** and a **main command post.** The command observation post, as the designation implies, is located close to the front and is sited to afford maximum observation of the unit area. It is generally manned by the commander, the deputy commander, the *zampolit,* the chief of intelligence, and the attached or organic artillery commander and is supported by a small communications and administrative support team. In maneuver regiments and battalions, the entire group is normally mounted in armored command vehicles for mobility and protection. The commander fights his unit from the command observation post.

The remainder of the staff is at the main command post, which is under the supervision of the chief of staff and is further to the rear than the command observation post. The main command post exercises administrative and logistics functions and is the center for routine reporting on the tactical situation.

Troop Leading Procedures

The process of preparing for a combat operation is referred to in the Soviet lexicon as *planirovanie operatsii* (planning of the operation).[11] It begins when a commander receives preliminary instructions (*predvaritelnoe rasporiazhenie*) from his higher headquarters.

The commander initiates his work by developing his concept of the operation (*zamysel operatsii*). The concept is worked out by the commander with the assistance of his principal assistant, the *zampolit.* It includes tasks for each subordinate unit and establishes the organization for combat by designating echelons and reserves. Tasks are generally classified in terms of whether they are immediate (*blizhaishie zadachi*) or subsequent (*promezhutochnie zadachi*). It is traditional, although not always true, that the concept of the operation is perceived as a series of steps (*etap*), one following the other, with immediate tasks being accomplished in the first steps, and subsequent tasks being included in later steps. Steps are usually defined in terms of time and terrain, while tasks are defined in terms of forces and firepower.

The staff does the basic work of developing the commander's concept of the operation into an operations order and of setting in motion the various actions necessary to execute it. The preferred method of staff work is the sequential method (*posledovatelnyi metod*), in which the higher staff finishes work on each portion of the order and then passes detailed instructions to subordinate units. When time is of the essence, as is often the case on the modern battlefield, the staff uses the parallel method (*parallelnyi metod*), in which the higher and subordinate staffs work at the same time.

Communications

The Soviet Army preaches that the state of communications, called the nervous system of command, largely predetermines the effectiveness of the employment of forces and weapons in combat and, eventually, the outcome of battle.[12] According to the chief of communications of the Soviet Armed Forces, Marshal of Signal Forces A. I. Belov, the key characteristics of combat communications systems are secrecy, reliability, survivability, and capacity.[13]

The Soviet Army is especially sensitive to the problems of communications security because of its historical experience. The greatest defeat in the history of Russian arms and one of the classic battles of annihilation in all of military history occurred in September of 1914 near Koenigsberg in East Prussia when a small German army totally destroyed a greatly superior Russian force. Modern Soviet historians attribute the defeat to a breakdown in Russian command authority and German interception of Russian orders transmitted by radio.[14] In studying World War II, historians discovered that 70 percent of the most reliable German intelligence on the Eastern Front resulted from interception of Soviet tactical radio communications.

Reliability is of particular concern because World War II combat experience demonstrated that unreliable and primitive Soviet communications robbed Soviet commanders of the flexibility to exploit unexpected opportunities in fluid battle situations. Much of the rigidity that characterized Soviet tactics on the Eastern Front was a result of attempts to compensate for inadequate tactical communications with detailed plans and inflexible orders.

Historical experience and a full appreciation of Western ELINT/ EW (Electronic Intelligence/Electronic Warfare) capabilities have combined to make modern Soviet combat commanders especially mindful of the vulnerabilities of their own electronic emitters. Soviet communications practices clearly demonstrate this concern in their heavy emphasis on communications discipline and security.

Soviet commanders are concerned about the capacity of modern tactical communications because increasingly sophisticated weapons systems, the higher tempo of modern battles, and the expansion of the battle area in depth, width, and altitude generate an ever increasing volume of traffic which must be transmitted in ever shorter periods of time over ever increasing distances. While these same challenges face all modern armies, the Soviet Army is developing its own unique responses. The ensuing explanation of how Soviet tactical communications operate is based primarily upon the communications for combat maneuver battalions, because it demonstrates the elements of a complete internal system and its interaction with higher, adjacent, and attached units.

Basic Communications Practices

The chief of communications is the staff officer directly responsible for planning, operating, and supervising unit tactical communications. He is subordinate to and answers directly to the chief of staff and, in combat, operates out of the main command post. The primary means of communications for highly mobile and widely dispersed forces is radio. However, it is a standard Soviet practice to limit the use of radios as much as possible and to make maximum use of other means such as wire, mounted messengers, audio and visual signals, and pyrotechnics. Responsibility for establishing and maintaining communications runs from higher to lower and from right to left. For specific communications planning, Soviet sources use standard procedures built around three types of combat operations: the march, the defense, and the offense.

The March

The preferred means of communications in units on the march are messengers and audio and visual signals. To preserve security, radio transmissions are limited to enemy contact; however, all receivers maintain listening silence and may receive, but not acknowledge messages. In daylight, signal flags are habitually used to pass commands along columns, and flashlights or illuminated wands serve a similar purpose during darkness. Where noise discipline is not a consideration, vehicle horns and other noise devices are used to pass prearranged signals.

Movement is regulated by traffic control posts set out by the advanced party in front of the main body. In marches conducted by division or higher headquarters, control posts are often manned by specially trained traffic regulator troops in distinctive black uniforms with white reflectorized cross belts. For independent movements by regiment or smaller units, organic troops can be assigned regulator duty.

Control posts regulate the march by controlling the direction, order, and rate of march, and the distance between units (Fig. 3.2). Preferably, control posts report to the headquarters controlling the march by wire, although occasionally radio is used. In many cases, they have no communications at all and report through motorized messengers moving along the route of march.

Communications with march units is usually by motor messengers, often on motorcycles, who deliver the mail while riding along the column. Another means is to transmit messages to traffic control posts to be handed to commanders as they pass. At halts, the battalion chief of staff usually "rides the circuit,"[11] visiting each march unit commander for personal communication. If time permits, foot or motor messengers may be dispatched to the battalion commander.

March security is heavily dependent upon reducing use of radios to the absolute minimum. Where reliance upon radio cannot be avoided, every effort is made to make transmissions from stationary sites remote from the route of march, as indicated in Figure 3.2. To enforce listening silence, it is standard practice in some units to require that microphones be disconnected until contact is made with the enemy.

The Defense

In the defense the preferred means of communications is wire, with radio serving as the alternate means. As during the march, radio stations maintain listening silence and may transmit only in event of enemy contact. Emergency messages such as warnings of CBR attack may be disseminated by radio, but stations do not generally acknowledge receipt.

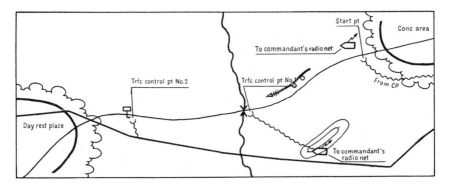

Figure 3.2.   Communications of a battalion on the march

Source: *Soviet Military Review*, no. 4, 1982.

As one of the first steps in organizing the defense, the chief of communications plans and establishes the wire net. At battalion, field wire may be used initially and is always used below company level. The basic wire system, however, uses battle cable in 100-meter lengths with quick-connects to link switchboards. Battalion installs the net, laying primary and alternate lines to each organic company and attached unit. Standard practice is to lay lines on the ground and to overhead them only where they cross vehicle tracks. When crossing roads, line crews will look for culverts and bridges to lay lines under rather than over the road.

Since a battalion net averages 10 to 12 kilometers of cable, maintenance of wire communications is a formidable and never-ending task. Although it is preferable to bury wire, the high tempo of modern combat seldom offers the time to complete this task, so it is standard practice to prepare slit trenches every 50 to 75 meters along communications lines to protect line crews from shell fragments and small arms. Reliability is improved by redundancy in laying more than one line to each switchboard, and by looping communications so that communications can be maintained by alternate switching. A type wire net for a motorized rifle battalion in the defense is shown in Figure 3.3.

Regiment lays landline communications to the battalion command post; however, battalions are responsible for installing and maintaining the regimental lateral lines to flanking battalions, in accordance with the right-to-left basic communications procedures. Battalions also

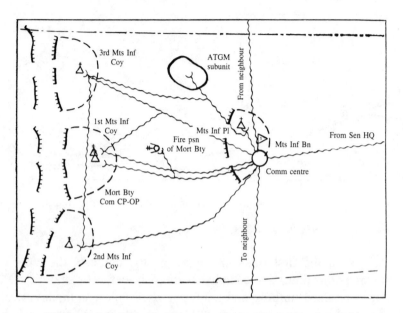

Figure 3.3.   Telephone wire communications schematic

Source: *Soviet Military Review,* no. 11, 1981, p. 20.

install and maintain landlines to regimental units in the battalion sector. Maintenance of regimental lines within a battalion sector, once the line is installed, is a battalion responsibility.

Radio is used to direct the battle after enemy contact is made if the wire lines are cut, as is often the case. The communications center for both wire and radio nets is at the battalion main command post where the chief of staff exercises staff supervison.

The Offense

Soviet commanders depend upon radio communications in offensive operations more than in any other battlefield situation. Even so, they go to great lengths to control and limit the volume of radio transmissions. Up to the time of departure, telephone landlines, traffic regulator posts, and messengers are used in a manner similar to that described for marches. Other signal means, such as prearranged pyrotechnics, searchlights, aircraft, or tracer fire, are used to supplement radio, but only radio has the flexibility and speed necessary to control a fast-moving combat situation.

The radio communications system of a Soviet maneuver battalion displays the basic structure and function of Soviet tactical radio communications. The system can be described as operating in four nets: a higher headquarters net, a battalion command net, a technical services net, and a fire support net. Each net comprises a number of subnets, and a battalion may operate on as many as sixteen separate frequencies.

Soviet radio communications practices include two modes of operation. In the standard mode, stations-maintain a receiver-transmitter on a frequency to routinely pass communications. If the station passing a message wishes a response, it ends the transmission with the word *priem* (transmit). Otherwise the addressee does not acknowledge receipt. The other mode involves switching to the frequency of the station to be contacted only long enough to pass specific information. This mode is often used in administrative nets or when a battalion commander wishes to communicate directly with a platoon commander, or a regimental commander with a company commander. It is also used for coordination between commanders of adjacent units.

The higher headquarters net for a maneuver battalion is the regimental net. The interface between battalion and regiment is depicted in Figure 3.4. The battalion commander and chief of staff both op-

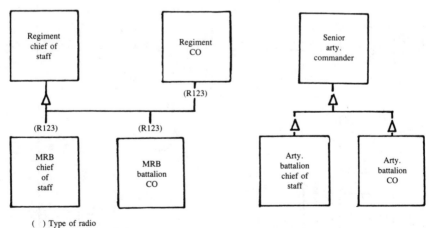

( ) Type of radio
△ Switch to net as required

Figure 3.4. Type communications net with regiment, Soviet reinforced motorized rifle battalion

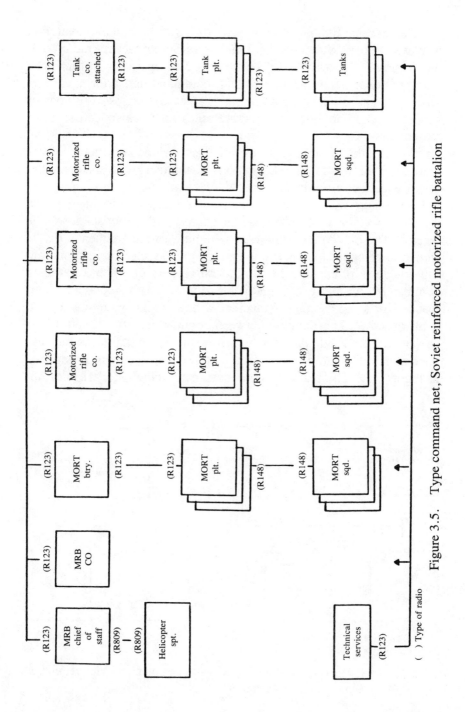

Figure 3.5.   Type command net, Soviet reinforced motorized rifle battalion

( ) Type of radio

erate FM radios on the regimental commander's frequency to pass commands and critical tactical information. Since the chiefs of staff normally operate at the main command posts, the battalion chief of staff may also enter the frequency of the regimental chief of staff to pass routine reports and administrative messages. This practice keeps routine traffic from cluttering the command net.

All organic companies and attached combat and combat support units operate on the battalion command frequency along with the chief of staff and the battalion commander. In turn, each company is as-

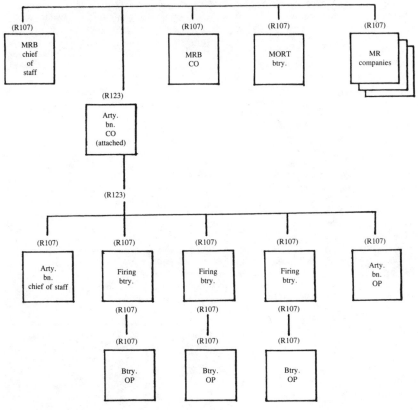

( ) Type of radio

Figure 3.6.   Type fire support net, Soviet reinforced motorized rifle battalion

Source: Deduced from Col. D. Moskalenko, *"Sviaz' Rabotala Ustoichivo"* ("Communications Functioned Steadily") *Voennyi Vestnik,* no. 4, 1982, p. 24.

signed company and platoon frequencies. Figure 3.5 is a schematic of the battalion command net. The technical service net has its own frequency but normally comprises only one station. Other stations requiring technical services support switch to that frequency as necessary.

The fire support net for a motorized rifle battalion comprises the battalion commander, the chief of staff, and the company commanders and operates on a frequency distinct from the command net. If

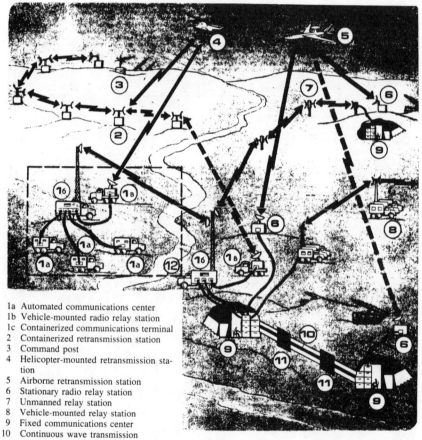

1a Automated communications center
1b Vehicle-mounted radio relay station
1c Containerized communications terminal
2   Containerized retransmission station
3   Command post
4   Helicopter-mounted retransmission station
5   Airborne retransmission station
6   Stationary radio relay station
7   Unmanned relay station
8   Vehicle-mounted relay station
9   Fixed communications center
10 Continuous wave transmission
11 Unmanned booster station
12 Mobile communications center

Figure 3.7.   Schematic of Soviet higher level communications

Source: *Tekhnika i Vooruzhenie*, no. 5, 1982, p. 46.

there is an attached artillery battalion, the artillery battalion commander also operates in this net, as well as in his own battalion net. Figure 3.6 is a schematic of a battalion fire support net.

Communications Beyond Regiment

The rather simple communications system for tactical units becomes more sophisticated at higher levels of command, as shown in Figure 3.7. As distances between terminal stations increase, directional microwave transmitters replace landlines and battle cable. For UHF and VHF transmissions, there are ground-mounted and airborne relay stations. Communications centers may be mounted in vehicles; however, they are often housed in sophisticated underground complexes, connected by cable to remote transmitting and receiving stations. These systems form the communications background behind the tactical communications system.

Conclusions

The Soviet command and staff system is the means by which Soviet commanders plan, direct, and fight the battle. While it does perform the same functions as the command and staff systems traditional in all other modern armies, it operates in a unique way. It reflects a specifically Soviet tension between distrust of the individual and the military requirement for unity of command. On the one hand, the guiding principle is *edinonachalie*. However, individuality is suppressed by a number of mechanisms designed to stress collective wisdom. Rather than imagination and initiative, the Soviet Army values precise execution of orders and grim determination to carry on whatever the odds.

Unity of command is a cardinal principle. However, authority and responsibility are generally narrowly defined and are vertically rather than horizontally executed. This vertical structure, along with the uniquely Soviet institution of the *zampolit*, provides senior commanders with a number of sources of information on, and means of influencing, events within subordinate units.

While the Soviet command and staff system has undeniable shortcomings and contradictions, experience in World War II and afterward clearly shows that it works. In combat, it is particularly effective in that it encourages commanders to fight the battle from positions well forward. The stern superior-subordinate relationship and emphasis on strict obedience to orders detract from flexibility and reinforce that determination to continue the fight regardless of circumstances.

For all its faults, the Soviet command and control system creates a tough, brave, well-disciplined foe who, though not likely to display brilliance or imagination, will be careful, calculating, well-prepared, and relentless. Command and control weaknesses have been traditional in Russian military history, but the current system results from the strenuous and long-term efforts of Soviet military planners to provide their commanders with effective equipment, operational techniques, and organization. C^3 can no longer be considered a major Soviet weakness.

Notes

1. Col. Ardant Du Picq, *Battle Studies*, transl. and ed. Col. John Greely and Maj. Robert C. Cotton, Harrisburg: Military Service Publishing Co., p. 219.
2. "Edinonachalie" ("One-Man Command"), *Sovetskaia Voennaia Entsiklopediia*, 8 vols., Moscow: Voenizdat, 1977, vol. 3, p. 301. See also definition of principle in Gen. Maj. S.N. Kozlov, ed., *Officer's Handbook*, Moscow, 1971. Published under the auspices of the U.S. Air Force, p. 4.
3. *Dictionary of Basic Military Terms*, Moscow: Voenizdat, 1965. Published under the auspices of the U.S. Air Force, p. 74.
4. Hedrick Smith, *The Russians*, New York: Quadrangle Books, 1976, p. 265.
5. Roy A. Medvedev, *Let History Judge*, New York: Alfred A. Knopf, 1972, p. 245. See also Robert Conquest, *The Great Terror*, New York: Macmillan Co., 1973, pp. 277–322.
6. A. Babenko, *Soviet Officers*, Moscow: Progress Publishers, 1976, p. 36.
7. Babenko, op. cit., p. 94.
8. Col. V. M. Bondarenko and Col. A. F. Volkov, eds., *Avtomatizatsiia Upravleniia Voiskami*, Moscow: Voenizdat, 1977, pp. 22–23.
9. Gen. T. E. Shavrov and Col. M. I. Galkin, eds., *Metodologiia Voenno-Nauchnogo Poznaniia*, Moscow: Voenizdat, 1977, p. 18.
10. Babenko, op. cit., p. 99.
11. *Sovetskaia Voennaia Entsiklopediia*, op. cit., vol. 6, pp. 349–50.
12. Marshal A. I. Belov, "Communications and Troop Control," *Soviet Military Review*, no. 4, 1980, p. 22.
13. Ibid., p. 24.
14. *Sovetskaia Voennaia Entsiklopediia*, op. cit., vol. 2, pp. 378–79.

CHAPTER 4

The Offense

> Only the offensive leads to the attainment
> of victory over the enemy.
>
> Col. A. A. Sidorenko

In the same way that Pearl Harbor taught the United States a stern lesson on the cost of a lack of vigilance, Barbarossa taught the Soviet Union a nearly fatal lesson on the cost of military unpreparedness. To avoid fighting another world war on Soviet soil, the Soviet Army has made the offensive the heart of its military doctrine.

Since the end of World War II, the Soviet Army has pursued the capability to launch and sustain an offensive with such single-minded intensity that the West is being forced into an increasingly divisive debate as to how—or even whether—it can stop the onslaught, should it come. In fact, a sort of symbiosis seems to be emerging wherein the growing Soviet offensive capability feeds development of increasingly sophisticated Western hardware designed to cancel Soviet offensive superiority, while the Warsaw Pact, in turn, continues to improve its offensive capability by fielding ever larger and better trained and equipped formations.

The Soviet devotion to the offensive does not simply reflect aggressive geopolitical intentions. It grows from a fervently held belief that if a war is to be fought, it must be won at least cost to the USSR, and that the only way to accomplish that task is to "smash the enemy forces and seize important territory."[1]

Three Concepts for the Offense

A study of official Soviet sources on offensive operations suggests that there are three basic concepts for conduct of the offense. Although official Soviet sources do not specifically identify these concepts as such, I refer to them as exploiting faults, attacking weakness, and attacking strength. Which concept is employed in a given situation depends upon the correlation of forces and on the actual battle situation at the specific time and location.

The concept of exploiting faults was developed in the early stages of World War II when the Red Army was attempting to stabilize the front and to assume the offensive.[2] As used here, *fault* refers to any opportunity created by weather, terrain, enemy error, or the combat situation to strike a painful blow at the enemy, without risking decisive engagement or defeat of Soviet forces. It is employed when the correlation of forces does not clearly favor Soviet forces, or is even against them. Its purpose is to gain the initiative by forcing the enemy to think defensively, and to gradually change the correlation of forces in favor of the Soviet Army through attrition and exhaustion of the enemy.

The classic and most often used concept for the offense is to attack weakness. It entails extensive maneuver to deliver the main blow at a weak point in the enemy's defense or upon the flanks or rear of the defender.[3] Attacking weakness requires what the Soviet Army assumes will be the most probable combat situation, in which the attacker has combat superiority but the defender also has strong and well-organized forces. Since it emphasizes speed, surprise, and maneuver more than massive numerical superiority, attacking weakness is especially relevant on a modern battlefield where weapons of mass destruction may be used.

Attacking strength is the shortest and quickest way to decisively win a battle; however, it is the least often used concept because it requires a significant combat advantage over an enemy whose main force is vulnerable to defeat. It entails a quick, heavy overpowering blow launched directly at the enemy's main strength at the outset of a campaign, with subsequent operations being devoted to deep exploitation and sweeping up the shattered remnants of the enemy force.[4] Soviet references to this type of operation talk of a slashing frontal blow (*rassekaushii frontal'nyi udar*) with the main effort being delivered over a wide front to shatter the defending force into isolated and disorganized groups to be bypassed in the process of achieving deeper objectives.[5] It was used in the late stages of World War II when the *Wehrmacht* lacked sufficient resources to develop mobile reserves and a defense in depth.

The concepts are not exclusive; any offensive campaign may employ a combination of them either sequentially or in concert. They all depend upon local combat superiority and effective intelligence. Intelligence, of course, means knowing the weather and terrain and the enemy's capabilities, deployments, and intentions. Combat superiority is a rather subjective evaluation of a quantitative comparison of enemy or friendly forces and a qualitative assessment of mobility, firepower, and other judgmental factors. It is usually described as the correlation of forces.

The Soviet Army expects to create or to improve the conditions favoring any of these concepts by using what it refers to as weapons of mass destruction: nuclear, chemical, or biological weapons. Nuclear weapons can be employed to dramatically alter the balance of combat power or to create weak points in an otherwise strong enemy defense. Chemical and biological weapons are especially useful for creating faults over a wide front in a well-organized enemy defense. Soviet maneuver forces mounted in armored, tracked vehicles that protect crews against the residual effects of weapons of mass destruction are especially suited to exploiting these conditions.

The application of these concepts on a modern battlefield implies a degree of aggressiveness, flexibility, and initiative on the part of Soviet commanders at all levels considerably beyond that which Western analysts have generally been willing to credit them with having. These concepts demand that Soviet commanders possess an in-depth understanding of their enemy's organization, weapons, and tactics and place a high premium on accurate and timely battlefield intelligence. The remainder of this discussion describes how these requirements are met in the planning and conduct of offensive operations by the Soviet Army.

Planning the Offense

The preceding chapter described the Soviet viewpoint that war is a phenomenon governed by "scientific" laws, principles, and rules and that the process of command is the objective application of these governing processes in the solution of specific military problems and tasks. This viewpoint suggests that decision making can be guided by use of algorithms and mathematical models carefully constructed to apply collective wisdom, historical experience, and objective data in a scientific way to any military situation.[6] Soviet sources refer to this scientific process in the terms *concept, algorithm,* and *decision.*

In this sense, *concept* refers to the volitional aspects of the mission assigned to a commander and to his understanding of the requirements it places upon his command. The term *algorithm,* defined as an orderly sequence of steps for making a decision, is a carefully structured decision-making process. *Decision* refers to how and when to implement and execute the concept. Soviet commanders are trained to apply this process in planning and executing the offense.

Concept

When a Soviet commander receives the order to attack, he understands that the fundamental mission is to kill or capture enemy troops and to destroy or seize enemy equipment within the assigned area and within a stated period of time.[7] The mission for the commander of a first echelon tactical unit normally comprises three elements: an immediate mission (*blizhaiashcha zadacha*), a subsequent mission (*posledyushchaia zadacha*), and a direction of further attack (*napravlenie dal'neishego nastupleniia*).[8] Regiments and divisions may also be assigned a mission of the day (*zadacha dnia*), which is literally the task to be accomplished within a twenty-four-hour period.[9] Within a mission statement there may be a group of specified tasks assigned in order of priority. As a rule, the primary task is the destruction of enemy nuclear weapons and their delivery capabilities.[10] The next task in order of priority is normally destruction of command and control facilities, and the remaining tasks are usually specific to that particular operation.

The priority of tasks is important to a commander both in planning and executing the attack. In planning, obviously, the weight and perhaps the timing of the operation will be ordered according to the priority of tasks. However, the priority of tasks can result in changes in the plan while the battle is in process. For example, if in the battle a tank battalion discovers the firing position of an enemy nuclear-capable artillery battalion, the commander is expected to redirect his operations at the destruction of that unit before continuing with the operation. The specification and ordering of these tasks is a way of building flexibility into an operational plan.

Algorithm

The Soviet Army believes that a properly constructed algorithm is a scientific system for considering all pertinent data in their proper sequence and relative importance, and for applying collective wisdom in battlefield decision making. It has only been recently, however, that a number of diverse Soviet sources have provided clues as to the content and structure of the algorithm used in offensive operations. A perception of the structure and content of the algorithm developed through inductive analysis is shown in Figure 4.1. In essence, the algorithm appears to be constructed to sequentially address the five considerations on the left side of Figure 4.1 and to integrate the responses into the commander's decision.

The Enemy

The Soviet Army's perception of the offensive includes three different military operations: meeting engagement (*vstrechnyi boi*), attack of a defending enemy (*ataka*), and pursuit of a withdrawing or retreating enemy (*presledovatelnyi boi*).[11] Each of these operations suggests a certain organization for combat (*boevoy poriadok*). The Soviet perception of *boevoy poriadok* addresses organization of forces to accomplish tasks, echelonment of forces including battle formations, and deployment.

Organization of forces is the structuring of subordinate units to tailor their capabilities to the requirements in their specific tasks. In this way, maneuver elements of tanks and motorized infantry may be combined with fire support and service elements according to need.

Echelonment of Forces

Echelonment of forces provides depth and flexibility to attacking formations. In the offense, it is standard practice to deploy in one, two, or three echelons. A single echelon is used on a wide front to place maximum combat power forward and is generally used against a relatively weak or disorganized enemy. The most often used formation is two echelons because it affords both heavy combat power forward, and depth. Three echelons are used only when terrain or tactical considerations constrict maneuver space or when speed of movement is paramount. It is the least desired formation.

An echelon is structured upon major subordinate units, battalions

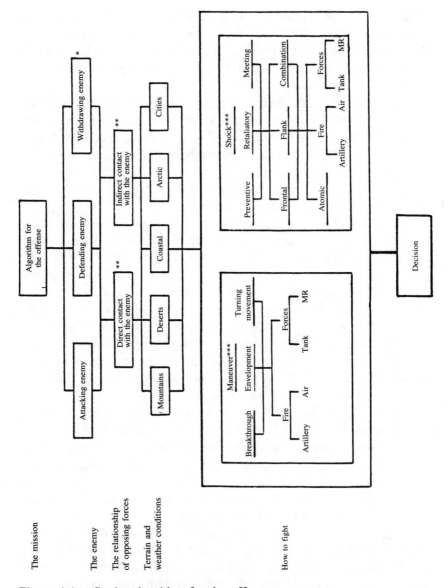

Figure 4.1.   Soviet algorithm for the offense
Sources: * Gen. Maj. Rimskii Korsakov, "*Osnovy Sovremennogo Nastupatel'nogo Boia,*"
            Voennyi Vestnik, no. 3, 1981.
         ** Col. A. A. Sidorenko, "*Nastuplenie,*" *Sovetskaia Voennaia Entsiklopediia,* 8
            vols., Moscow: Voenizdat, Vol. 5, pp. 518–22.
        *** Gen. Maj. I. Vorob'ev, "*Oruzhia i Taktika,*" *Krasnaia Zvezda,* 12 January
            1982, p. 2.

for a regiment or regiments for a division. Since individual commanders must normally decide their own *boevoy poriadok,* echelonment is seldom uniform. For example, a regiment may be deployed in two echelons while its subordinate battalions are in one, two, or three echelon formations.

In the Soviet view, forces in echelon are committed forces, regardless of whether they are in contact with the enemy, because each echelon has an assigned mission and tasks. Often, second and third echelons have the same mission as the first echelon but are assigned a task of adding depth to the battle by exploiting the success of the first echelon, or of maintaining the momentum of the attack by replacing or reinforcing a first echelon force.

In the Soviet Army, a reserve is a small, uncommitted force constituted to deal with unexpected contingencies, usually defined as enemy counteractions. If a Soviet commander constitutes a reserve, it is normally two subordinate units lower. For a battalion, the reserve is normally a platoon; for a regiment, a company. The reserve may, however, be reinforced with special capabilities such as antitank weapons or engineer troops. In the offense, a reserve is seldom constituted in other than a single-echelon formation.

There are ways to vary a single echelon to conform to the enemy or the terrain. Figure 4.2 depicts an on-line formation (*v liniu*), an incline left (*ustup v levo*), and an incline right (*ustup v pravo*).

The Soviet Army believes that modern battle, especially in the first stage of the war, will most likely be characterized by meeting engagements because of the great maneuverability of forces and the range and firepower of modern weapons.[12] Combat will comprise a number of intense battles between separate forces committing to battle from the march over a wide front and in confusing situations where there are no clearly defined front lines.

Figure 4.3 depicts the Soviet perception of the battlefield. This schematic is worth careful study because it shows the Soviet perception of a meeting engagement and of a modern battlefield with more clarity than a volume of words. To begin with, the direction arrow in the left corner clearly implies an East-West (Warsaw Pact–NATO) conflict, and the mushroom clouds indicate use of tactical weapons of mass destruction. The integration of air, missile, tank, motorized rifle, artillery, and airborne forces into a combined air-land battle with deep attack of the enemy's follow-on echelon illustrates the Soviet concern with the concept of a combined arms commander, described

ON LINE	INCLINE RIGHT	INCLINE LEFT

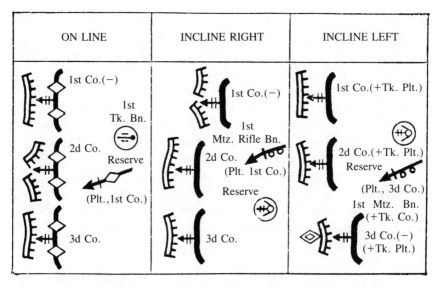

FIGURE 4.2   SINGLE ECHELON FORMATIONS

Source: *Sovetskaia Voennaia Entsiklopediia*, Moscow: Voenizdat, Vol. 1, p.533.

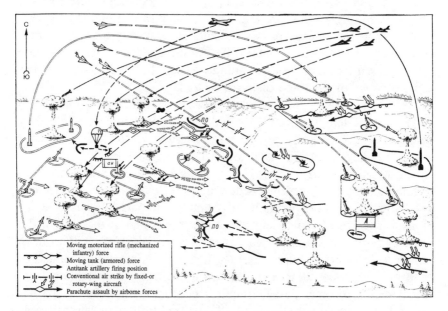

Moving motorized rifle (mechanized infantry) force
Moving tank (armored) force
Antitank artillery firing position
Conventional air strike by fixed-or rotary-wing aircraft
Parachute assault by airborne forces

Figure 4.3.   Schematic of a Meeting Engagement

Source: *Sovetskaia Voennaia Entsiklopediia*, Moscow: Voenizdat, Vol. 2, p. 406.

in Chapter 3. It depicts forces entering battle from the march and the extensive use of maneuver to strike the enemy flanks and rear.

Many actions are occurring simultaneously on this battlefield. The overall flow of the battle is the sum of many smaller engagements of subordinate units. Some forces are attacking, while others are involved in meeting engagements. Still other forces are pursuing defeated enemy groups, while some forces are temporarily on the defense. All of the basic forms of combat action are represented: attack, meeting engagement, pursuit, and defense.

An attack, *ataka,* is defined as the employment of fire and maneuver in combination to destroy the enemy. In the ground forces, the term is used generally to refer to tactical combat operations against an occupied enemy position or installation. The enemy force is fixed, or on the defense, while Soviet forces possess the initiative, and are on the offensive.

A meeting engagement, *vstrechaushchii boi,* occurs when both enemy and friendly forces are on the offensive, and meet while on the move. According to current Soviet military theory, this is the most likely form of combat under conditions where weapons of mass destruction may be, or are, being employed. A meeting engagement is characterized by an obscure and rapidly changing situation, and relatively short but intense battles as both sides swiftly build up forces in contact to gain and maintain the initiative. Commanders operate with exposed flanks and expect little assistance from adjacent or higher units because of time and distance factors.

An unfavorable outcome of the meeting engagement may force Soviet troops temporarily to assume a defensive posture while they reorganize to launch an attack, as described earlier. A successful meeting engagement may lead to a pursuit.

A pursuit (*presledovatelnyi boi*) is defined as an attack on a retreating enemy to complete his destruction. Soviet sources recognize two types of pursuit: parallel and frontal.[13] A parallel pursuit envisions a high-speed movement along the flanks and at the rear of the enemy to surround him. It was often used in World War II in deep winter to prevent retreating German forces from reaching wooded or built-up areas where they could achieve a margin of protection from the elements. Frontal pursuit requires continuous attacks on the enemy's flanks and rear to force him to turn and fight under unfavorable circumstances.

The Relationship Between Opposing Forces

Whether opposing forces are in contact is a matter of concern with regard to how time and space factors affect the capability to plan the battle, organize for combat, and deploy forces in battle. The rule of thumb defining direct contact is that the enemy is within range of organic weapons. Under this definition, a regiment might be in direct contact although its organic battalions and companies are not. Units not in direct contact have more mobility as they have no responsibility for conduct of the battle in progress. The impact of these time-distance factors on the planning and preparation for battle are rather specifically defined in nomographs that tell Soviet commanders how soon they will engage the enemy and to what extent they can deploy their forces under various conditions.[14] Figure 4.4 is a sample of this type of computation.

Terrain and Weather Conditions

Terrain and weather are categorized under six specific conditions: normal or usual, which applies to Central Europe as a whole, and five special conditions defined as mountain, desert, coastal, arctic, and cities.[15] Each condition has specific influences on the organization for combat and how the battle is fought.

Mountain Warfare

The way the Soviet Army solves the problems of combat in special weather and terrain conditions is most apparent in the case of mountain warfare, because it has recently become a subject of some interest. Undoubtedly, problems encountered in Afghanistan account for much of this interest, but certainly not all of it. It is also possible that there has been a conscious reassessment of relative threats and a focusing of greater concern on the Soviet southern border, which is lined with mountains from the Black Sea to the Sea of Japan. While Afghanistan is probably not the sole reason for recent Soviet interest in mountain warfare operations, it probably exposed operational weaknesses in this environment.

Since serious Soviet concern with mountain warfare is a fairly recent phenomenon, there is no single authoritative source on the subject. There is, however, a rapidly growing library of varied sources that, when taken as a whole, give a rather clear picture of how moun-

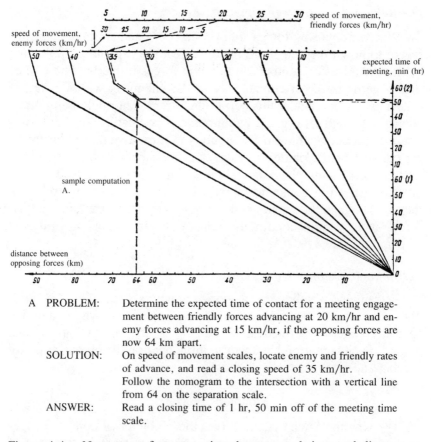

A PROBLEM: Determine the expected time of contact for a meeting engage-
                ment between friendly forces advancing at 20 km/hr and en-
                emy forces advancing at 15 km/hr, if the opposing forces are
                now 64 km apart.

   SOLUTION: On speed of movement scales, locate enemy and friendly rates
                of advance, and read a closing speed of 35 km/hr.
                Follow the nomogram to the intersection with a vertical line
                from 64 on the separation scale.

   ANSWER: Read a closing time of 1 hr, 50 min off of the meeting time
                scale.

Figure 4.4.   Nomogram for computing the expected time and distance to
               the probable line of contact with the enemy

Source: A. Ia. Vainer, *Takticheskie Raschety* (*Tactical Computations*), Moscow: Voenizdat,
          1982, p. 45.

tain warfare techniques are derived and of Soviet concepts for the
conduct of mountain warfare.

It appears that data on operations in Afghanistan are being subjected to careful scrutiny in the various branch service schools in the
USSR to discover problems in technology and techniques. The results
of this analysis are used to develop concepts for operations in mountains, not against guerrillas or irregular forces, but against conventional ground forces. These concepts are then tested in maneuvers in

the mountainous regions of the USSR, especially in the Carpathian Military District, in Turkmenistan, and in Central Asia. In fact, the Soviet Army has established a mountain warfare training center in the Central Asian Military District.[16] The results of maneuvers are then reported to the military schools for evaluation, and the process is repeated as revised concepts are tested until satisfactory results are achieved.

The most notable characteristic of the emerging Soviet operational concept for mountain warfare is the reliance upon air mobility and airborne weapons systems to maintain the momentum of the offensive. An assault is used to seize key terrain in front of the advancing mechanized forces to facilitate their advance or to block the movement of defending forces. Armed helicopters are used for close-in fire support because of their flexibility, while fixed-wing aircraft assume the role at longer ranges because high performance and range make them more survivable.

Colonel A. A. Sidorenko, in writing about the offense in the *Soviet Military Encyclopedia,* characterizes mountain warfare as an intense struggle for routes of communications, communications network centers, roads, and mountain passes. Operations are normally slower and less deep than on level areas. To seize commanding heights and to strike the defender on the flanks or in the rear, turning movement detachments (*obkhodiaushchii otradi*) are deployed by air.

For close-in operations, generally within 20 kilometers of friendly troops, detachments are normally air landed on or near the objective by helicopter. As the distance from friendly forces increases, or if objectives are defended, it is more usual to rely upon airborne units delivered by parachute. Since airborne units are mechanized, landing zones may be as far as 10 kilometers from the objective, although the preference is for closer landing zones.

Descriptions of such operations often show platoon-size detachments; however, the norm appears to be to use company- or battalion-size units for these missions. Link-up with ground forces for heliborne detachments normally takes place in less than twenty-four hours, while airborne units may operate independently for forty-eight hours or longer.

The limitations of terrain on maneuver in mountainous regions favor deep echelonment of forces. It is the standard example for deploying in three echelons.

The development of Soviet mountain warfare techniques is noteworthy for two reasons. First, it is a good demonstration of the deliberate and systematic Soviet methodology for problem solving in military affairs. Second, it clearly shows that the Soviet Army is not allowing Afghanistan to distract attention from what it obviously feels to be the more basic concern of security on its Chinese and West European frontiers.

Desert Warfare

Soviet experience in desert operations goes back to the mid-1930s when the new Soviet state was attempting to establish its authority over Central Asian regions of the former czarist empire. It also had some experience in desert operations in the waning days of World War II against the Japanese in East Asia, and some Soviet officers have had opportunity to observe the problems of desert warfare in support of their clients in Africa and the Middle East.

Soviet desert warfare operations are characterized by attacks on wide frontages and on several axes, with operations oriented on terrain important for sustaining life. The Soviet Army perceives desert warfare as a number of widely dispersed small unit actions to seize water sources, on the assumption that control of the water supply will quickly defeat the enemy.

Maneuver in desert regions requires deep echelonment to cover the flanks and to defeat enemy counterattacks on the widely dispersed first echelon forces. The operational characteristics of desert regions favor the creation of combined forces groups to engage in large-scale maneuvers to strike the rear and flanks of the enemy.

Coastal Operations

The Soviet Army has three classifications of amphibious operations: strategic—the landing of forces to establish a new theater of military operations, operational—landings in an established theater of military operations to support operations of a front or army, and tactical—landings to support operations in coastal regions by regular forces. All Soviet wartime experience in amphibious warfare has been tactical, and the size and structure of Soviet Naval Infantry and the amphibious forces of other Warsaw Pact armies strongly imply that the most likely use of these forces in any general war will be in the tactical mode. However, the Soviet Army has experimented with amphibious operations at the operational depth, in exercises such as ZAPAD 81 and SHIELD 82.

Operations in coastal regions are normally carried out by unified ground and naval forces. The naval contingent protects the open flanks of the ground forces from attack from the sea and supports the advance of ground forces with naval weapons. Naval forces may also conduct tactical landings to seize key objectives that facilitate the advance of the ground forces. Amphibious operations are normally coordinated with helicopter and parachute operations to disrupt enemy defenses, or they may be mounted against islands and peninsulas that control the access to the coast from sea or land.

In Soviet military literature, amphibious operations in coastal regions, airborne operations, and helicopter assault operations are generally referred to under the rubric of *desantnaia operatsia*—landing operations. In fact, the primary difference between operations in normal conditions and operations in coastal regions is the addition of the amphibious dimension to landing operations.

Arctic Warfare

Geography and history have combined to give the Soviet Army more experience in large-scale operations in arctic conditions than any other army in the world. Geographically, most of the Soviet Union lies north of the fiftieth parallel, placing it roughly in the same climatic zone as Alaska and northern Canada. Winter in the vast expanses of Siberia, an area roughly twice the size of the continental United States, is routinely marked by temperatures more than twenty degrees below zero Fahrenheit. In history, the legendary Russian winters were major factors in the defeat of two would-be conquerors from the West—Napoleon and Hitler.

Their experience in large-scale operations in the vast trackless expanses of northern Europe has led the Soviets to the conclusion that the most important factors are avenues of movement along roads, valleys, and frozen rivers, and across frozen lakes and swamps. Frozen waterways are especially suited to maneuver of forces in winter warfare, according to Soviet views, and during World War II the Red Army was repeatedly able to surprise the *Wehrmacht* by launching surprise attacks over seemingly impassable ground. Soviet ground forces have mastered sophisticated techniques for reconnaissance of frozen waterways for routes that will support heavy tactical vehicles and for locating and reinforcing weak spots in the ice.[17]

The unique characteristics of winter operations arise from the scarcity of roads and airfields, deep snow, the cumulative effects of extreme cold on men and equipment, short periods of daylight, and the influence of polar electromagnetic phenomena on communications and navigation. The sum of these characteristics necessitates fewer and simpler military missions for troops, reduction of tempo and speed of operations, and limited depth and breadth of operations in space and time.

Combat operations in polar regions are generally conducted by small units dispersed over a wide front and require a large second echelon to replace first echelon units that are quickly worn down by the harsh effects of climate and terrain. Immediate objectives are normally to seize and secure key population centers and communications centers to control movement and resources important to survival in the region. Principal forms of maneuver are the envelopment and the turning movement. Depth is added to the battlefield by use of airborne and airmobile troops to seize key objectives in the enemy rear.

It is interesting that the Soviet concept of arctic warfare is similar in many ways to its concept of desert warfare. Both concepts stress the concern for climate and terrain on equipment. In both instances, a critical objective is to seize and secure the basic life-sustaining areas in the region by widely dispersed, independent actions.

Combat in Cities

The Red Army had extensive experience in combat in cities in World War II. Two of the major battles of that war on the Eastern Front—Stalingrad and Berlin—were probably the largest and most extensive military operations in cities in the history of war. The effect of these experiences is apparent in Soviet training today. For instance, the standard obstacle course that all Soviet soldiers negotiate at least weekly as part of their physical training is designed to build skills specifically suited to combat in cities. It includes vaulting low obstacles, climbing walls, walking balance beams, diving under low doors, and jumping through windows.

In offensive operations, Soviet commanders prefer to avoid extended combat in built-up areas, because it slows the rate of advance. Where possible, the practice is to use turning movements to isolate enemy forces in towns and cities and to bypass them, leaving their destruction to be accomplished by following forces. However, the Soviet Army realizes that it cannot always bypass large cities (defined as those with more than 100,000 inhabitants) and that in certain conditions, as in desert, arctic, and mountain warfare, the built-up area itself may be the objective.

The organization for combat for attacking built-up areas differs from that in other terrain conditions.[18] The building blocks are motorized rifle units reinforced with other arms. The key organization is the motorized rifle battalion, which is organized for combat into an assault group (*shturmovaia gruppa*). Companies organize one or two platoons into attack groups (*gruppa zakhvata*), and at least one support group (*gruppa obespecheniia*).

Attack groups, reinforced with attached tanks and sappers, are the combat elements that close with the enemy and seize and secure specific objectives. The support group, with attached mortars and artillery pieces, provides direct and close-in fire support to the attack groups. Individual howitzers from the regimental artillery battalion or division artillery regiments are normally attached to the support groups and are employed in the direct fire role—the armored, self-propelled M-1974 122mm howitzer, organic to motorized rifle regiments, and M-1973 152mm howitzer, organic to maneuver divisions are ideally suited to this role.[19]

At battalion and below, the standard formation is a single echelon, with a small reserve withheld to deal with unexpected developments. At regiment and division, the standard formation is two echelons, with the second echelon having the mission of opening a new axis of attack at the proper time or of replacing or reinforcing a first echelon battalion. Rear area security, damage control, and operation of routes of evacuation and supply are functions of division rear service elements.

The key objectives in an attack on a built-up area are those locations and installations that ensure control of the population and movement through the city. These include radio stations, telephone centrals, public utilities, bridges, and transportation centers. The concept of the battle is to first isolate the built-up area with surrounding forces from division or army and then to systematically divide and isolate the defenders in ever smaller groups, until they are weak enough to be destroyed.[20]

The Elements of Battle

Having addressed the operational conditions, the next step in the problem-solving process is to decide how to fight the battle. Soviet commanders are trained to view the conduct of the offense as the application of the two elements of battle: maneuver (*manevr*) and shock (*udar*).[21]

Maneuver

Soviet commanders understand *maneuver* to mean organized movement in combat to concentrate the forces and means necessary to strike a decisive blow on the enemy.[22] It includes maneuver of troops (*manevr voiskami*) and maneuver of fire (*manevr ognem*).[23] Tank and motorized rifle troops are the maneuver forces, while artillery, rocket troops, armed helicopters, and ground attack aircraft constitute the fire to be maneuvered.

The theory of mechanics tells us that all mechanisms, no matter how complex, are merely applications of three simple machines: the wheel, the lever, and the inclined plane. A similar observation applies to the element of maneuver in Soviet offensive operations. No matter how complex the operation, the element of maneuver is the individual or combined use of three basic forms of maneuver: the breakthrough (*proryv*), the turning movement (*obkhod*), and the envelopment (*okhvat*).[24]

The *proryv*, or breakthrough, has captured the imagination of Western military observers of the Soviet army as though it were a sort of Russian art form. This fascination is based largely on lurid tales by German officers who fought in World War II on the Eastern Front about stupendous artillery barrages followed by massive waves of Russian soldiers and tanks washing over German defenses like some angry sea, relying upon sheer mass rather than intelligent application of force to defeat the enemy.

Concern over Soviet numerical superiority vis-à-vis the West continues to breathe life into this dramatic perception. Understandably, the Soviet Army has done nothing to dispel the myth even though the truth is a bit more mundane. Soviet military sources define the origin of the breakthrough as a solution to the problem of attacking a strong, well-organized enemy defense in depth that lacks an open flank.[25] In their view, the *proryv*, as depicted in Figure 4.5, is a means of creating an open flank when none exists, or when the attacking forces cannot exploit existing open flanks.[26] In World War II, German tactical skill and shortcomings in Soviet mobility, operational capabilities, and logistics often caused conditions favoring a *proryv*.

Present-day Soviet military theory holds that the conditions requiring breakthrough are generally unlikely to exist on the operational or strategic scale, because the use—or threat of use—of weapons of mass destruction forces the enemy to disperse and prevents him from forming a solid front in depth.[27] In this case, the Soviet practice is to attack from the march, exploiting the gaps in the defense to maneuver into the depth of the battle area and to attack the enemy from the flank and rear, a reinforcement for their interest in the meeting engagement.

On a tactical level, Soviet commanders recognize that a specific mission or situation may require an attack on a fortified region wherein they must penetrate the enemy's defense to rapidly destroy him.[28] In this case, the preferred solution is to use weapons of mass destruction to create a gap and to quickly exploit it with highly mobile tank and mechanized forces advancing at a rapid rate of speed. If nuclear,

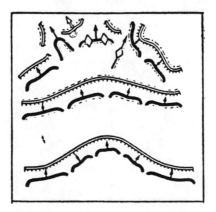

Figure 4.5   The breakthrough

Source: Gen. Maj. V. G. Reznichenko, ed., *Taktika,* Moscow: Voenizdat, 1966, p. 67.

chemical, or biological weapons are not used, heavy concentrations of conventional munitions are delivered on identified enemy defensive positions by artillery, rocket launchers, and aircraft. Fire strikes are rapidly exploited by mounted tank and motorized rifle formations that close with the enemy at the fastest possible rate of speed from widely dispersed attack positions.

Major General Reznichenko asserts that on the modern battlefield, the lack of a continuous front and the substantial dispersion of forces and the resulting presence of open flanks and large intervals between units are conducive to maneuver, to the execution of bold envelopments and deep turning movements to the flanks and rear of the enemy, and to the delivery of unexpected and decisive strikes from various directions.[29] His perception of the appearance of a modern battlefield is shown in Figure 4.6.

The Soviet Army believes, then, that the principal forms of maneuver in a modern war will be turning movements and envelopments, not breakthroughs. Rather than striking an enemy frontally or attacking his strength, the decisive blow will be delivered to the rear and flanks of the enemy. The basic essence of these forms of maneuver is shown schematically in Figure 4.7.

The essential difference between the *okhvat* (envelopment) and the *obkhod* (turning movement) is the depth of the maneuver force. In an envelopment, the maneuvering force moves in a relatively shal-

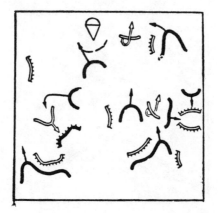

Figure 4.6.   Soviet perception of a modern battle field

Source: Gen. Maj. V. G. Reznichenko, ed., *Taktika,* Moscow: Voenizdat, 1966, p. 67.

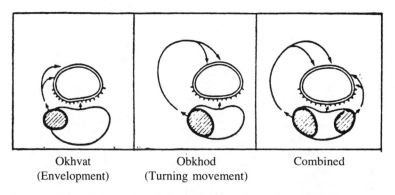

Okhvat   Obkhod   Combined
(Envelopment)   (Turning movement)

Figure 4.7.   Schematic of the envelopment and turning movement

Source: Gen. Maj. G. Reznichenko, *Taktika*, Moscow: Voenizdat, 1966, p. 64.

low and constricted envelope. The size of the envelope may vary according to terrain, weather, type of unit, and other factors, but the principle is that the enveloping force remains in range of direct support and under continuous control of the parent unit. While envelopments may be conducted at any tactical or operational level, they are the most predominant form of maneuver at battalion level and below.

In a turning movement, the maneuvering force moves in a wide and deep envelope that resembles an independent, or at least semi-independent, operation. Its maneuver is sufficiently wide and deep that it cannot be directly supported by the parent unit. While any size unit can conduct a turning movement, it is more prevalent at levels above battalion, where units have a better capability to operate independently.

Maneuver of fire is in some aspects more complex than maneuver of forces. It includes the displacement of fire means so that targets are within range, trajectories are compatible, and weapons characteristics are fully exploited. For direct fire weapons it includes overcoming problems of enfilade and dead space, and for indirect fire weapons, the problems of mask. Maneuver of fire also addresses the command and control problems for shifting, lifting, and adjusting fires and the timing of displacement of fire elements to ensure continuous support. Figure 4.8 is one of the nomograms used in making these computations.

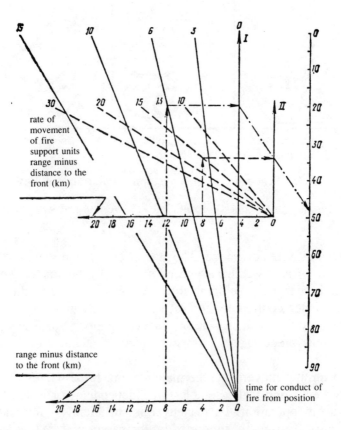

rate of
movement
of fire
support units
range minus
distance to the
front (km)

range minus distance
to the front (km)

time for conduct of
fire from position

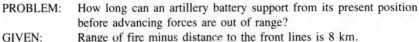

PROBLEM: How long can an artillery battery support from its present position
             before advancing forces are out of range?

GIVEN: Range of fire minus distance to the front lines is 8 km.
             Speed of movement for displacing artillery is 15 km/hr.
             Rate of advance of maneuver elements is 6 km/hr.

SOLUTION: Plot range vs. speed of advance on the I axis.
             Plot range vs. speed of displacement on the II axis.
             Connect intercepts on I and II axes.
             Read answer of 48 minutes off of conduct of fire axis.

Figure 4.8.   Nomogram for calculating the continuity of fire from the same
              position

Source: A.Ia. Vainer, *Takticheskie Raschety,* Moscow: Voenizdat, 1982, p. 64.

Shock

The other element of battle in the Soviet view is *udar*. The word has been translated into English as both "shock" and "strike," but an accurate translation of the word as a military term is difficult because the concept is rarely used in Western military thought. The Soviet Army defines it as the specific form of battle resulting from the effective employment of the various means of combat.[30] Specifically, it refers to the physical and psychological effect of violence on the enemy capability to fight. In this sense, it can be understood as being similar to the shock action ascribed to armored warfare by the U.S. Army.

The Soviet view, however, is rather wider. It holds that shock comprises three sources: nuclear shock (*iadernyi udar*) caused by use of atomic weapons, fire shock (*ognevoy udar*) caused by conventional munitions delivered by ground weapons or aircraft, and troop shock (*udar voisk*) caused by tank and motorized rifle troops. Shock is not only characterized by how it is caused, but also by where it is delivered. In this sense, it is called frontal, flank, or combined. In this way, the effects of surprise are encompassed by the concept of shock action.

The concept of shock action is the combined effect of violence and surprise on the enemy. In planning an offensive operation, Soviet commanders plan and execute the operation in such a way as to achieve the maximum possible shock action on the enemy. The purpose of shock action is to break apart enemy units so that the attacking forces, in the process of achieving deeper objectives, can isolate small, disorganized enemy groups between a number of axes of advance on a wide front for later defeat in detail. This concept of shock action is especially adaptable to the frontal strike used when the correlation of forces is clearly to the advantage of the Soviet forces.[31] In this usage, the objective is to shatter (*rassekat'*) the enemy main force at the outset of the operation.

Decision

The algorithm results in a decision according to which the Soviet commander selects his course of action, which is guidance for his staff and which forms the concept (*zamysel*) for his subordinate commanders. Under ideal conditions, where time is not a critical factor, this process follows the *posledovatel'nyi* (or sequential process) described in Chapter 3. Normally, however, the parallel method is used.

While the degree to which the decision is worked out and the detail in which it is expressed depend on the time available, it must, as a minimum, prescribe the enemy's strength, activity, and location; the employment of maneuver and shock; fire support; the direction of the main and secondary (if any) efforts; and the organization for combat. It may include other data such as boundaries and phase lines and special communications instructions.

Conduct of the Offense

Those who have experienced the terrors of the battlefield know that nothing ever seems to go as planned. One reason is that plans are predictions of the future, and the unknown and the unexpected always intrude upon expectations. Another reason is that warfare is a human experience, and the individuals on both sides who plan, direct, and fight the battle react in unique ways to the chaotic, complex, and emotional crises that battle forces upon them.

It is therefore optimistic in the extreme to assume that Soviet commanders will blindly adhere to stereotyped offensive operations or that Soviet combat operations will exhibit standardized patterns that lend themselves to templating. Such simplistic views dangerously underestimate the professionalism of Soviet officers and betray a lack of understanding of the complex dynamics of the modern battlefield.

Nonetheless, Soviet soldiers, like those in all armies, will tend to act in battle as they are trained to, and while it is objectively impossible to press individual Soviet commanders into some standardized mold, it is possible on a more sophisticated level to understand the principles that they are trained to apply in conducting the offense. The great captains in military history are commanders who possessed this knowledge of their enemy and exploited it to their advantage.

Authoritative Soviet sources generally describe the conduct of the offense in terms of the violence of the battle, the continuing struggle to gain and maintain the initiative, and continuity of battle in both space and time. These perceptions are best defined in what the Soviet Army refers to as the principles of military art, discussed in their general sense in Chapter 1. Their application at the operational-tactical level in offensive operations has some unique and specific values that define the Soviet conduct of the offense.

Surprise

There is, to begin with, a major Soviet concern with the element of surprise, which is viewed as having both a passive and an active aspect. It is significant that there are three Russian words translated as meaning surprise: *surpriz, neozhadennost', and vnezapnost'*. The word in Russian that encompasses the idea of surprise in all its aspects is the cognate *surpriz*. This blanket term is seldom used by military writers, except in the most general discussions.

The second word, *neozhadennost'*, is a compound word that denotes "surprise" in terms of "unexpected." The word appears in Soviet military jargon in a passive sense to describe the situation or enemy action. For instance, commanders must be prepared to respond to unexpected situations caused by terrain, weather, or the enemy. Combat readiness includes being prepared to meet enemy action from an unexpected direction, in an unexpected place, or at an unexpected time.

The third word, *vnezapnost'*, is another compound word that denotes the idea of being beyond comprehension or understanding. It is used in Soviet military jargon to describe the Soviet use of surprise against the enemy. *Vnezapnost'* goes beyond the idea of merely the unexpected; it includes the concept of stunning or paralyzing the enemy by the violence and speed of the attack, as well as by surprising him by its direction and time.[32] In this active sense, surprise is an application of *udar*, or shock, one of the two elements of battle discussed in planning the offensive.

Initiative

Like surprise, the principle of initiative has both a passive and an active aspect. In its passive aspect, Soviet commanders are expected to display initiative by executing their orders regardless of the situation. It has the meaning of grim determination in relentless pursuit of the objective more than that of imaginative problem solving or flexibility. In its active aspect, initiative means making the enemy think defensively by continually attacking or at least threatening to attack. This concept of seizing the initiative is also occasionally referred to as *aktivnost'*, sometimes translated as "combat activity," which means keeping the pressure on the enemy.[33]

Coordination

The principle of *vzaimodeistvie*, or coordination, is the application of combat strength in time and space to achieve maximum shock effect and surprise. Its application in the offense includes the delivery of the maximum quantity of supporting fire in the shortest possible period of time with no interval between the shifting of supporting fires and the closing on the objective of maneuver forces. Attention to these time and space factors is another way of attaining the element of shock.

Mass

The principle of mass is the application of the main and secondary axes of advance. In Soviet military jargon, *massirovanie* includes both quantitative and qualitative aspects. The quantitative aspect measures combat power in the traditional sense of relative sizes of forces and quantities of weapons. The qualitative aspect, which is increasingly important in modern warfare, includes consideration of the range and firepower of weapons and the mobility of ground-gaining forces. The application of these qualitative factors as they impact on the effects of time and space is achieved primarily by maneuver, the other element of battle.

Simultaneous Destruction

The conduct of the offensive attempts the simultaneous destruction of the enemy to the entire depth of the battle area. This principle requires the simultaneous deep attack on the enemy's combat, combat support, and combat service support capabilities to take away his initiative and freedom of maneuver. Deep attack includes conventional artillery and air-delivered munitions, described in Chapter 7, but also requires the extensive use of landing operations (*desantnaia operatsia*). In coastal areas, this includes use of amphibious assault to support operational and tactical plans. In all instances, it includes the integration of air assault by parachute or helicopter-delivered forces to support attack on the main axis.[34] In general, helicopters are used to deliver troops to shallow objectives (less than 20 kilometers from the front, where they can be supported by artillery) and where time factors are short (link-up within less than twenty-four hours, and preferably sooner than that). Heliborne operations normally involve company- or battalion-size motorized rifle elements less their combat vehicles delivered on or immediately adjacent to their objective. Parachute operations normally use company- to regiment-size operations to depths greater than 20 kilometers where they may operate up to three days before link-up. Because they usually drop with their organic combat vehicles, the BMD, landing zones may be 5 to 10 kilometers from objectives, and missions often include raids on command and control and fire support activities, as well as seizing and holding key terrain.

Soviet military writings strongly imply that, while Soviet landing forces (both airborne and amphibious) are national strategic assets in peacetime and in power projection scenarios, their principal function in general war will be operational-tactical. For instance, the depiction in Figure 4.4 of a meeting engagement specifically shows parachute forces in the battle. Discussion of the employment of airborne forces in such official publications as *Voennyi Vestnik* and *Krasnaia Zvezda* heavily stresses tactical operations by small units in support of ground operations by conventional tank and motorized rifle formations.

Moral-Political Factors

A standard theme in all Soviet tactical writings is a concern with what are called the moral-political factors. In Soviet military jargon, this applies to the discipline and determination of friendly troops, including cultivation of hatred for the enemy.[35] It also includes psychological operations against the enemy and the population in the battle area.[36] SPETZNAZ forces (discussed in Chapter 6) play a major role in the application of this principle on the battlefield.

Command and Control

The application of the principle of command and control was covered in Chapter 3. Particularly in offensive operations, this principle stresses that in the absence of orders to the contrary, the plan is to be followed as written. In a sense, the Soviets' concern with detailed planning and their perception of initiative as grim determination are means of ensuring continuity of operations regardless of what happens to communications or command and control facilities.[37] As explained in Chapter 3, Soviet commanders assume that they may have to carry on the battle with forces at hand and with a minimum of contact with higher headquarters.

Security and Rear Support

It is interesting that Soviet military theory includes security and rear support under the same principle of military art. Security includes all of the concepts of *maskirovka,* hiding one's own capabilities and intentions to mislead the enemy. Rear support means provision of adequate logistics support for the operation. Logistics is discussed in some detail in Chapter 6.

Reconstitution of Combat Capability

Reconstitution of combat capability is best understood as the application of the Soviet Army's concept of expending units in combat and replacing them, rather than sustaining units in combat. Standard operating procedures within all Soviet combat and combat support formations include procedures for reorganizing in response to heavy combat losses. Rather than expecting replacements for casualties and losses in major items such as tanks or armored vehicles, Soviet commanders assume that battalions may have to organize into companies and companies into platoons as the battle progresses. When second echelon units replace first echelon units, the expended units may be cannibalized to reconstitute new formations that are enhanced with whatever replacements are available.

During World War II, the Soviet practice of reconstitution of forces and creation of new formations from the remnants of old ones occasionally caused German intelligence to overestimate actual Soviet order of battle. This practice is also a basis of the Soviet peacetime habit of maintaining category II and III divisions at less than 100 percent equipment and personnel strength. It is suggested here that the assumption that all of these units are to be filled out by mobilization is not necessarily correct. Some, in concert with remnants of first echelon forces, may be used to reconstitute combat capability. Such a concept is entirely justified by Soviet military practices and, if true, has some significant implications for Western assumptions concerning strategic warning, mobilization, and reinforcement time.

Summary

The basis of Soviet devotion to the offensive is a deeply held determination to fight the next world war, should it come, on everyone else's territory. It also reflects an absolute belief that wars are fought to be won and that the definition of winning is destroying enemy forces and occupying enemy territory. Only the offense can achieve these goals.

The Soviet concept of the offense comprises three basic approaches. The first is to attack strength, which entails a single decisive blow to shatter the enemy's capability to resist. It depends upon the attacker possessing overwhelmingly superior force. The second and most often used approach is to attack weakness. It too depends upon a superior attacking force, but it also depends upon maneuver to gain an additional advantage over a strong enemy. The third approach is to exploit faults. It entails using offensive action to seize the initiative while avoiding decisive engagement until the correlation of forces clearly favors the attacker.

The process of planning for the offense is a scientifically constructed algorithm that ensures the logical consideration of relevant factors in their relative order. The result is a plan of battle described in terms of the two elements of battle: maneuver and shock. Maneuver describes the echelonment of forces and the three basic forms of maneuver—the breakthrough, the envelopment, and the turning movement. It concentrates the forces and means necessary to destroy the enemy. *Udar*, or shock, is the physical and psychological effect of violence on the enemy, that which destroys his ability or will to resist. It is the short, violent period of actual decisive battle.

Conduct of the battle is the execution of the plan. It is described as a violent struggle in space and time to gain and maintain the initiative that continues until the enemy is destroyed. Soviet commanders are taught to conduct the offense by applying basic principles to the specific mission and situation. The principles stress surprising and stunning the enemy, seizing and maintaining the initiative, and coordinating combat forces to mass superior combat power at the proper time and place.

Conclusions

Soviet combat operations lean heavily upon offensive operations as the only way to achieve victory. Even in the initial phases of a war and in conditions where the correlation of forces is clearly not in their favor, Soviet commanders are trained to think and act in terms of the offense, to seize the initiative and to turn the momentum of combat to their favor.

With the detailed attention to the problems of planning and control so typical of all aspects of Soviet life, the Soviet Army has instituted a methodology for planning offensive operations that applies its definition of science and ensures a logical and structured decision-making process. This process is expressed in an algorithm that, with the addition of the proper nomographs and other formulae and data tables, is suited to machine intelligence, computer logic, and automated decision making.

In the conduct of the offense, Soviet commanders are trained to concentrate upon the application of carefully formulated principles to expand the time and space parameters of the battle. The application of these principles is to the two elements of battle: maneuver and shock. Maneuver concentrates the quantitative and qualitative factors that constitute combat power at the correct time and place. Shock causes the physical and psychological destruction of the enemy by compressing violence into short periods of time, increasing the speed or tempo of combat, and surprising the enemy by the time, direction, and intensity of the attack.

To the degree that the Soviet concept of the offensive is structured to consider certain factors and not others, and to the extent that the principles guiding the conduct of the offense tend to exclude other considerations, it is valid to raise the criticism of stereotyped operations robbing commanders of initiative. Practically speaking, however, the validity of this criticism is dubious. To begin with, there is a great deal of latitude left to commanders within the constraints placed upon them, and an individual commander's perceptions of the situation will vary input to algorithms and the application of principles.

The Soviet view is that the "scientific" approach to the offensive disciplines and streamlines the planning and conduct of the battle by focusing mental and physical resources upon what is relevant. The Soviet Army believes that its "scientific" approach makes its military science superior to ours.

Whichever viewpoint the reader takes, one point should be certain. Plans to defeat a Soviet offensive that assume rigidly standardized formations and waves of neatly arrayed forces making easy targets are a naive prescription for defeat. Wishful thinking and notional enemies are not substitutes for hard facts. In fact, the Soviet Army requires its commanders to exercise a high degree of initiative by deliberately building flexibility into the planning and conduct of the offense through devices such as specific tasks set in order of priority, to be executed as opportunities arise. Other factors reducing the validity of templates or patterns include task organization and variations in formations at all levels.

The moral of the myth of Achilles, however, is that no human endeavor is without exploitable flaws. In the case of the Soviet concept of the offensive, the sophisticated defender who understands the Soviet decision-making process may be able to influence it in his favor by varying the input by his own actions. This is an application of Sun Tzu's admonition to "know thy enemy and know thyself. . . ."

Notes

1. Col. A. A. Sidorenko, *The Offensive,* Moscow: Voenizdat, 1970. Translated and published under the auspices of the U.S. Air Force, p. 1.
2. Otto Chaney, *Zhukov,* Norman: University of Oklahoma Press, 1974, pp. 93–96.
3. A. A. Sidorenko in *Sovetskaia Voennaia Entsiklopediia,* 8 vols, 1976–1980, Moscow: Voenizdat, vol. 5, p. 52.
4. For a general discussion of this concept, see Nathan Leites, "The Soviet Style in War" in *Soviet Military Thinking,* ed. Derek Leebart, Washington D.C.: National Defense University, 1981, pp. 186–92.
5. A. I. Radzievskii, *Proryv (Breakthrough),* Moscow: Voenizdat, 1979, p. 166.
6. V. V. Druzhinin and D. S. Kontorov, *Concept, Algorithm, Decision,* Moscow: Voenizdat, 1972. Translated and published under the auspices of the U.S. Air Force, pp. 1–5.
7. *Sovetskaia Voennaia Entsiklopediia,* op. cit., vol. 1, p. 512.
8. Ibid., p. 513.
9. Ibid., vol. 3, p. 365.
10. Ibid., vol. 1.
11. Gen. Maj. Mikhailovskii and Col. A. Zotov, *"Voprosii Taktiki v Sovetskaia Voennaia Entsiklopediia"* ("Questions on Tactics in the Soviet Military Encyclopedia"), *Voennyi Vestnik,* no. 11, 1980, pp. 38–39.
12. *Sovetskaia Voennaia Entsiklopediia,* op. cit, vol. 2, pp. 406–7.
13. *Sovetskaia Voennaia Entsiklopediia,* op. cit., vol. 6, p. 511.
14. See, e.g., Col. A. Ia. Vainer, *Takticheskie Raschety (Tactical Computations),* Moscow: Voenizdat, 1982, pp. 44–46.
15. *Sovetskaia Voennaia Entsiklopediia,* op. cit., vol. 5, pp. 521–22.
16. *Krasnaia Zvezda,* 15 January 1983, p. 1.
17. See, e.g., William P. Baxter, "Soviet Norms for Driving Tanks in Winter," *Military Review,* September, 1980.
18. Gen. Maj. A. K. Shovkolovich, Col. F. I. Konasov, and Col. S. I. Trach, *Boevye Deistvaiia Motostrelkogo Batal'ona v Gorode (Combat Actions of a Motorized Rifle Battalion in Cities),* Moscow: Voenizdat, 1971, pp. 27–58.
19. See, e.g., William P. Baxter, "Soviet 122mm S. P. Howitzer," *Field Artillery Journal,* January/February 1980.
20. *Sovetskaia Voennaia Entsiklopediia,* op. cit., vol. 5, pp. 522–23.
21. Gen. Maj. I. Vorob'ev, *"Oruzhia i Taktika"* ("Weapons and Tactics"), *Krasnaia Zvezda,* 12 January 1982, p. 2.
22. *Sovetskaia Voennaia Entsiklopediia,* op. cit., vol. 5, p. 114.
23. *Vorob'ev,* op. cit.

24. Ibid.

25. Radzievskii, op. cit., p. 3.

26. *Sovetskaia Voennaia Entsiklopediia*, op. cit., vol. 6, p. 576.

27. Ibid.

28. Ibid.

29. Gen. Maj. Reznichenko, ed., *Taktika (Tactics,)* Moscow: Voenizdat, 1966, p. 63.

30. Vorob'ev, op. cit.

31. Radzievskii, op. cit., p. 166.

32. *Sovetskaia Voennaia Entsiklopediia*, op. cit., vol. 2, p. 161.

33. *Sovetskaia Voennaia Entsiklopediia*, op. cit., vol. 1, pp. 510–11.

34. Col. Gen. A. A. Lomov, ed., *The Revolution in Military Affairs*, Moscow: Voenizdat, 1973. Translated and published under the auspices of the U.S. Air Force, p. 149.

35. A. A. Grechko, *The Armed Forces of the Soviet Union*, Moscow: Progress Publishers, 1977, pp. 288–89.

36. Gen. Maj. V. V. Milovidov, ed., *Problems of Contemporary War*, Moscow: Voenizdat, 1972. Translated and published under the auspices of the U.S. Air Force, pp. 195–96. See also pp. 211–12.

37. Ibid., p. 197. See also Lomov, op. cit., p. 172.

CHAPTER 5

The Defense

> The defense is necessary when it is impossible or inadvisable to attack.[1]
>
> Col. G. Ionin

Of the two aspects of battle recognized in Soviet military science, the offense and the defense, Colonel Ionin's lukewarm endorsement of the defense emphasizes Soviet preference for the offense. It is, of course, an inherent characteristic of the profession of arms, regardless of nationality, to attack rather than to defend, and in this sense, Colonel Ionin is merely displaying a prejudice characteristic of his profession.

However, the Soviet Army is even more ambiguous toward the defense than are most other armies. The Soviet preoccupation with the offense is evident in the relative lack of effort expended in training in and studying defensive warfare. For example, the Soviet military press has not published any major theoretical works on the defense to compare with *The Offensive* by Colonel Sidorenko or *The Breakthrough* by A. I. Radzievskii, and the quantity of work in the professional military journals reflects a remarkable neglect of the defense. In fact, this neglect is so noteworthy that some authoritative Western analysts of Soviet military affairs have suggested that the defense is becoming a forgotten art in the Soviet Army.[2]

Aside from strictly military reasons, the Soviet preference for the offense is predicated upon Marxism-Leninism, which predicts that if a new world war occurs, it must mercilessly and irrevocably sweep capitalism from the face of the earth.[3] A defense, no matter how masterfully executed, can hardly be expected to achieve such a grandiose objective. There also appears to be an emotional aversion to the defense buried in the Soviet psyche. Savkin hints at this in warning that a defensive psychology breeds passiveness in troops and encourages an attitude of retreat and defeat in commanders.[4]

Savkin's concern is supported by investigations in another branch of Soviet military science, military psychology. In espousing Pavlov's proposal that external conditions can condition men to react in reflexive ways, Soviet military psychology suggests that the natural human tendency to avoid danger can only be inhibited through training.[5] By implication, passiveness and an attitude of retreat and defeat are best overcome by conditioning officers and men in the offense.

The indifferent Soviet attitude toward the defense evidenced by Colonel Ionin, then, results from a combination of influences. There exists a preference for the offense that is traditional in the military profession as a whole, regardless of cultural or ideological differences between nations. In the Soviet Army, this military tradition is reinforced by Marxist-Leninist ideology and the Soviet view of military psychology. The practical results of this preference for the offense are reflected physically in the organization and equipment of the Soviet Army and in the structure of Soviet military thought.

It is a dangerous error, however, to underestimate Soviet skills in defensive warfare. Russians have a justly earned reputation for ferocity and tenacity in the defense that has cruelly punished many would-be conquerors from the east, the west, and the south. In a sense, the current Soviet bias against the defense is ironic when considered in terms of the epic defensive battles of Leningrad, Moscow and, of course, Stalingrad that broke the back of the Nazi war machine that had conquered most of continental Europe. Thus, while it is obvious that the Soviet Army does not like to be on the defensive, Russian history shows that it will be a fierce enemy all the same.

While the defense is not as popular in the Soviet Army as the offense, it is not in the nature of the Soviet military profession to leave important problems unattended. Recognition of the difficulties of modern defensive warfare led the prestigious Frunze Military Academy, under General Reznichenko, to appoint a collection of professional military scholars to examine and solve the problems of modern defensive warfare at the tactical level.[6] The results of their investigations were subjected to field trials in Soviet exercises, especially in Exercise Karpaty in 1977, which tested various concepts for organizing the ground, and in Exercise Berezina in 1978, in which various concepts for organization of units for defensive combat were tested.[7]

The Soviet Perception of Defensive Warfare

Soviet professional military jargon uses two words generally translated into English as "defense." As is often the case, some meaning and a lot of understanding are lost in the process of translation because the two words convey significantly different meanings to Russian readers. One term, *zashchita,* is a compound word that literally means "as a shield." In Soviet military usage, it conveys the idea of defense in the passive context of protection. The other term, *oborona,* is also a compound word, apparently derived from words meaning "against harrow." *Harrow,* in this context, is used in its ancient meaning of "destruction" or "plunder." Thus, *oborona* conveys the idea of defense in the active sense of resistance or opposition and includes the concept of striking out at the enemy as well as of fending off his blows.

In official Soviet military usage, *zashchita* is used to describe purely defensive actions such as CBR defense or self-defense. On the other hand, operational terms such as Ministry of Defense, civil defense, antiaircraft defense, and defense (as opposed to offense) are all based upon the active term *oborona.* While etymology is not a topic in this book, it is important to understand that the Soviet military perception of defense includes the concept of offense. In the Russian language, the word *defense, oborona,* is a general term that encompasses the much narrower concept of offense, rather than being its antonym, as is the case in English.

Purpose of the Defense

The Soviet Army states that the purpose of the defense is to halt the offense of a superior enemy force, to inflict severe losses on it, to secure critical terrain and locations, and to create favorable conditions for assuming the offensive.[8] Since it defines a successful defense as one that creates conditions favorable for the offense, the Soviet Army conducts the defense in a way that destroys the enemy's equipment and exhausts and bleeds white his formations.[9] To the Soviet Army, a defensive battle is a battle of attrition.

In the Soviet view, a successful defense requires more than simply halting an enemy offensive or holding critical terrain. As the root of the word *oborona* implies, it must also inflict constant pain and strain on the enemy. This is the conceptual link to the offensive concept of attacking weakness, described in Chapter 4.

Classification of Defensive Operations

Technically, the term *defense* is used in Soviet tactics, operational art, and strategy to describe one of the two classifications of military operations, the other being offense.[10] In this sense, defense includes not only the traditional holding of ground but also retrograde operations, which are further classified as either retreat or withdrawal.

A retreat, *otstuplenie,* is an operational-strategic maneuver conducted at army or above to trade space for time by moving into the depth of friendly territory. It is executed to achieve a better posture for subsequent operations.[11] A retreat can only be ordered by the national command authority, and divisions or lower units participate only as part of the larger formation.

Divisions and below may execute a withdrawal, *otkhod,* (literally, to step backwards) to avoid destruction by superior enemy forces, to gain time, or as an economy of force measure to redeploy forces to another axis.[12] A withdrawal must be approved by a commander at least two echelons above the withdrawing unit and can only be executed if specifically ordered. For example, if a battalion is to execute a withdrawal, its commander must receive a specific order from his regimental commander that has the approval of the division commander.

It should be noted that a Soviet tactical commander does not simply request permission to withdraw; he asks his commander to order him to withdraw. It is also important to understand that a commander cannot order the withdrawal of a subordinate unit without the approval of his commander. While this process is cumbersome, it serves the Soviet Army's purpose of discouraging too much willingness to give ground. It is also an excellent example of the concept of *otvetsvennost'* (responsibility) in Soviet command, described in Chapter 3. The process leaves no doubt as to who is responsible for Soviet forces giving ground to an enemy, and the swift and brutal nature of Soviet military justice, described in Chapter 2, serves to stiffen the resolve of even the most timid Soviet commander. In the Soviet Army, there is neither a professional nor even a personal future in being too eager to withdraw.

While it may seem unusual to the Western military profession to spread responsibility up the chain of command, it is entirely consistent with Soviet military traditions and practice; it is an institutionalized expression of the characteristic of Soviet military service described by Andrew Cockburn in his book *The Threat: Inside the Soviet Military Machine.*[13] Cockburn dwells to some degree on the negative influences of the practice, but the Soviet military profession sees it in a positive light as providing a specific guide to behavior which, in the chaos of battle, contributes to steadfastness and unity of effort.

It would be erroneous, however, to conclude that the Soviet concept of the defense is inflexible or that it stifles initiative. When the defensive plan calls for a withdrawal, as for a covering force or as part of a maneuver plan, the responsible commander has the flexibility to execute by virtue of the approval of his defense plan. In the Soviet mind, this concept actually encourages initiative in the Soviet view of grim determination, explained in Chapter 3.

In summary, Soviet defensive operations can be described as temporary measures marked by a basic unwillingness to give ground and by continual attempts to inflict heavy losses on the enemy. Their purpose is to change the correlation of forces in favor of the Soviet Army so that it may assume the offensive.

Characteristics of Defensive Operations

The Soviet Army stresses that successful defensive operations must display two characteristics: *aktivnost'*, generally translated into English as "combat activeness," and *ustoichivost'*, traditionally translated as "steadfastness."[14] As is often the case, these translations do not convey the full meanings of the terms, and they actually confuse the issue. Since these terms define the perception of Soviet commanders as to what characterizes a successful defense, it is important to understand their specific meaning in Soviet military jargon.

The Soviet *Dictionary of Basic Military Terms* defines *aktivnost' oborony*, combat activeness in the defense, as destruction of enemy weapons of mass destruction, conduct of fire strikes, and combining use of maneuver and obstacles to break up the attack.[15] Other Soviet sources expand on this definition by including the requirements of repelling the attack and destroying the attacker, imposing the will of the defender on the attacker, and creating conditions favoring the offensive.[16] In short, Soviet commanders understand *aktivnost'* as meaning aggressively seeking to cause enemy casualties and losses and to seize the initiative. It is perceived as using aggressiveness as a force multiplier to compensate for a temporary insufficiency in forces and means.[17]

The *Dictionary of Basic Military Terms* defines *ustoichivost' oborony* as exploiting firepower, maneuver, and terrain to defeat superior enemy forces and to hold the defended area.[18] Firepower contributes to steadfastness by destroying attacking enemy forces, and maneuver contributes to steadfastness by increasing the depth and density of the defense in the area of the enemy's main effort.[19] Conceptually, steadfastness, *ustoichivost'*, entails the attacking enemy force literally getting "wedged into" (*vklinivatsia*) the defense, where it can be pounded to pieces by the defenders.[20] In the Soviet view, steadfastness in the defense is an obstinate determination not to give ground.

A Soviet commander receiving the order to conduct a defense understands that the defense is an expedient and temporary situation and that he will sooner or later resume the offensive. He knows that defensive operations are not related to extended position warfare and are not part of a static situation, but exist as a temporary, local condition on an extended and dynamic battlefield.

The Defensive Battlefield

The Soviet view of the contemporary defensive battlefield is that it exists as part of the offensive battlefield described in Chapter 4. The Soviet Army believes that the defensive battlefield will be characterized by combined arms operations with diverse means of combat being engaged in intense and transient battles that will rapidly and sharply change the situation.[21] The course and outcome of the defense will not come about as the result of a single engagement but will be determined by the sum of the results of these seemingly random battles.

It is important to understand this view of the nature of the contemporary defensive battlefield because it explains why the Soviet Army has moved away from traditional dependence upon stylized defensive deployments with defined frontages for various types and sizes of combat units and with prescribed distances between positions, and now favors application of general rules to specific situations. As in the offense, the causes of these changes are a sum of a number of influences generally described as the power of weapons of mass destruction, the lethality and range of modern conventional weaponry, and the impact of technology on military capabilities. The concept of set-piece combat on a templated battlefield reached its zenith in the latter stages of World War II and held on until the mid-1950s, when it was formally abandoned.[22]

Planning the Defense

The process of planning a defensive mission is one of applying the rules and principles of Soviet tactics to a specific military task and situation. The same basic pattern of concept-algorithm-decision that applies to the offense, described in the preceding chapter, applies to the defense as well.

Concept

The volitional aspects of the mission of a combat unit ordered to conduct a defense begin with the general missions of killing enemy troops, destroying their equipment, and exhausting their capability and desire to fight. The general mission is elaborated upon by the specific defensive missions assigned to each commander. Each mission includes a group of specified tasks in order of priority.

The general defensive missions normally comprise the following four tasks in order of priority:

- Destroy enemy weapons of mass destruction and their delivery means
- Destroy enemy command, control, and communications
- Locate and destroy enemy tank reserves
- Destroy forces in contact

Other tasks and their priorities specific to the given mission are defined in the operations order.

The tasks and their priorities are important because they tell commanders how to employ their time and resources and guide them in resolving conflicting requirements. For example, a Soviet commander whose reconnaissance has located an enemy 155mm howitzer battery and a tank battalion assembly area, but who has sufficient assets to destroy only one target, would know to expend those assets on the artillery battery because of its CBR capability. It is important to remember that the set tasks are not a priority of work in preparing the defense, as in preparing obstacles, building field fortifications, and improving lines of communication. They are operational priorities guiding conduct of the defensive battle.

An interesting aspect of the order of priority of tasks is that the weight of the defensive is focused in the depth of the enemy formation, not at the line of contact. Nuclear capable weapons and units, command posts, and reserves are all going to be located well behind the FEBA. Only forces in contact, the fourth and lowest priority, are at the front. The concept of deep attack, or of holding the second echelon at risk, was well established in Soviet defensive tactics decades before it gained popularity in U.S. defensive doctrines.

In addition to assigning tasks, the order for the defense may assign a priority to work to be done in preparing the defense. While the priority of work is scenario-dependent, Soviet sources indicate that three requirements usually receive the greatest emphasis. The first priority is usually preparation of obstacles and barriers, because they form the basis of the defense and they increase the destructive effect of fire on the enemy.[23]

The second priority of work is selection of regions, upon which the steadfastness of the defense depends.[24] This work includes organization of the ground through reconnaissance and selection of defensive belts and strong points and physical construction of defensive positions, which begins as soon as they are designated. The ancient Russian tradition of going to Mother Earth for protection in battle is very much a part of modern Soviet military practice. Soviet norms state that protective shelters reduce vulnerability and thereby decrease losses in personnel and equipment to the effects of nuclear explosions by a factor of three, and to the effects of conventional weapons by a factor of seven or more.[25] Field fortification, in the Soviet view, has the effect of a force multiplier.

Maskirovka (translated as "camouflage" but actually including all active and passive measures for concealment, cover, and deception) is an integral part of organization and preparation of the ground.[26] *Maskirovka* includes passive measures to conceal friendly dispositions from the enemy through the use of natural and artificial camouflage materials and techniques, and the use of security measures to frustrate enemy collection efforts. The concept of *maskirovka* is not, however, only or even primarily, a passive effort to deny information to the enemy. Indeed, it includes extensive and often sophisticated efforts to overload the enemy's intelligence with misleading or spurious data.

The third priority is normally the communications network to support movement of reserves and supply and evacuation. A particular concern in preparation of the communications network is support of the movement of counterattack forces. Routes are generally marked and cleared of obstacles that might impede the rapid deployment of the counterattack force.

Schematically, the priority of work is from front to rear, from the areas in front of the defensive position to the support areas. It must be remembered, however, that priorities are not sequential: work progresses in all areas at the same time, but emphasis and scarce resources, such as engineer support, are committed by priority.

Algorithm

The Soviet faith in the use of algorithms as an objective, scientific form of logic for combat decision making applies to the defense as well as to the offense. Because of the bias for the offense in the Soviet military profession, discussions of the decision-making process are generally presented from that aspect, and much less is written about the defense. What is written about defensive operations, however, implies that there is a decision-making model for defense and that its structure closely approximates that for the offense presented in Chapter 4 (Fig. 4.1). Analysis of available data suggests that the algorithm for the defense resembles the structure depicted in Figure 5.1.

The Enemy

As in the offense, the first problem is to define the relationship to the enemy. In the Soviet view, the defense is justified under four general conditions:

- To repulse an expected enemy counteroffensive
- As the outcome of an unsuccessful meeting engagement
- To protect the flanks or rear of a major unit on the offense
- To defend a coastline against amphibious attack[27]

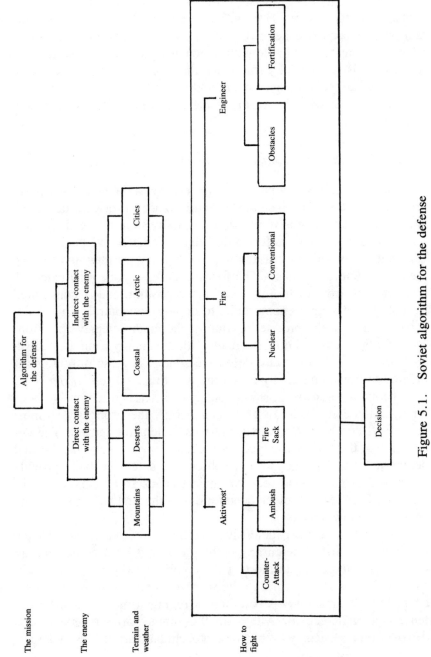

Figure 5.1.   Soviet algorithm for the defense

Preferably, a unit will assume the defense when it is not in direct contact with the enemy. However, this condition generally will pertain only to second echelon forces. There are occasions, however, when units engaged in battle with the enemy may have to assume the defense. This is especially true when there has been an unsuccessful outcome of a meeting engagement; and it may also apply when a unit in direct contact with the enemy is included in the defensive system of a larger unit.

Normal Terrain and Weather Conditions

When not in direct contact with the enemy, a defense is generally organized in depth and includes a security zone, a forward defensive zone, and a main defensive position. For a division, the security zone may extend 20 kilometers forward of the main defensive position and is manned by small units tasked to provide early warning and to slow the enemy rate of advance. The forward defense zone may extend 5 kilometers in front of the main defensive position and is constituted to force the attacking enemy units to deploy prematurely and to deceive them as to the precise location of the main defensive position. By definition, units in direct contact with the enemy cannot establish a security zone or a forward defensive zone. They can only do so if ordered to break contact by executing a withdrawal (otkhod).

The main defensive position comprises a series of defensive belts arranged in depth.[28] The first belt is generally the strongest and most important, and is located along the most defensible terrain. The destruction of the enemy is expected to occur in front of, or in, the first defensive belt. The second and subsequent defensive belts provide depth to the defense and security against attack from unexpected directions. They serve to block penetrations of the first belt or as staging areas for counterattacks.

As a rule, the main defensive position is organized to provide depth and all-around defense. Depth is achieved by deep echeloning of defensive forces, with most of the combat power in the first echelon, and most of the armor in the second echelon to provide mobile counterattack capability. A battalion or regiment may organize a defense in a single echelon with a small combined arms reserve if it is deployed on a secondary avenue of approach, has suffered heavy losses, or is unable to organize in depth due to heavy enemy pressure.[29] The rule, however, is two echelons, and levels above regiment are always in two or more echelons.

In reality, echelonment in the defense results in an extremely complex and dense defensive deployment. For example, there are tactical (division and below) first and second echelons, operational (army) first and second echelons, and strategic (front) first and second echelons. A strategic first echelon would be two or more armies of a front, and an operational first echelon would comprise two or more divisions of an army. The tactical first echelon consists of two or more first echelon regiments of first echelon tank or motorized rifle divisions. The tactical first and second echelons in turn comprise the first and second echelons of the battalions and regiments.

Generally, defensive belts correspond to echelons, but this is not a hard and fast rule. Defensive belts are organized along defensible terrain and comprise a series of mutually supporting defensive positions or strong points reinforced with obstacles and supported by fire. Defensive belts are the organization of the ground. Echelons, on the other hand, are the organization of units for combat. The first defensive belt is usually occupied by the first echelon, while the second and subsequent defensive belts are prepared by the second echelon and may be occupied permanently or on order, as part of the defensive plan of maneuver.

A defensive belt is not a continuous line of troops, but comprises a number of strong points, normally constructed around a reinforced company, that are mutually supporting by fire. Under current norms, a motorized rifle company may occupy a strong point 1000 meters wide and 500 meters deep, with 300 meters between platoons. Platoon positions are self-contained and are organized so that the company and the platoon can fight in any direction. Norms specify that gaps between companies may be 1 to 1.5 kilometers. Gaps between units are covered by fire and are protected by obstacles and patrols. In addition, second echelon units may be placed to provide defense in depth in gaps between first echelon units. Figure 5.2 is a schematic of a motorized rifle battalion in a single echelon defense. In this instance, the battalion commander has constituted a reserve from a platoon of a rifle company. Figure 5.3 is a schematic of a reinforced tank battalion in two echelons. In this case, there is no reserve; how-

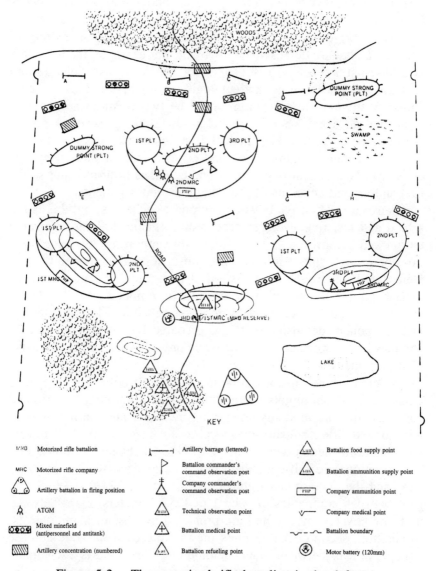

KEY

MRB	Motorized rifle battalion		Artillery barrage (lettered)	Battalion food supply point
MRC	Motorized rifle company		Battalion commander's command observation post	Battalion ammunition supply point
	Artillery battalion in firing position		Company commander's command observation post	Company ammunition point
	ATGM		Technical observation point	Company medical point
	Mixed minefield (antipersonnel and antitank)		Battalion medical point	Battalion boundary
	Artillery concentration (numbered)		Battalion refueling point	Motor battery (120mm)

Figure 5.2.   The motorized rifle battalion in the defense

Source: DDB-1100-197-78; "The Soviet Motorized Rifle Battalion," DIA, September 1978, p. 94.

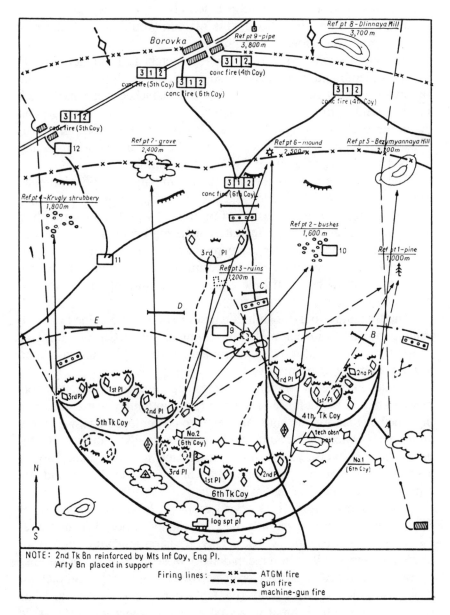

Figure 5.3.   Tank Battalion in the Defense

Source: *Soviet Military Review*, No. 6, June 1983, p. 14.

ever, a platoon from the second echelon company is deployed in the
security zone. In all likelihood, this platoon would become the battalion reserve when forced to withdraw.

A platoon strong point is up to 400 meters in frontage and 300
meters in depth and comprises squad positions, positions for organic
armored personnel carriers, and locations for attached weapons.[30] Each
squad defends a front of approximately 100 meters, structured around
the armor-protected firepower of the BMP, which is normally positioned approximately 50 meters behind the squad positions. Figure
5.4 is a schematic of a squad defensive position.

The normal process is for the squad commander to position each
squad member on the ground, and for the troops to prepare their individual firing positions. A connecting trench with dugouts providing
overhead cover and primary and alternate firing positions for the BMP
are prepared. The final step is to prepare communications trenches
for supply and evacuation and to permit covered movement within
the platoon strong point. If time and assets permit, alternate and supplementary positions are prepared.

The trenching tools of individual soldiers are supplemented with
vehicle-mounted pioneer tools and engineer support in the form of
demolitions and earth-moving equipment. If available, tank-mounted
dozer blades are also employed.

In addition to echelonment of forces and defensive belts, it is normal practice in the defense to constitute an antitank reserve comprising attached and organic antitank means to be deployed against enemy
armor penetrations. The antitank reserve normally occupies an *ognevoy rubezh* (literally, fire line) preselected to block likely armor
avenues of approach.[31] Fire lines may be located in the second defensive belt or between defensive belts.

The antitank reserve is a key element in the defense because of
Soviet concern for the threat posed by enemy armor. For instance,
the Soviet Army calculates that a U.S. division attacking on a front
of 25 kilometers will offer a mean density of sixteen tanks per kilometer of front, and if it attacks on a narrower front of 15 kilometers,
this density increases to twenty-five tanks per kilometer of front. This
is obviously a potent threat to a first echelon Soviet motorized rifle
battalion.

Another means of responding to a threat is the Soviet concept of
an *ognevoy meshok* (fire sack),[32] in which a first echelon battalion

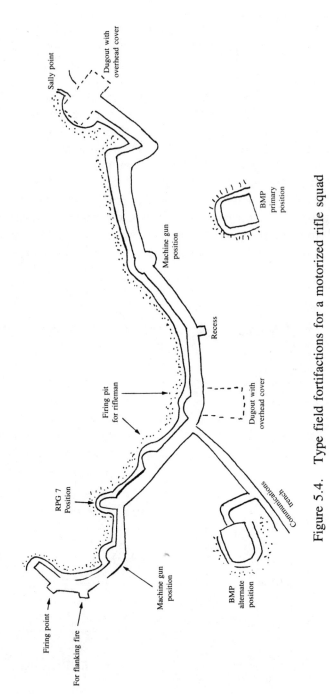

Figure 5.4.   Type field fortifactions for a motorized rifle squad

deploys so as to channel the attacking enemy into a pocket in the center of the battalion position, where they will be blocked by obstacles and destroyed by concentrated fire from the front, flanks, and rear. A schematic of a fire sack is at Figure 5.5.

The fire sack resembles the U.S. mobile defense in some superficial aspects but differs fundamentally in that the killing ground is created prior to the battle by deliberate deployment rather than by maneuver, and in that destruction of the enemy is achieved by sudden, overwhelming firepower rather than by counterattack.

By nature, a fire sack is a two-echelon deployment for a battalion. The precise configuration depends upon terrain, but the optimum width, according to Soviet norms, is 1.5 times the effective range of the principal antitank weapon available.[33] A typical fire sack is 2 or 3 kilometers wide and 1 to 2 kilometers deep. The fire sack is an ap-

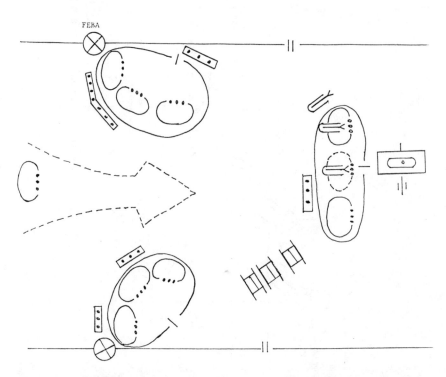

Figure 5.5.   Schematic of Reinforced Motorized Rifle Battalion Deployed in a "Fire Sack" Defense

plication of the concept of getting the enemy wedged, or stuck, in the defense so that he can be shattered by fire.

A high density of fire (*plotnost'*) is achieved by layering of fire. This is an interesting Soviet perception of fire planning which seeks to increase the volume of fire by vertical as well as horizontal deployment of weapons. Essentially, longer-range weapons such as the ATGM, (antitank guided missiles) artillery in direct fire roles, and antitank guns are placed at longer ranges from the killing ground and on the highest ground to deliver plunging fire upon the enemy, while tanks and shorter-range weapons are emplaced closer to the killing ground with more attention to flanking and grazing fire.

In both the antitank reserve and in the fire sack, it is the Soviet practice to employ a mix of what are referred to as general and special antitank means.[34] General means include weapons capable of destroying tanks but having other primary battlefield roles. They include missiles, tanks, aircraft, and artillery. Special means are weapons designed specifically to engage tanks by direct fire. They include antitank guided missiles, antitank guns, recoilless rifles, and antitank rockets, grenades, and mines. It is interesting that the Soviet army perceives tanks as a general, rather than special, antitank means. Unlike the U.S. Army, the Soviet Army considers antitank artillery, either towed or self-propelled, and ATGMs as the principal antitank weapons. Tanks deployed in the first echelon are used as mobile antitank guns because Soviet norms state that tanks firing from deliberate positions can defeat two or three times their number, but if employed in a mobile counterattack role, they must have numerical superiority over the enemy tanks.[35] The effectiveness of antitank means can also be multiplied by a factor of two to three if positions are fortified.

Antitank weapons are also integrated into the antitank defense according to weapons characteristics. The impact of one characteristic, range, is displayed in Figure 5.6. Essentially, it shows that ATGMs are most effective at ranges from 500 meters to 3000 meters, while guns are effective at ranges less than 2000 meters, and infantry weapons are effective at less than 1000 meters. It is important to remember that these figures are planning guidelines only. They assist in fire planning by assuring the most efficient use of all available weapons, but they do not preclude any particular weapons system from engaging targets outside of its envelope when that is possible.

The Soviet penchant for relying upon "scientific" calculations in planning a battle applies in the defense as well as in the offense. Figure 5.7 shows a nomogram used to calculate the number of anti-tank weapons required to conduct an effective defense. Actually, the nomogram should be used in combination with a sophisticated model of the data in Figure 5.6 depicting the capabilities of various antitank means that might be available. By manipulating these data, Soviet commanders can determine the optimum density, mix, and deployment of antitank means to defeat the expected tank threat.

Special Terrain and Weather Conditions

Soviet military science recognizes five special terrain and weather conditions as having unique effects on how military operations are

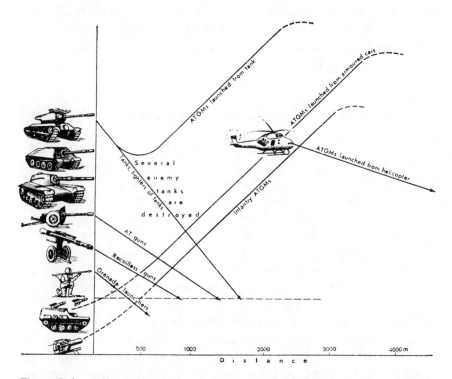

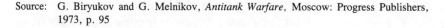

Figure 5.6.   Effectiveness of various means used against attacking medium tanks versus range

Source: G. Biryukov and G. Melnikov, *Antitank Warfare*, Moscow: Progress Publishers, 1973, p. 95

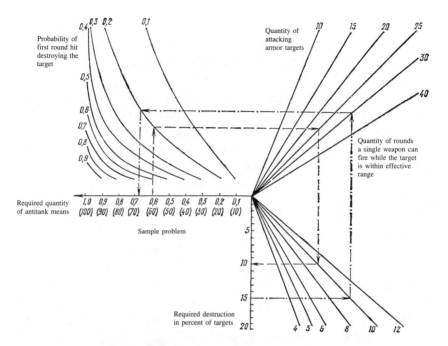

Problem: How many antitank means are needed to destroy not less than 60% of
           the attacking enemy tanks?
Given: Expected quantity: 25.
           Probability of first round hit: 0.2.
           Rate of fire while target is in range: 10.
Solution: Find required destruction and read up to probability of first round hit.
           Read across to expected quantity of tanks. Read down to rate of fire.
           Read across to quantity of antitank means.
Answer: 10 antitank means are required.

Figure 5.7.   Nomogram for computing the required quantity of antitank means

Source: Col. A. Ia. Vainer, "Takticheskie Raschety," Moscow: Voenizdat, 1982, p. 54.

conducted. These conditions are defined as mountain, desert, coastal,
arctic, and cities.

The defense in mountainous terrain is structured to block avenues
of approach for the attacking enemy, leaving gaps between units to
be protected with reconnaissance and barriers.[36] Fire planning is based
upon engaging the enemy at maximum range with layered fire, as in
the fire sack. A successful defense in mountainous regions depends
upon occupation of commanding heights that dominate passes, road

junctions, and other centers of communications. Due to the dispersion of forces and the effects of terrain, most artillery is attached to first echelon units. Terrain restricts counterattack routes to roads, valleys, or ridgelines.

In desert terrain, defending forces are widely dispersed and concentrated around vital regions, such as communications centers and water sources.[37] In desert operations, large mobile reserves are maintained to engage enemy forces attempting to penetrate between strong points. Gaps are covered by extensive reconnaissance, and strong artillery reserves are used to reinforce mobile forces. A major concern in all desert operations is ensuring sufficient supply and distribution of water for friendly forces, while denying it to the enemy.

The Soviet concept for defense in arctic conditions is similar to that in desert conditions in many specifics. It entails concentrating the defense on avenues of approach to vital areas, usually defined as communications centers, leaving large unoccupied sectors between strong points to be covered by patrols and observation points. Soviet experience has shown that the sparse transportation infrastructure defines key terrain more than physical geography. The tempo of operations is greatly slowed by requirements to supply water to troops and to keep them warm.

Defensive combat in cities is a Soviet speciality, developed from long experience in World War II in such epic battles as Stalingrad, Leningrad, Odessa, and Sevastopol. The concept is to organize strong points in width and depth, usually based upon city blocks and major buildings.[38] Each block is organized to resist attack from all sides and to fight independently. Armored vehicles, including tanks and BMPs, are usually located inside the block, where they can maneuver to any threatened side to fire along streets or across open areas.[39] Sewer systems are exploited for ambushes and as communications systems. Command and logistics operate from basements of buildings, riflemen from first floors for grazing fire, and crew-served weapons from upper floors to increase the density of fire by adding plunging fire. Most of the artillery is deployed in the first echelon and has a major direct fire role in defending against enemy armor. Engineer priorities are to convert buildings into strong points, to create obstacles, and to keep communications routes open.

In recent years, the Soviet Army has shown increasing interest in the problems of defending a coastline against amphibious assault.

Lacking historical experience in any but the most minor amphibious operations, Soviet perceptions of the amphibious threat certainly are based entirely upon an appreciation of the U.S. amphibious capability. As a result, the Soviet concept of defending a coastline is an adaptation of traditional Soviet tactics, modified by an understanding of Western practices, to a new situation. The Soviet Army describes its concept for defense of a coastline as "defense on an extended front established by forces not in direct contact with the enemy."[40] The concept of an extended front means deployment in a single echelon with a small reserve. "Not in direct contact with the enemy" implies deployment of a security echelon, extensive barrier planning, a detailed fire plan, preparation of alternate positions, and an extensive *maskirovka* effort. The basic tactical unit is a motorized rifle battalion reinforced with at least an artillery battalion, a tank company, an antiaircraft platoon, and a sapper platoon. Consider, for example, a reinforced motorized rifle battalion deployed in defense of a coastline. Soviet sources hold that such a force can successfully defend a beach against assault by a U.S. Marine Amphibious Unit (MAU). In this configuration, a Soviet motorized rifle battalion would probably defend on a front of about 5 kilometers. Although its combat power is less than that of a MAU, the Soviet battalion would expect its prepared positions to reduce the attacker's superiority, and would expect to prevent the MAU from organizing its combat power ashore by engaging it at sea and defeating the first wave before the second wave can reach the shore. Soviet commanders are aware of the threat of heliborne operations, but they assign the mission of destroying them to the regiment or division second echelon, and they believe that defeat of the over-the-beach force is the key to a successful defense of the coast.

An interesting Soviet practice in coast defense is the extensive use of devices to aid ground forces in delivering accurate fire on offshore targets. Buoys, rafts, and other floating markers are anchored at various positions to provide reference points for sectors of fire, for range estimation, and for reference in adjusting artillery and mortar fire.

Decision

In the defense, a Soviet commander's decision involves solving two major problems: organization of the ground and organization of his forces. Organization of the ground is generally described as defining the defensive belts. Organization of forces is generally defined as echeloning of forces and *boevoy poriadok,* or task organization of subordinate elements. Implementation of the commander's decision is by assignment of tasks and definition of the priority of work.

In organizing the ground, Soviet commanders are primarily concerned with control of dominant terrain, which is understood as that which ensures control and use of the area and that which controls or blocks enemy avenues of approach. In both instances, dominant terrain may include not only militarily important high ground, but also other features such as communications centers and road networks permitting movement and use of the geography.

Organization of forces is guided by the defensive principles of *aktivnost'* and *ustoichivost'*. Both principles generally favor defense from prepared positions with the majority of forces and means well forward. The general rule is to deploy in two echelons on main avenues of advance for the enemy, and in one echelon across secondary avenues. *Boevoy poriadok,* or task organization, is based upon creation of battalion and company strong points that are mutually supporting but that can defend against attacks from all sides. Their function is less to maneuver to meet the enemy attack than to hold in the face of it. Mobile reserves serve to reinforce against enemy success and to maintain *aktivnost'* by aggressive patrolling and counterattacks. Fire planning includes combined arms, with tanks, mechanized infantry, and antitank means being combined in company teams and artillery and air defense added at battalion level. Other combat support means, such as engineers and CBR defense, are added at regiment and above.

The Soviet system for command, control, and communications in the defense is discussed in Chapter 3. A reason why the Soviet Army considers landline to be the primary means of communications in the defense should be apparent from its tactics for conduct of the defense. Position defense in well-prepared field fortifications lends itself to greater reliance upon wire and less upon radio.

Conclusions

Of course, it is undeniable that the Soviet military profession possesses a strong aversion to the defense and has a clear bias for the offense for professional, political, and psychological reasons. However, this examination clearly shows that Nathan Leites's observation that the defense is a lost art in Soviet military doctrine is a bit optimistic. General Reznichenko's collective of military scholars at the Frunze Military Academy successfully completed their task of creating effective modern Soviet defensive tactics, and their field-tested findings now guide the Soviet Army in defensive operations.

In execution, the Soviet concept of the defense is structured to provide a coordinated and unified defense in width and depth, but at the same time to ensure that individual company and battalion strong points are capable of resisting even if isolated and surrounded. It is also important to understand that the rather elaborate set of norms, rules, and nomographs described here represents the concept of a defense and tells the Soviet commander how to most efficiently *plan* the use of his assets. Fighting the defensive battle is quite another thing, however. At that point, everyone from the individual soldier to the senior commander digs in and holds on, no matter what happens, and every opportunity to kill the enemy and to destroy his equipment is exploited. Collective wisdom embodied in rules and norms applies to planning and directing the battle. The Soviet concept of initiative, however, applies to fighting the battle.

Modern Soviet defensive tactics are crafted to exploit the capabilities of contemporary Soviet military technology and organization. In a deeper sense, however, they reflect the traditional Russian military traits of grim determination and stubbornness that have ultimately defeated would-be conquerors from Charles XII of Sweden through Hitler. For all its new weaponry and techniques, the Soviet Army of today still ascribes to the ancient Russian defensive tradition of spilling prodigious quantities of its own blood in exchange for imposing even greater carnage and destruction on its enemy. History tells us that those who make war with the Russian bear must be willing and able to pay the cost.

Notes

1. Col. G. Ionin, "Sovremennaia Oborona" ("Modern Defense"), *Voennyi Vestnik*, no. 4, 1981, p. 18.
2. See, e.g., Nathan Leites, "The Soviet Style in War" in *Soviet Military Thinking*, ed. Derek Leebaert, Cambridge: Harvard University Press, 1981, pp. 204–15.
3. Gen. Maj. A. S. Milovidov, ed., *The Philosophical Heritage of V. I. Lenin and Problems of Contemporary War,* Moscow: Voenizdat, 1972. Translated and published under the auspices of the U.S. Air Force, p. 17.
4. V. Ye Savkin, ed., *The Basic Principles of Operational Art and Tactics,* Moscow: Voenizdat, 1972. Translated and published under the auspices of the U.S. Air Force, p. 250.
5. V. V. Shelyag, A. D. Glolochkin, and K. K. Platonov, eds., *Military Psychology,* Moscow: Voenizdat, 1972. Translated and published under the auspices of the U.S. Air Force, pp. 65, 80, 285.
6. Gen. Maj. L. Korzun, *"Razvitie Taktiki Oboronitel'nogo Boia Motostrelkovykh i Tankovykh Podrazdelenii v Poslevoennye Godi"* ("Development of Motorized Infantry and Tank Unit Defensive Tactics in the Post-war Period"), *Voenno-Istoricheskii Zhurnal,* no. 10, 1980, p. 39.
7. Ibid., p. 41.
8. Ionin, op. cit.
9. Col. V. Tums, *"Aktivnost' Oboroni"* ("Aggressiveness in the Offense"), *Voennyi Vestnik,* no. 3, 1980, p. 38.
10. Gen. Maj. Mikhailovskii and Col. A. Zotov, *"Voprosii Taktiki v Sovetskoi Voennoi Entsiklopedoi"* ("Questions on Tactics in the Soviet Military Encyclopedia"), *Voennyi Vestnik,* no. 11, 1980, pp. 38–39.
11. *Sovetskaia Voennaia Entsiklopediia,* 8 vols., 1976–1980 Moscow: Voenizdat, vol. 5, p. 171.
12. Ibid., p. 172.
13. Andrew Cockburn, *The Threat: Inside the Soviet Military Machine,* New York: Random House, 1983, pp. 52–76.
14. Tums, op. cit.
15. *Dictionary of Basic Military Terms,* Moscow: Voenizdat, 1965. Published under the auspices of the U.S. Air Force. Translated by the DGIS Multilingual Section, Translation Bureau, Secretary of State Department, Ottawa, Canada, p. 8.
16. Tums, op. cit.
17. Ionin, op. cit., p. 16.
18. *Dictionary of Basic Military Terms,* op. cit., p. 227.
19. F. D. Sverdlov, *Takticheskii Manevr (Tactical Maneuvers),* Moscow: Voenizdat, 1982, p. 135.

20. Ibid., p. 133.

21. Ionin, op. cit., p. 14.

22. Korzun, op. cit., pp. 34–35.

23. Ibid., p. 35. See also Gen. Maj. I. Vorobev, "Oruzhie i Taktika" ("Weapons and Tactics"), *Krasnaia Zvezda*, 12 January 1982, p. 2.

24. Gen. Lt. Kir'ian, ed., *Voenno-Tekhnicheskii Progress i Vooruzhennye Sili SSSR (Military-Technical Progress and the Soviet Armed Forces)*, Moscow: Voenizdat, 1982, p. 247.

25. Ionin, op. cit., p. 15.

26. Ibid. See also *Dictionary of Basic Military Terms*, op. cit., p. 118.

27. *Sovetskaia Voennaia Entsiklopediia*, op. cit., vol. 1, p. 246.

28. Ionin, op. cit., p. 16.

29. Ibid.

30. Col. L. Merzylak, "IFVs on the Defensive," *Soviet Military Review*, no. 8, 1983, p. 20.

31. *Sovetskaia Voennaia Entsiklopediia*, op. cit., vol. 6, p. 13.

32. Ibid., p. 12.

33. G. B. Biryukov and G. Melnikov, *Antitank Warfare*, Moscow: Progress Publishers, 1973, p. 107.

34. Ibid., p. 68.

35. Ibid., p. 72. See also p. 97.

36. *Sovetskaia Voennaia Entsiklopediia*, op. cit., vol. 5, p. 663.

37. Merzylak, op. cit.

38. Col. Z. Zotov, "Defense of a Town," *Soviet Military Review*, no. 6, 1982, p. 48.

39. Merzylak, op. cit.

40. Gen. Maj. Shevchenko, "*Kontrataka*" ("Counterattack"), *Voennyi Vestnik*, August 1981, pp. 39–43.

CHAPTER 6

Supporting Operations

Not by bread alone

Dudintsev

In his 1956 book, *Not by Bread Alone,* the Soviet writer Dudintsev used this biblical passage as a metaphor to explain that, while strong black bread springing from the earth of Mother Russia is the staff of life, more is needed to survive and thrive. Applying the metaphor to the Soviet Army, the "bread of life" is its tank and motorized rifle forces maneuvering against the enemy, supported by the fires of artillery, rockets, and aircraft. Like salt in bread, however, other elements are needed to survive in battle and win.

The most prominent of these elements are collected in this chapter. Since this book is technically structured to respect Soviet military thought, each of the headings in this chapter should properly have its own chapter. In the interest of style and brevity, however, they are gathered here under the single heading Supporting Operations. Some would argue that air defense, landing operations, combat engineers, and CBR warfare are not combat support since they involve combat to some degree. From a Soviet standpoint, however, they can be categorized as supporting operations because they are not missions in themselves, but contribute to the success of maneuver forces in the offense and defense.

Air Defense

The Red Army's experience at the hands of the German *Luftwaffe* in the early stages of World War II was a painful lesson in the havoc that tactical air power can create in ground forces operations. Its own employment of air power, and analyses of operations in recent local wars in Asia and the Middle East have reinforced the Soviet Army's respect for the threat from the sky.

The Soviet Army's response to the threat of tactical air power is to blanket the battlefield with an impressive quantity of sophisticated air defense weapons, and to provide an extensive organization to control and direct the battle against intruding enemy aircraft. The Soviet concept of air defense is reflected in the missions and organization of Soviet air defense. It includes the active and passive aspects of defense described in Chapter 5.[1] The passive aspect of *zashchita* includes all of the actions of *maskirovka* (concealment and deception), movement, and dispersion that, in combination, make ground forces hard to find and hard to hit. The active aspects of *oborona* include the air battle, air defense by missiles and guns, and even creating "ambushes" to draw enemy aircraft into killing grounds of antiaircraft fire.

The Organization and Missions of Soviet Air Defense

In the past few years, Soviet air defense has undergone an extensive reorganization that has decentralized and streamlined command and control. In place of National Air Defense (*PVO Strany*) and Air Defense of Ground Forces (*PVO SV*), there is now Air Defense Forces (*Voiska PVO*) and Troop PVO (*Voiskovaya PVO*).[2] Organizationally, Air Defense Forces is one of the five Soviet Armed Forces, and exercises administrative and logistical control and support functions for all PVO forces. Operationally, Air Defense Forces is divided into the four branches shown in Figure 6.1. The ZRV comprises the missile units deployed in military districts, groups of forces, and fronts. It is the ground component to PVO. APVO is the interceptor component of PVO and operates in coordination with missile units. RTV mans early warning and air surveillance radars, while the rear service troops provide supply, administration, and maintenance for PVO materiel and units.

Troop PVO provides ground antiaircraft defense for the ground forces at army level and below.[3] Its organization is shown in Figure 6.2. While Troop PVO functions as a branch of the ground forces, PVO-specific logistics and administration are provided by PVO Forces Rear Services. Non–PVO-specific support is supplied by the ground forces.

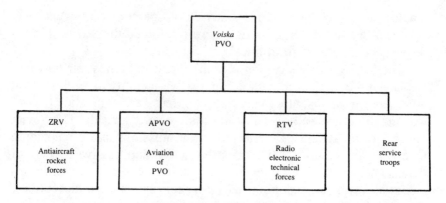

Figure 6.1.   Organization of Soviet antiaircraft defense forces

Source: *Spravochnik Ofitsera Protivovozdushnoi Oborony,* Moscow: Voenizdat, 1981, pp.
5–8.

Air Defense Forces apparently operate at theater level and supply
air defense assets, such as the air defense brigade at army/*front* level.
Although the Front Commander may not have assigned APVO
interceptor aircraft under his control, he may use frontal aviation fighters
for this purpose if he desires.

Troop PVO provides tactical air defense for ground forces at di-

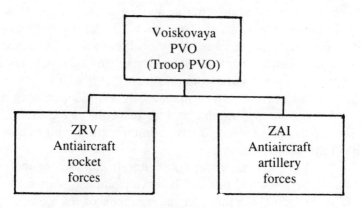

Figure 6.2   Organization of Troop PVO

Source: *Spravochnik Ofitsera Protivovozdushnoi Oborony,* Moscow: Voenizdat, 1981, pp.
6–7.

vision and below. Its capabilities are reinforced and supplemented by air defense forces at army and *front*. All these assets are integrated into a single air defense zone that engages enemy aircraft operating within the battle area. The Soviet concept of this integrated air defense is depicted in Figure 6.3.

The impetus for air defense is from rear to front. Early warning and tracking radars organic to Air Defense Forces monitor enemy air activity in the battle area and are used in planning and directing the air battle. Air threats of primary concern to strategic level commanders are engaged by fighter aircraft of APVO or the missile systems organic to ZRV.

Air interceptors are closely controlled from the ground, and operations follow the four-stage scenario shown in Figure 6.4.[4] In stage 1, the air control post guides the interceptors to a tactically advantageous position in relation to the target by a flight plan that avoids

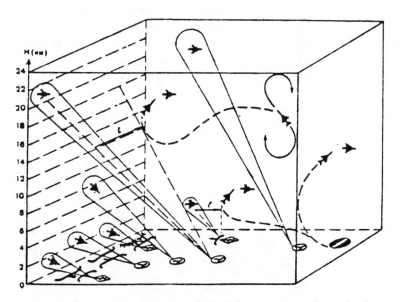

Integration and deployment of air defense systems in a single zone by front, depth, and altitude (ℓ = safety space)

Figure 6.3.

Source: Gen. Col. of Artillery Levchenko, ed., *Protivovozdushnaia Oborona Sukhoputnykh Voisk*, Moscow: Voenizdat, 1979, p. 188.

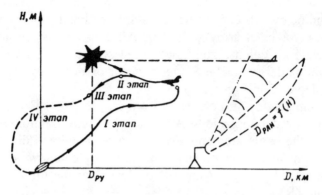
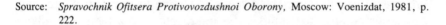

Figure 6.4.   Stages of a fighter interceptor mission

Source: *Spravochnik Ofitsera Protivovozdushnoi Oborony*, Moscow: Voenizdat, 1981, p.
           222.

the threat of other friendly antiaircraft systems. In stage 2, the pilot
takes over and uses visual or on-board electronics to execute the attack. In stage 3, the pilot maintains contact with the target until a kill
is ensured. In stage 4, the air control post again assumes control and
guides the interceptor back to the airfield.

Antiaircraft Rocket Forces (ZRV) follows a different scenario. Areas
assigned to its coverage are divided into the three parts shown in Fig-

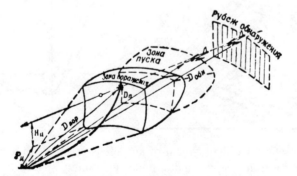

Figure 6.5.   Combat zones for an antiaircraft rocket complex

Source: *Spravochnik Ofitsera Protivovozdushnoi Oborony*, Moscow: Voenizdat, 1981, p.
           264.

ure 6.5. The initial contact point is called the acquisition line. This is an arc near the maximum range of the weapon's target acquisition and guidance radar. At the point where an enemy aircraft crosses that line, the tracking and firing sequence starts. As the target approaches the launch site, it enters the launch zone, an area beginning beyond the maximum effective range of the weapon, defined by the speed and path of the target and the weapon capability as being where a launch will generate a target hit. The destruction zone is that space defined by weapon characteristics as where destruction of the target may occur.

The strategic assets overreach and reinforce the air defense capabilities of operational commanders at *front* and army. At both levels there are assigned air defense brigades armed with surface-to-air missiles (SAMs). Although *front* commanders do not generally have APVO interceptor aircraft under their control, they may employ the fighter assets in their subordinate tactical air army in the air defense role. Likewise, there is some information suggesting that army commanders may use assigned armed helicopters against enemy helicopters, if the situation so warrants.

Army and *front* air defenses overreach and reinforce the tactical air defenses of divisions. Tank and motorized rifle divisions have organic SAM regiments equipped with mobile missile systems to provide area defense within the division zone. Since they are operating under a blanket of strategic and operational air defenses from theater, *front*, and army, division commanders are free to concentrate their air defenses in those areas and around those installations that are of primary concern to their tactical missions.

The antiaircraft battery organic to maneuver regiments uses mobile gun and missile platoons to provide short-range point air defense to key regimental installations or units. These weapons systems can operate from fixed sites or while on the march and are reinforced by the area coverage from division and higher assets.

Motorized rifle battalions have an organic antiaircraft platoon mounted in personnel carriers. This platoon is equipped with shoulder-fired heat-seeking missiles to engage low-flying aircraft. It provides the battalion with immediate close-in defense against air attack. Tank battalions have no organic dedicated air defense capability. For defense against air attack, they rely upon the 12.7mm antiaircraft machine gun mounted on the turret of each tank.

Control of the Air Defense Battle

The first problem in the air defense battle is to differentiate between friend and foe, or to avoid the tendency to shoot everything down and sort it out later on the ground. This control problem is addressed at regiment and above by centralizing and coordinating air defense through the air defense staff element at each headquarters. These staff elements are linked in a dedicated communications net that connects firing units, staff elements, and surveillance systems in a quick response network assisted by automation at every level.

It should not be surprising that this control system is governed by a decision-making algorithm, described in Figure 6.6. Interestingly, this algorithm functions by filtering out aircraft positively identified as friendly, leaving all others to be displayed as hostile. The two principal methods of identifying aircraft are electronically through IFF (identification, friend or foe) or by comparison of flight data with flight plans.

In part, this characteristic justifies the Soviet system of strict controls over air operations and the flights of every aircraft. Any aircraft not following an authorized flight plan is liable to be shot down. In the Soviet view, defense against enemy air attacks takes precedence over flexibility in friendly operations. This attitude also has some application in understanding how a tragedy like the downing of KAL Flight 007 on September 1, 1983, could occur. Since it was not friendly, it was regarded as hostile. The Marxist dialectic does not admit to intermediate conclusions.

The lowest level having a dedicated air defense staff to centrally control and coordinate air defense operations is the maneuver regiment. At battalion level and below, air defense operations are independent, meaning that they are not subject to centralized control.[5] Each company establishes an air observation post with communications and optical instruments to scan the sky for hostile aircraft. Upon locating an approaching aircraft, the air observation post normally uses pyrotechnics to alert the unit to take protection measures. In tank units, the commander of each tank will lay the antiaircraft machine gun in the direction indicated by the air observation post and establish a curtain of fire over the company position. In motorized rifle companies and noncombat headquarters, there is a duty platoon assigned to establish the curtain of fire with its individual small arms. If attacked by armed helicopters, tanks or armored vehicles may en-

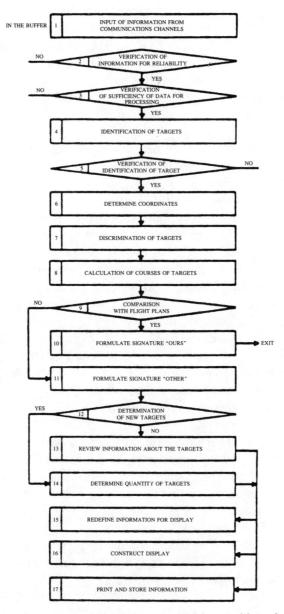

Figure 6.6.   Structural scheme of AAA decision-making algorithm

Source: Gen. Col. of Artillery Levchenkog ed., *Protivovozdushnaia Oborona Sukhoputnykh Voisk*, Moscow: Voenizdat, 1981, p. 223.

gage attacking aircraft with main guns and vehicle-mounted ATGM.

At this level, air observation posts use communications to report enemy air activity and to receive warning of friendly or enemy air activity in the vicinity. Protection of friendly aircraft may be achieved by directing certain air observation posts not to engage any aircraft during a prescribed time period. Another method is to use prearranged light or pyrotechnic signals to identify friendly aircraft, since air observation posts lack IFF.

Obviously this fire cannot be carefully aimed and is not likely to be effective in terms of downed aircraft. The Soviet intention, however, is not so much to shoot down aircraft, as to distract air crews to reduce the accuracy of air-delivered weapons or to force enemy aircraft into the envelope of more sophisticated weapons. This latter intent is occasionally used to create air ambushes wherein ground fire is used to deflect enemy tactical aircraft into preselected killing zones comprising large numbers of antiaircraft weapons that simultaneously engage unsuspecting aircraft from several directions.

While Soviet antiaircraft defense concepts have been developed from successful experience in World War II, they have not been effectively tested against modern aircraft over a battlefield approximating that which might be found in a future general war. Vietnam did not provide the density or mix of weapons that might be expected; nor did the VC have the requisite command and control systems. The various Middle East wars have been too short to provide conclusive answers.

However one argues the case on technical grounds, it is undeniable that losses in aircraft and crews have affected operations through the political process. On December 3, 1983, a fleet of twenty-eight U.S. aircraft attacking hostile positions in Lebanon lost two aircraft and had one damaged in a raid that was at best a qualified success. Participating U.S. pilots explained the problem as resulting from the unprecedented density and high volume of antiaircraft fire. From the Soviet point of view, there is strong evidence that, while there is room for technological improvements in weaponry, their concept is valid. Soviet air defense greatly attenuates the threat to ground forces from the air.

Landing Operations

The Soviet military lexicon defines a landing (*desant*) as any military operation in which specially trained or dedicated forces are deployed upon territory under enemy control to conduct military operations.[6] The generic term does not differentiate by scale of operation or by means of delivery forces; it specifically refers to operations against enemy-controlled territory. Since the front lines or the battle area is territory where opposing forces are contending control, landing operations imply delivery of combat forces into the enemy rear.

Categorization of Landing Operations

Obviously, the definition of what is rear area and what is battle area is a matter of scale. A first echelon battalion rear area, for example, is in the front line battle area of an army. For this reason, the principal means for categorizing landing operations is according to the command level at which they are conducted: strategic, operational, or tactical. Briefly, strategic landings are conducted against the enemy homeland or vital regions to force him out of the war or to open a new front. Strategic landings may comprise air landings, sea landings, or a combination of both in a single operation.

Operational landings are planned and executed by *front* or army commanders to influence the battle at the operational level. They employ assets assigned to the *front* or army to attack enemy nuclear weapons or command installations, or to deny him use of critical areas such as ports or communications centers. Operational landings are generally executed by naval infantry or airborne forces or by a combination of the two.

Tactical landings employ naval infantry, ground forces, or airborne forces to seize objectives in the enemy rear important to the mission of a tactical (division or below) commander. The landing force is platoon- to regiment-size and is delivered by ship, parachute, or helicopter to execute a mission of immediate importance to the tactical commander. Link-up with the main force usually takes place within a period of several hours or days.

Besides scale, landing operations are classified by the means for delivering the landing force. Amphibious landing operations (*morskaia desantnaia operatsiia*) are generally conducted by naval infantry over a beach. Air landing operations (*vozdushnaia desantnaia operatsiia*) are conducted by parachute or helicopter forces or by air landed troops. Soviet writings indicate that amphibious landing operations often include an air landed component and that an air landing operation can contain a sea component, although the latter appears to be a rare occurrence. Either way, the overall operation is categorized by the major component of the landing force.

Capabilities of Landing Operations

Historical precedent, force structure, and military writings all strongly imply that tactical landings are the predominant form and role for Soviet landing operations. Soviet military historians do not lay serious claim to Soviet forces ever having conducted strategic landing operations, citing World War II experience as the primary examples of operations at this scale. Virtually all of the historical examples in Soviet literature are tactical or, optimistically, operational-tactical in scale.

The Soviet Navy does not possess a particularly impressive amphibious landing capability. Naval infantry comprises some 13,500 troops organized into five brigades supported by a total of eighty-four amphibious assault and support ships.[7] This force capability is diluted by its being widely dispersed between four operational fleets, with two brigades being assigned to the Pacific Fleet, and one each to the Northern, Baltic, and Black Sea fleets. In theory, it would be possible to concentrate ships and troops for a large-scale operation, but time and distance factors present formidable problems in marshaling forces and means and in preserving secrecy. Training strongly suggests that these amphibious forces are intended to provide tactical and operational-tactical capabilities for Soviet ground forces operating along coastlines washed by seas where their parent fleets sail.

The Soviet parachute landing capability is concentrated in eight airborne divisions supported by a fleet of 1700 transport aircraft.[8] Commanded by Gen. D. S. Sukhorukov, this force is apparently dedicated to the Soviet strategic reserve in peacetime. The strategic capability of Soviet airborne forces is greatly enhanced by their centralized command and control and air mobility. In a general war, however, their employment in strategic operations would be severely constrained by the need to reinforce or link up with airborne troops either by sea or by land. Training appears to concentrate upon company- through regimental-size operations in direct support of ground forces, indicating that wartime employment would likely be in tactical or operational-tactical missions.

In his book *Inside the Soviet Army*, Viktor Suvorov claims that there is an airborne assault brigade comprising one helicopter assault regiment of sixty-four transport helicopters and three airborne infantry battalions subordinate to each *front*.[9] In addition, it is standard Soviet practice to train one battalion of every motorized rifle regiment in helicopter assault operations. These ensure that all Soviet operational and tactical commanders down to regiment have an organic air assault capability. Suvorov claims, and Soviet military writings confirm, that the principal use for these forces is to secure key terrain in front, and on the flanks, of advancing ground forces in the main effort.

SPETZNAZ Operations

In addition to the conventional combat capabilities in Soviet airborne and naval infantry forces, there is a rather shadowy group of special mission forces generally referred to by their Russian acronym, SPETZNAZ. These are highly trained and motivated troops organized into special units, called diversionary (*diversant*) brigades.[10]

Although *diversant* operations are not specifically landing operations, they may be infiltrated by helicopter, by parachute, by sea, or by other means in company-size or smaller units. *Diversant* units carry out raids and sabotage operations against nuclear weapons delivery and storage sites and communications and command installations, and spread panic and confusion among rear troops and the local populace. Suvorov, in particular, dwells on the employment of special SPETZNAZ assassination teams targeted on key military and political leaders. SPETZNAZ operations are normally planned and coordinated at the operational or strategic level.

Conduct of an Air Assault

An air assault can be conducted by landing troops in transport aircraft or helicopters (*vysadka*) or by parachute assault (*vybroska*).[11] Landing in transport aircraft is normally a strategic or operational mission and assumes control of the landing field by friendly forces. This is the method by which Soviet airborne troops were delivered in Prague in 1968 and in Afghanistan in 1979.

Helicopter landing operations are normally tactical or operational missions planned and executed at *front*, army, or division level. *Front* commanders employ their assigned airborne assault brigades. At army, assigned *armeiskaia aviatsiia* (army aviation) provides aircraft, while troops are drawn from the specially trained motorized rifle battalions in the army second echelon division. Division commanders receive aircraft support from army assets and use troops from a division second echelon motorized rifle battalion.

Since helicopter assault troops are lightly armed and lack ground mobility, objectives generally appear to be within 20 kilometers of the line of contact and are usually undefended, or lightly defended, terrain features selected because they directly contribute to the rapid advance of the regiment making the main effort. Fire support generally comes from armed helicopters and long-range artillery, and a link-up with advancing troops usually takes place within a matter of hours.

Airborne assault by parachute forces is either a strategic or an operational mission at *front* level. Strategic airborne operations usually involve division or multi-division operations planned at theater or national level, and are relatively rare. Airborne training appears to concentrate heavily on operational missions by battalion- to platoon-size elements with missions to attack enemy nuclear weapons storage and delivery sites or command and control facilities. As a rule, airborne operations are deeper than heliborne operations, and drop zones may be 10 to 20 kilometers from the objective.

A typical airborne raiding force is an airborne company reinforced with antitank guided missiles and sappers.[12] Although an airborne company is small in numbers, comprising six officers and seventy-nine enlisted men, it is highly mobile in its eleven organic BMD-1 armored fighting vehicles and its firepower is considerable, considering the cannon and machine guns mounted on the BMD. In total, the combat power and mobility of an airborne company closely approximates that of a motorized rifle company.[13]

The standard jump altitude is 150 to 300 meters, and the drop zone is normally secured by a small reconnaissance and security force preceding the main element by about fifteen minutes.[14] Heavy equipment and crew-served weapons precede personnel during the drop.

Troops organize on the ground on their vehicles, which are equipped with small radio homing beacons to assist troops in locating them even in the dark.[15] In addition, three R-255 PP radio receivers in each squad permit passing voice instructions by radio to almost every other airborne soldier.[16] The norm for a company to reorganize on the ground

and clear the drop zone is sixty minutes, with individual squads and
platoons departing as soon as they are assembled.

The conduct of a typical raid by an airborne company is shown
in Figure 6.7. Platoons move from the drop zone to attack positions
by separate routes, organizing on the march. Land navigation is assisted by the gyrocompass and land navigation instruments mounted
in each vehicle.[17] The company commander normally precedes the
rest of the company to make his final reconnaissance of the objective,
and issues last-minute changes in orders by radio.

The assault is normally an attack on converging axes, and there
is no reserve, although a small force may be used to isolate the objective. Prearranged radio code words and pyrotechnics are the standard means used for coordination and control.[18]

On order, the company withdraws from the objective and individual vehicles march to an assembly area where the unit reorganizes.
The assembly area is approximately 2 kilometers from the objective
and in the opposite direction from the drop zone. After reorganizing,
the company exfiltrates or seeks to link up with advancing friendly

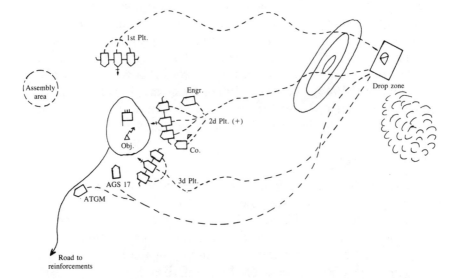

Figure 6.7.   Schematic of an airborne raid on a command and control in-
                stallation

ground forces, unless it has a secondary mission. A company force can expect to spend a period of up to three days on a mission of this type.

The Threat from the Sky and Sea

The specter created by some analysts of thousands of Soviet super soldiers swarming over the rear areas and homelands of the United States and its allies is dramatic, but greatly overdrawn. These highly trained units are carefully targeted against well-researched low-risk, high-return objectives that clearly contribute to the immediate mission. The Soviet concept is better viewed as the insertion of a carefully placed needle rather than the blast of a shotgun.

The needle is not likely to kill, but it can cripple the enemy so that conventional maneuver forces can quickly and efficiently dispatch him, and this is exactly what Soviet landing operations are about. Like everything else in Soviet operations, they complement the assigned tasks of the maneuver forces.

While one should avoid overstating the threat, it is an equally dangerous error to underestimate it. Any commander facing Soviet forces who thinks that his rear is secure or who does not take stern measures to defend key installations and areas is likely to suffer a devastating lesson. At the very least, friendly forces must be prepared to respond to the confusion that even small units or the threat of their use can create. An example of how dangerous this can be took place in December of 1944, when a handful of Nazi paratroopers under Col. Otto Skorziny created havoc in the rear of American forces greatly out of proportion to their actual numbers or deeds.

Combat Engineers

In World War II, the Red Army continually faced the problems of space and time in the struggle against the German invaders. The trackless expanse of the Central European Plain translated war into battles on an epic scale, while the primitive transportation network severely curtailed the movement and supply of the huge armies. At the same time, the networks of the great river systems of Eastern Europe gouged out a seemingly endless array of natural barriers on an average of one every 30 kilometers.

At the front, masses of Soviet infantry assaulted the rivers using bundles of brush wrapped in ponchos for buoyancy, while tanks and guns crossed on crude rafts laboriously constructed of locally available timber. In the rear, long columns of motley transport struggled along an inadequate road network in a futile effort to feed the guns and tanks with enough ammunition and fuel to maintain the offensive.

In the early stages of the war, the great defensive battles of Leningrad, Moscow, and Stalingrad called forth prodigious efforts to construct field fortifications and barrier systems to rob the *Wehrmacht* of its superior battlefield mobility. These systems were created by the physical labor of millions of civilians and soldiers equipped with only the most primitive hand tools, axes and shovels, and other implements found in farms and factories.

While these efforts in World War II were indeed heroic achievements, they dictated a grinding, slow battle and the massing of vast numbers of men and quantities of materiel. Soviet officers recognized that these deficiencies were incompatible with modern warfare on a nuclear battlefield and, with typical deliberation, set about solving the problem by providing combat forces with a quantity and quality of combat engineer support certainly equal to the best in the world.

A beginning step was to reduce the need for special engineer support. Motorized rifle troops, reconnaissance troops, airborne troops, and some artillery have been equipped with amphibious tracked vehicles that permit river crossings and high cross-country mobility without engineer bridging. Another approach was to equip tanks with a snorkel so that they can ford deep rivers underwater.

Organization and Technology of Combat Engineers

The real solution, however, required that tactical maneuver forces be equipped with efficient combat engineer support. To this end, the Soviet Army has organized and equipped its combat engineers with an impressive array of sophisticated and specialized technology.

The engineer battalion organic to tank and motorized rifle divisions is organized into five companies as shown in Figure 6.8. Each company is trained and equipped to perform certain specified tasks. The engineer company provides general engineer support and mechanized mine-laying capabilities. The technical company provides earthmoving and construction capabilities for field fortifications and barriers and runs the division water point. The road construction com-

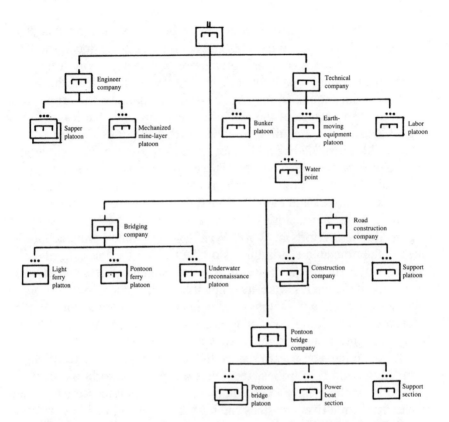

Figure 6.8.   Engineer battalion, motorized rifle and tank divisions

pany is equipped to repair and maintain supply routes and roads in the division rear. The bridging company supports river crossings by division first and second echelon elements. It has two ferry platoons and an underwater reconnaissance platoon of scuba divers to reconnoiter fording and ferry sites. The pontoon bridge company provides pontoon bridge support for the division second echelon and the division rear.

Tank and motorized rifle regiments have an organic engineer company that is a scaled-down version of the division engineer battalion. It is organized as shown in Figure 6.9. The sapper platoon is trained to perform general engineer tasks and is equipped with mechanized mine-laying and mine-clearing equipment. The bridge platoon has tank-launched and vehicle-launched dry-span bridging capabili-

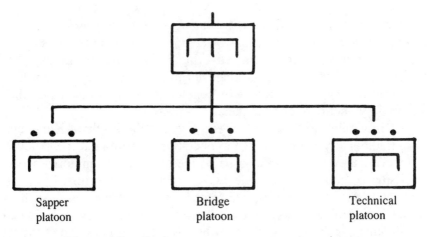

Figure 6.9.   Engineer company, maneuver regiments

ties. The technical platoon is equipped with ditching and earth-moving equipment and can operate a water point.

Employment of Combat Engineers

The general rule is to centralize control and tasking of engineer troops according to their specialties. Actual work, however, may be decentralized by assigning priorities to tasks in support of one or another subordinate element.

The general rule is not without exceptions, however. One major exception is that sapper elements are often attached to reconnaissance units and to tank and motorized rifle companies or battalions on missions that take them far from the main body, as in the advance guard. Normally these elements comprise a sapper squad from the sapper platoon of the regimental or division engineer company. For special missions, such as reconnaissance of crossing sites, divers from the underwater reconnaissance platoon or other specialists may be attached to maneuver elements.

Another exception to the standard practice of maintaining centralized control of engineer assets is the formation of engineer task forces to perform specific missions in support of a given operation. The most often used examples of these temporary engineer groups are mobile obstacle detachments and movement support detachments.

Mobile obstacle detachments (*podvizhnyy otryad zagrazhdenii*, or POZ) are temporary formations of engineer troops organized to construct artificial barrier systems covering exposed flanks and gaps between units.[19] POZ are task-organized to block avenues of approach for enemy tanks in the attack or counterattack or to cover breaches caused by enemy nuclear strikes.

Historically, POZ were first employed at the Battle of Kursk and are traditionally employed at the operational (army and *front*) level; however, they now may also be formed by tank or motorized rifle division commanders.[20] While POZ are comprised primarily of engineer forces, they may be reinforced with other elements, such as mine-laying helicopters, and their actions are certainly coordinated with other capabilities, such as artillery-scattered mines and chemical contamination.

POZ closely cooperate with antitank reserves in establishing the fire line (*ognevoy rubezh*) or fire sack (*ognevoy meshok*) described in Chapter 5. While their principal weapons are antitank mines, they also use demolitions on a large scale to create ditches and deadfalls, and employ construction equipment to close defiles or block routes through built-up areas.

Movement Support Detachments (*Otryad Obespecheniya Dvizheniya* or OOD) are temporary engineer task forces formed to facilitate the maneuver of first echelon combat forces in the attack, movement to contact, or withdrawal.[21] OOD normally operate in front of the main body to clear natural or man-made obstacles or to find, improve, and mark alternate routes.

If necessary, OOD may include combat or reconnaissance elements for their own security, and their actions are always closely coordinated with advance guards or reconnaissance troops. In CBR warfare conditions, OOD will include CBR reconnaissance and decontamination elements to find, mark, and clear routes through contaminated areas.

OOD are not line of communications troops. They are organized only to facilitate the continuous movement of first echelon combat forces. Any obstacle that cannot be overcome quickly with available means is bypassed and reported for removal by follow-on engineer assets. In the case of major barriers such as rivers, the OOD locates and reconnoiters the site for the assault crossing by lead combat elements, but organization and preparation of crossing sites for the main body are not part of its duties.

River Crossing

Ideally, Soviet commanders desire to cross rivers "from the march" (*s khodu*) to deprive the enemy of the opportunity to develop a coherent defense and to maintain the momentum of the offensive. In this instance, reconnaissance elements seek undefended, or lightly defended, areas where first echelon motorized rifle battalions can quickly establish defensive positions on the far bank after a "headlong dash" across the river in their organic amphibious carriers.[22] The assault crossing by a motorized rifle battalion establishes a bridgehead 3 kilometers deep, enough to prevent accurate antitank fire on the crossing site, and 2 to 3 kilometers wide.[23] The follow-up crossing by tanks and wheeled vehicles then proceeds as means come available.

If enemy defenses are too strong to permit a crossing from the march, the alternative is a forced crossing (*forsirovanie*). In this type of operation, tanks and self-propelled artillery are deployed forward to blanket forward defenses with heavy fire while motorized rifle troops cross screened by smoke and covered by friendly fire, and supported by armed helicopters and strike aircraft. In concert with airborne or heliborne forces, they secure a departure area (*iskhodnoe polozhenie*) on the far bank to a depth permitting the unobstructed crossing of other combat and combat support elements, and large enough to accommodate a buildup of sufficient forces to resume the offensive.[24]

Engineer troops participate in clearing natural and artificial obstacles on both riverbanks and in the initial reconnaissance, selection, and preparation of crossing sites. While the initial assault is primarily a combat operation, the crossing of the main body is an engineer function.

A critical factor in maintaining the momentum of the attack is the time it takes to cross the main body. Not surprisingly, Soviet engineers use a nomogram, such as that in Figure 6.10, to determine the number and types of crossing means required. Using the table in the center of the diagram, the engineer officer can calculate that to cross a river 200 meters wide with a flow of 1 meter per second will require nine minutes for a PTS amphibian, twelve minutes for a GSP medium ferry, and fifteen minutes for a 60-ton heavy ferry. If there are twenty-seven loads to cross by PTS (point C), and there are six PTS available, the crossing will take forty-seven minutes. Obviously, this nomogram can be used a number of ways to balance crossing means, loads, and time to achieve optimum use of assets.

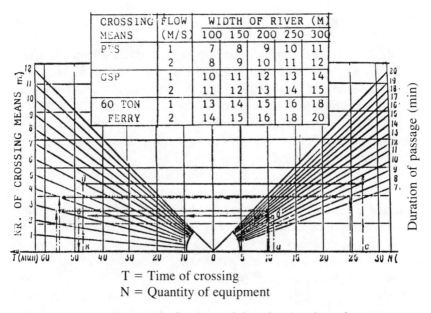

CROSSING MEANS	FLOW (M/S)	WIDTH OF RIVER (M)				
		100	150	200	250	300
PTS	1	7	8	9	10	11
	2	8	9	10	11	12
GSP	1	10	11	12	13	14
	2	11	12	13	14	15
60 TON FERRY	1	13	14	15	16	18
	2	14	15	16	18	20

T = Time of crossing
N = Quantity of equipment

Figure 6.10.   Auxiliary table for determining the duration of a passage

Source: Col. G. Nashchyekin, *Raschyety Pri Ryeshyenii Inzhyenyernykh Zadach* ("Computations For Solving Engineering Problems"), *Voennyi Vestnik,* no. 5, May 1981, p. 33.

A schematic for a river crossing is shown in Figure 6.11. Of course, not every operation will be supported by all means, but there will certainly be more than one means available to support an operation, and the same crossing means may be used at more than one site, depending upon equipment availability and river characteristics. The distance between sites is not fixed but should be such that two sites cannot be closed by a single attack. This generally is taken to require a minimum separation of 1500 meters. Each site operates independently, with a site commander on the near riverbank to speed the crossing and to control activity at the bank, and a deputy site commander on the far bank to expedite activity at that point. There is also a recovery vehicle at each site to evacuate broken or damaged equipment and to keep the site in operation. Each site also has a designated holding area or assembly area in a concealed location approximately a kilometer from the site. Site commanders use landline communications to call individual loads forward at a rate assuring continuous

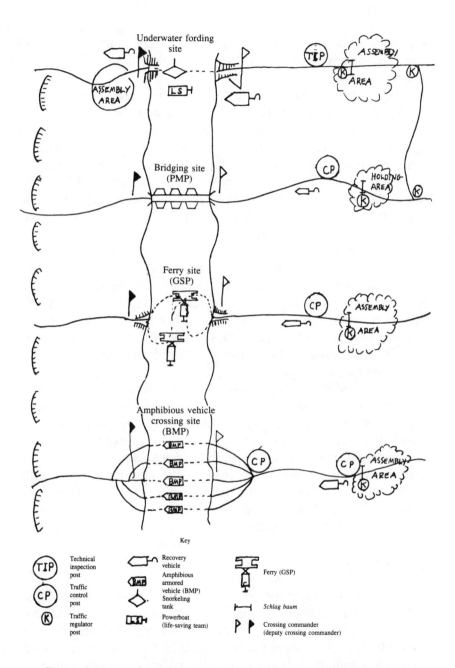

Figure 6.11.   Schematic of an engineer river crossing operation

Source: N. I. Dalinin and V. P. Kutsenko, eds., *Voennaya Inzhenernaya Podgotovka (Military Engineer Training)*, Moscow: Voenizdat, 1982, pp. 214–19.

operation of the site without massing equipment in the open. Traffic control posts are normally operated by specially trained and equipped traffic regulators.

At the deep fording site, tank crews install the snorkel and seal the vehicle in the assembly area. This is a complicated process that takes an hour or more, and each tank is checked at a technical inspection post before it approaches the river. Tanks cross single file while divers in a launch look for breakdowns. If a vehicle halts, divers connect cables from a recovery vehicle to the tank, and it is towed out of the water. On the far bank, a concealed assembly area is designated. Here crews prepare their vehicles to go into action, a process that takes up to thirty minutes.

At pontoon bridge sites, columns of vehicles move across at constant speed, maintaining intervals that prevent any section of the bridge from being overloaded. A key consideration for the site commander and his deputy is to maintain constant speed on the bridge to avoid structural stress by surge. At ferry sites a key consideration is to avoid massing vehicles on the near bank waiting to cross. On the far bank, vehicles are dispatched individually as they land; march units do not reform on the riverbank.

Crossing sites for amphibious vehicles usually comprise several crossing points for individual vehicles, separated by 50 to 100 meters. Each point has its own route, and entrance and egress points on the riverbanks may be improved by construction engineer work. Vehicles are prepared for amphibious operation in the assembly areas by the crew and are dispatched to the crossing site to cross in waves rather than in column. After departing the assembly area, movement is continuous. Crossing units deploy, swim the river, and reform in column on the far bank without halting.

CBR Warfare

The Soviet Army refers to chemical, biological, and radiological (nuclear) weapons under the generic term "weapons of mass destruction" (*orudie massovykh porazhenie*) or by the undistinguished acronym OMP. It accepts as fundamental truth that these weapons have caused a revolution in military affairs and have ushered in a fundamentally new method of combat in which they are the main means of waging war.[25]

Perceptions and Control

Although they have tremendous influence on the battlefield, it appears that employment of these weapons is planned and controlled at the strategic, operational and, only occasionally, at the operational-tactical levels.[26] The impressive array of battlefield nuclear delivery systems is virtually all organic to army or *front*. The only weapon in the division inventory is the FROG-7 or SS-21 system.

The multiple rocket launchers in the division BM-21 battalion are capable of delivering chemical munitions, but the authority to employ these weapons does not seem to extend below division. While Soviet sources discuss extensively and in considerable detail battlefield operations under conditions of nuclear or chemical warfare, they virtually never mention biological warfare. Apparently, the Soviet Army considers biological weapons to be unsuited for tactical employment on the battlefield. They are probably reserved for strategic employment deep in the enemy rear or in his homeland. The health and medical problems in the Soviet Army, discussed in Chapter 8, lend support to this observation, and it is consistent with the rather spotty reports on employment emanating from Afghanistan and Southeast Asia.

CBR Defense

While Soviet commanders below division do not control the employment of chemical or nuclear weapons, they certainly expect that operations will be supported by OMP, and they assume that they will be subject to attack by enemy nuclear and chemical weapons. Soviet combat vehicles and special purpose vans are equipped with collective protection systems that permit crews to survive and function in a contaminated environment. Individual troops have protective masks and clothing, and training in their use is extensive.

Every maneuver regiment has a chemical defense company comprising a reconnaissance platoon and a decontamination platoon.[27] The four BRDM-2 RKh armored reconnaissance vehicles of the reconnaissance platoon have internally mounted alarm systems for detection and monitoring of chemical and radioactive contamination, and external flag emplacers to mark contaminated areas. The decontamination platoon is equipped with two manually operated DKV decontaminating sets, one DDA-53 vehicle-mounted decontamination apparatus to clean clothing and small equipment items, and three ARS-14 truck-mounted decontamination systems. The ARS-14 is a versatile piece of equipment that can wash contaminants from a road using pressure dispensers under the bumper or can decontaminate large pieces of equipment using eight pressure hoses. The decontamination platoon can decontaminate one tank or motorized rifle company without refill.

The division chemical defense battalion is an expanded version of the chemical defense company at regiment. It has a reconnaissance platoon with nine BRDM-2 RKh, two decontamination companies, and maintenance and service capabilities. In addition to the equipment found at regiment, each decontamination company has two TMS-65s, jet engines mounted on trucks that generate steam for rapid decontamination of large pieces of equipment. The TMS-65 is also used to generate aerosol smoke.

Employment of OMP

While Soviet lower level tactical commanders do not expect to be involved in planning, allocating, and controlling the employment of chemical or nuclear weapons, they do expect to exploit or benefit from their use. In the offense, nuclear weapons may be used to create a gap in enemy defenses for first echelon regiments making the division main effort, and a maneuver battalion may be the exploiting force for a friendly nuclear strike. It appears that chemical weapons will be employed to suppress enemy defenses so that maneuver elements may fight through them without dismounting. They will also be used to create obstacles to the deployment of enemy reserves. Soviet decontamination and reconnaissance capabilities ensure that these areas will not impede the maneuver of their own forces.

In the defense, nuclear weapons may reinforce the fires of a first echelon regiment, especially against enemy tank reserves. Chemical or nuclear weapons may be used to protect an open flank. Nuclear weapons may also be employed against an enemy force that penetrates the first defensive belt, but it does not appear that chemical weapons are to be used within friendly defensive positions.

The CBR Debate

Western analysts and, occasionally, Soviet military specialists periodically engage in debates as to whether or under what circumstances weapons of mass destruction might be used on the battlefield. For the Soviet tactical commander, these discussions are rather similar to intercourse between elephants in that they take place way over his head, and his only concern is to avoid being trampled in the excitement. Journeyman combat commanders will not risk their careers, commands, or lives on assumptions that their enemy will not employ such devastating and decisive tools of war, and they certainly do not intend to be caught short if their own seniors suddenly sacrifice moral squeamishness to battlefield pragmatism.

For these reasons, Soviet tactics, particularly at the lowest levels, do not make the sharp distinction between nuclear and nonnuclear warfare that is traditional in the West. Soviet commanders assume that, if OMP have not been used in battle, their use by one or both sides is imminent, and their forces must be configured for that reality.

Conclusions

Soviet combat support operations provide the salt in the bread to enable Soviet combat forces to survive and win on the battlefield. The Soviet "scientific" approach to warfare so often referred to throughout this book has forced a proportional development of combat support capabilities to complement tactical fighting capabilities of the fighting units.

The narrow preoccupation of Western intelligence analysis of Soviet combat capability with technical description of weapons characteristics and quantification of weapons and forces has obscured the fact that the Soviet Army views this balanced development of combat and combat support means and capabilities as its way of achieving combat sustainability, flexibility, and survivability. It is the Soviet perception of an integrated force structure.

Notes

1. Gen. Col. of Artillery Levchenko, ed., *Protivovozdushnaia Oborona Su-khoputnykh Voisk* (*Antiaircraft Defense of Ground Forces*), Moscow: Voen-izdat, 1979, p. 72.
2. *Spravochnik Ofitsera Protivovozdushnoi Oborony* (*Antiaircraft Officer's Handbook*), Moscow: Voenizdat, 1981, p. 5.
3. Ibid., p. 7.
4. *Spravochnik Ofitsera Protivovozdushnoi Oborony*, op. cit., p. 223.
5. Lt. Col. Iu. Dyadyun, *"Zenitnye Podrazdeleniya v Oborone Noch'yu"* ("Antiaircraft Units in Defense at Night"), *Voennyi Vestnik*, no. 6, 1983, p. 75.
6. *Sovetskaia Voennaia Entsiklopediia*, 8 vols., 1976–1980, Moscow: Voenizdat, vol. 3, p. 152.
7. *The Military Balance 1982–1983*, London: International Institute for Strategic Studies, 1982, p. 16.
8. Ibid., p. 14.
9. Viktor Suvorov, *Inside the Soviet Army*, New York: Macmillan Co., 1983, pp.74–75.
10. For a detailed discussion of the origin and functions of SPETZNAZ units, see John J. Dziak, "Soviet Intelligence and Security Services in the Eighties: The Military Dimension," *Orbis*, no. 4, Winter 1981, 771–86.
11. *Sovetskaia Voennaia Entsiklopediia*, op. cit., vol. 3, p. 155.
12. See, e.g., Guards Capt. B. Kozyulin, *"Rota Zakhvatyvaet Punkt Uprav-leniya"* ("A Company Seizes a Command Post"), *Voennyi Vestnik*, February 1980, pp. 39–41.
13. DDB-1100-333-82, "Soviet Divisional Organizational Guide," DIA, July 1982, p. 93.
14. DDB-1100-2-82, "The Soviet Airborne Forces," DIA, April 1982, p. 13.
15. Ibid., p. 14.
16. Guards Maj. A. Taratyto, *"Chtoby Upravlenie Bylo Nadezhnym"* ("Re-liable Communications Were Insured"), *Voennyi Vestnik*, no. 2, February 1983, p. 38.
17. M. I. Kuznetsov, V. K. Presnov, and L. I. Surat, *Tankovye Navigat-sionnye Systemy* (*Tank Navigation Systems*), Moscow: Voenizdat, 1978, pp. 82–83.
18. Kozyulin, op. cit.
19. *Sovetskaia Voennaia Entsiklopediia*, op. cit., vol. 6, pp. 374–75. See also Col. F. D. Sverdlov, *Takticheskii Manevr* (*Tactical Maneuvers*), Mos-cow: Voenizdat, 1982, p. 88.
20. *Basic Dictionary of Military Terms*, Moscow: Voenizdat, 1965. Pub-

lished under the auspices of the U.S. Air Force, translated by the DGIS Multilingual Section, Translation Bureau, Secretary of State Dept., Ottawa, Canada, p. 161. See also *Sovetskaia Voennaia Entsiklopediia,* op. cit.

21. *Sovetskaia Voennaia Entsiklopediia,* op. cit., vol. 6, pp. 169–70.

22. Lt. Col. A. Gusev, *"Motostreklovyi Batal'on Forsiruet Reku"* ("Motorized Rifle Battalion Forces a River"), *Voennyi Vestnik,* no. 9, September 1983, p. 41.

23. V. U. Zelenskii, A. A. Chistov, and G. S. Chalkov, *Technicheskoe Obespechenie Tankovykh i Motostrelkovykh Podrazdeleni V. Sovremennom Boyu (Technical Support of Tank and Motorized Rifle Units in Modern Combat)*, Moscow: Voenizdat, 1982, p. 122.

24. *Sovetskaia Voennaia Entsiklopediia,* op. cit., vol. 8, p. 306.

25. *Marxism-Leninism on War and the Army,* Moscow: Progress Publishers, 1972. Published under the auspices of the U.S. Air Force, p. 253.

26. *The Revolution in Military Affairs,* Moscow: Voenizdat, 1973. Translated and published under the auspices of the U.S. Air Force, p. 150.

27. DDB-1100-333-82, op. cit., p. 24.

CHAPTER 7

Fire Support

Speed the artillery!

Peter the Great

T he first great Russian artilleryman was Czar Peter the Great, who ruled from 1682 to 1725. Starting with a virtually nonexistent technology, he created a mining industry to provide metal, a metallurgical industry to cast the cannon and build gun carriages, and schools to train artillerymen. By 1705, the quality of Peter's guns and the skill of his cannoneers were the equal of any in Europe.[1]

Since that time, Peter's command to "speed the artillery" has become a fundamental of Russian military tradition, and artillery in the Soviet Army is called the "king of battle." During World War II, the Red Army measured artillery "density" (*plotnost'*) by the number of weapons per kilometer of front. In the later stages of World War II, it was normal to have a density of two hundred to three hundred tubes per kilometer of front to support an offensive operation.[2] These masses of artillery fired carefully preplanned thunderous barrages that literally tore the ground asunder and shredded German defenses.

This traditional love affair between Russians and artillery continues to be manifested in the Soviet Army of the 1980s. It is apparent in the increasing quantity and improving quality of artillery weapons and supporting equipment and in the growing sophistication in techniques for its employment.

Modern technology has not only improved field artillery but has added a new dimension to the capabilities of fire support in the form of fixed-wing and rotary-wing aircraft. Finally, rocket artillery reinforces and supplements other fire support means at the tactical, operational, and strategic levels.

The integration of these diverse capabilities into a unified fire support plan for an operation is a major task for combined arms commanders and is fundamental to the success of the operation. Fire support capabilities and their use are the subjects of this chapter.

Field Artillery and Rockets

The application of rapid changes in modern science and technology to the solution of military problems on the battlefield is causing what the Soviet Army calls "a revolution in military affairs." This revolution has overtaken Soviet artillery weapons, tactics, and techniques.

Field Artillery Weapons and Equipment

In the field of weapons and equipment, the Soviet Army is returning to the use of self-propelled (SP) artillery in place of towed pieces. Although the Red Army used some SP artillery in World War II, it apparently abandoned that approach after the war in favor of towed artillery, which offered, among other things, the advantage of a greater number of pieces at a cheaper price. Indeed, an article in the November/December 1975 issue of the U.S. Army's *Field Artillery Journal* asserted that "Soviet artillery is mainly towed, with an almost total lack of self-propelled pieces."[3] It is ironic that at the time this article was printed, the new Soviet M-1974 122mm SP howitzer and the M-1973 152mm SP howitzer were replacing their towed counterparts in motorized rifle and tank divisions.

The M-1974 (Fig. 7.1) is now the standard piece in the artillery battalions organic to motorized rifle regiments and seems to be replacing its towed predecessor, the 122mm D-30 as fast as production permits. It comprises a 122mm howitzer in a fully enclosed revolving turret mounted on a full-tracked high-speed amphibious chassis. The light armor protects the system components and the four-man crew from radiation, small arms fire, and shell fragments, and a collective protection system provides defense against CBR contaminants.[4]

Soviet sources advertise the M-1974 as a weapon for future wars, and indeed the description is apt. The cross-country mobility and amphibious capability of the M-1974 enable it to accompany motorized

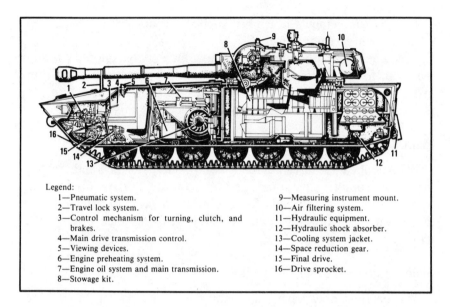

Legend:
1—Pneumatic system.
2—Travel lock system.
3—Control mechanism for turning, clutch, and brakes.
4—Main drive transmission control.
5—Viewing devices.
6—Engine preheating system.
7—Engine oil system and main transmission.
8—Stowage kit.
9—Measuring instrument mount.
10—Air filtering system.
11—Hydraulic equipment.
12—Hydraulic shock absorber.
13—Cooling system jacket.
14—Space reduction gear.
15—Final drive.
16—Drive sprocket.

Figure 7.1.   Cutaway view of the M-1974 122mm SP howitzer

Source: William P. Baxter, "Soviet 122mm Self-Propelled Howitzer," *Field Artillery Journal,* January/February 1980, p. 36.

rifle troops mounted in BMPs. Armor protection, a low silhouette, and direct fire sights allow the M-1974 to displace close to front line troops and to engage the enemy with direct fire if necessary. An onboard land navigation system that tracks azimuth and geographic coordinates assists in land navigation during marches and displacements and also, by using back azimuth and distance modes, greatly reduces the requirement for time-consuming survey.[5]

The M-1973 152mm howitzer was designed to replace the towed D-20 152mm towed howitzer in division artillery regiments. Like the M-1974, it is full-tracked and armor-protected with the howitzer mounted in a turret with 360° rotation. Instrumentation is also similar to that found on the M-1974.[6] The principal differences in operating characteristics are the caliber of the piece and the fact that the M-1973 is not amphibious. Presumably, the Soviet Army is not concerned about the lack of amphibious capability because of the range of the piece and the bridging capability of the division.

Improvements in Soviet artillery are not limited to division level, but also include new army and *front* level capabilities, such as the nuclear-capable 203mm SP howitzers and 240mm mortars.[7] These weapons systems reportedly began to appear in the Group of Soviet Forces, Germany (GSFG) in 1980; however, little is known about them as of yet.

The only standard Soviet artillery piece that has no SP counterpart is the M-46 130mm gun organic to army and *front* level artillery units. This long-range, high-velocity gun with its distinctive limber, has had a long period of service extending back to 1950. It can fire a 65-pound projectile to a range of 27 kilometers. One can speculate that the new 203mm SP howitzer may replace the M-46, but there is no evidence to support this speculation at this time.

At the same time that the Soviet Army was fielding its new family of self-propelled artillery, it also introduced a supporting vehicle designated the MT-LB.[8] This vehicle, built on a chassis similar to that of the M-1974, provides a command observation post (COP) and a fire direction center (FDC) with the mobility, amphibious capability, and armor protection necessary to accompany maneuver elements. All versions of the MT-LB are apparently equipped with ground navigation systems similar to those on the M-1974 howitzer. The version used for a COP apparently also has rangefinders and night vision devices, and the FDC version appears to be equipped with an electronic computer.[9] Another version of the MT-LB mounts a counterbattery radar. These armored, full-tracked vehicles have mobility and amphibious capabilities that enable them to keep pace with the maneuver elements of the division.

In addition to a long-standing tradition of calling tube artillery the "king of battle," the Soviet Army, since the early days of World War II, has been the world's leading proponent of rocket artillery. Although recent developments in tube artillery may have been more dramatic, rocket artillery is also experiencing some significant improvements. Basically, rocket artillery in the ground forces falls into one of two categories: systems for area suppression and systems for delivery of mass destruction weapons. Within the former category, the BM-21 is found in the division that launches the famous "Katusha" rockets. The eighteen truck-mounted launchers in a division, each capable of firing a ripple of forty 122mm rockets to a range of 20 kilometers, can deliver a powerful HE or chemical strike on any area target and are a significant means of reinforcing the tube artillery capability of the division.[10] This venerable MRL, first seen in 1964, appears to be the standard system in Soviet division, although Czechoslovakia introduced a variation with an automatic reload capability mounted on a Tatra truck in 1974.

The USSR is fielding a new MRL, variously referred to as the BM-27 or the M-77. While many details of the system are as yet unknown, it is reportedly replacing the BM-21 in Soviet artillery divisions and brigades at army and *front*. The BM-27 is a significant improvement over the BM-21 in almost all respects.[11] It is mounted on the same ZIL-135 20-ton 8×8 chassis as is the FROG-7, giving it excellent cross-country and highway mobility. With each launcher is a companion vehicle, also a ZIL-135 variant, that can provide a single automatic reload in approximately twenty minutes.

The projectile is a 240mm spin-stabilized heavy artillery rocket with a solid fuel propellant. The rocket is 4.8 meters long, weighs 300 kilograms, and has an effective range up to 40 kilometers. Warheads are HE, fragmentation, and chemical, and many include a scatterable mine warhead.

The launcher comprises two rows of six bands and one row of four bands, each 5 meters long, that can be elevated up to 50 degrees and traversed up to 240 degrees. The firing sequence is either single or ripple at one round per second. No photographs of the BM-27 have as yet been released.

The mass destruction delivery systems in ground forces include the FROG-7 in division, the SCUD-B at army/*front,* and the SCALE-BOARD at theater of military operations (TVD) level. These vehicle-mounted surface-to-surface missile systems are apparently being replaced by newer, longer-range systems. The FROG-7 is to be replaced by the SS-21, the SCUD-B by the SS-X-23, and the SCALE-BOARD by the more accurate SS-22.[12] Although few operational details are known about these new systems, it is certain that they will be more reliable and have greater accuracy and range. As in the case of their predecessors, their principal function is to attack point targets with nuclear or possibly chemical weapons.

This discussion of the quantity, types, and distribution of Soviet artillery assets is summarized in Table 7.1. It is obvious that the Soviet artillery park is supplied with a large quantity of modern ordnance that can provide effective fire support to maneuver elements. This summary also exposes one of the characteristics of Soviet artillery, and of all Soviet military materiel, a tendency toward specialization.

Table 7.1
Artillery Assets, Soviet Ground Forces

Organization Level	Supporting Arty.	No.-Type/Wpn.
Motorized Rifle		
Regiment	Battalion	
	3 Btry. 122mm How.	18 - M-1974/D-30
Tank/Motorized Rifle		
Division	Regiment	
	2 Bn. 122mm How.	36 - M-1974/D-30
	1 Bn. 152mm How.	18 - M-1973/D-20
	1 Bn. MRL	18 - BM-21
	1 Bn. Msl.	4 - FROG-7/SS-21
Army*	Artillery Brigade	
	1 Bn. 152mm How.	18 - M-1973/D-20
	1 Regt. 130mm Gun	36 - M-46
	1 Bn. MRL	18 - BM-21/BM-27
	203mm SP (?)	
	240mm Mortar (?)	
Front*	Artillery Division	
	1 Bn. SS Missiles	12 - SCUD-B/SSX-23
	1 Regt. 152mm How.	36 - M-1973/D-20
	1 Regt. 130mm Gun	36 - M-46
	1 Bn. MRL	18 - BM-21/BM-27
	203mm SP (?)	
	240mm Mortar (?)	
Theater (TVD)*	Brigade	
	SS Missiles	9 - SCALEBOARD/S-22

*Type Organization: No standard organization established at these levels

Unlike U.S. and NATO practices, where there is a trend toward fewer types of weapons with multiple uses, the USSR prefers a number of different weapons, each designed to perform in a specific role.

The M-1974 howitzer, for example, is well suited to the mission of accompanying maneuver regiments, while the M-1973 howitzer is less well suited to that role, but an excellent division piece. The BM-27, as an area coverage weapon, is an excellent asset for an army or *front* commander to employ to screen an exposed flank during a rapid advance, especially if used to scatter mines or persistent chemicals.

The lesson is that understanding the Soviet Army is not simply a problem of systematically evaluating the characteristics of one or another weapon; it also requires that the threat be examined from a systemic, or generic, standpoint of how weapons systems interact on the battlefield. Thus interaction is not only a function of technology but also of techniques and tactics, and it is these latter functions that must now be addressed.

Artillery Employment

There is a long-standing and heated debate among analysts as to whether Soviet military developments are driven by technological changes bringing forth new tactics or by new tactics creating the need for new technologies. Engineers boast that state-of-the-art technology, by providing new capabilities, creates tactical change. Others fervently believe that operational need creates the impetus for technological development. The argument, although philosophically interesting and bureaucratically important in the intelligence and scholarly communities, is of no practical value in understanding Soviet military capabilities. In the real world, it is enough to remember that technology and tactics have a symbiotic relationship: changes in either one drive changes in the other.

In the Soviet artillery, technological changes are accompanied by corresponding changes in tactics and techniques of employment. Traditionally, the Soviet Army has tended to resolve the conflicting requirements of centralized control—the massing of artillery assets to support the main effort—and responsiveness—the requirement to shift artillery assets to address unexpected demands—in favor of centralized control. Soviet military planners have realized, however, that strict centralized control is simply not adequate for mobile warfare on the fluid battlefield that they envision as characterizing future wars.

At the same time, tradition and concern for the reliability of the extensive communications net necessary to operate a flexible and decentralized system such as that derived by the U.S. and British armies have caused Soviet military planners to develop their own unique compromise between the competing demands of centralization and responsiveness.

The Soviet solution to this problem is to build fire support around the artillery battalion (*divizion*). A battalion is defined as comprising twelve to eighteen guns organized into three firing batteries and the necessary command and control and support elements.[13] Modern technology has permitted the use of computers to centralize and automate the fire control system.

Why the battalion is considered the basic artillery element has to do with a number of interrelated factors. One factor is the Soviet perception of the nature of targets on a modern battlefield. The Soviet military believes that, in general, targets are too hard, too dispersed, and too mobile to be easily destroyed by a fire strike of less than a battalion. An example of Soviet calculations is shown in Table 7.2, which gives Soviet norms for destruction of various types of targets. As this table shows, a battery takes ten minutes to complete a mission to destroy a single ATGM, while a battalion can complete this same mission in two minutes. In both cases the total number of rounds is the same, forty (rounded off to the nearest equal whole number per tube). For the types of targets listed, a battery mission runs from seven minutes for the softest target to thirty-three minutes for the hardest target, while a battalion firing the same missions requires from two to ten minutes.

The concern with time to complete the mission has three motivations.[14] The first is to preserve the momentum of the attack. For example, a platoon engaged by an enemy ATGM has, according to Soviet norms, a total of three to five minutes to make its decision for maneuver, depart its covered position, and move to the fire safety line.[15] If it takes ten minutes to fire the mission, the attack is held up for five to seven minutes, and friendly troops risk greater losses. The second reason has to do with the perceived threat from U.S. counterbattery fire. The Soviet Army believes that U.S. counterbattery radar can locate its guns and initiate a counterbattery fire mission in three and a half to four minutes.[16] The third concern, which is not as decisive as the first two, is that mobile armored forces can maneuver out of the target area within a period of about five minutes, thus neutralizing the full destruction power of the fire strike if it takes too long to complete the mission.

There are, however, exceptions to the rule on battalion level fire missions. In the defense it is still a standard practice to assign battery barrages and concentrations for defensive fire planning. Another exception is built around what the Soviet Army refers to as the psychological effect of artillery fire, the temporary disruption of unit cohesion and effectiveness caused by artillery. For example, the Soviet Army envisions the standard deployment of a U.S. mechanized infantry battalion as occupying an area up to 3 kilometers wide and 2.5 kilometers deep, with two reinforced companies forward and one company in reserve. The commander of the artillery battalion in a

Table 7.2
Destruction of Type Targets by a Battery and Battalion

Targets	Battery—6 Weapons							Battalion—18 Weapons				
	Expenditure for Destruction	Rounds per Tube	Performance Time	Registration Time	Time to Adjust Fire	Total Time for Fire Mission	Density of Fire on Target	Rounds per Tube	Performance Time	Time to Adjust Fire	Total Time for Fire Mission	Density of Fire on Target
ATGM single weapon	40	7	1.5	A6	2	10	10	2	0.5	1.5	2.0	27
Radar site	40	7	1.5	B3	2	7	11	2	0.5	1.5	2.0	27
Single armored target	80	13	2.0	A6	3	11	16	5	1.0	1.5	4.0	40
Mech. inf. plt.—1 hectare psn	112	19	4.0	B3	5	12	12	6	1.0	1.5	4.0	56
Mech. inf. co.—3 hectare psns	340	56	16.0	B3	14	33	11	19	4.0	1.5	10.0	38
Bn. CP unfortified—2 hectare	100	16	3.0	B3	4	10	14	6	1.0	1.5	4.0	50
TOW plt. unfortified—1 hectare	112	19	4.0	A6	5	15	12	6	1.0	1.5	4.0	56
90mm AT gun plt. deployed on line—3 hectares	340	56	16.0	B3	14	33	11	19	4.0	1.5	10.0	38

A = Burst adjustment
B = Rangefinder
Source: Gen. Lt. of Artillery E. V. Stroganov, "Ognevoi Udar" ("Fire Strike"), Voennyi Vestnik, no. 11, 1980, p. 69.

Soviet MRR, in planning the fire support for his regiment, would impose a series of barrage lines (in this case, six) as shown in Figure 7.2. Based upon the expected level of resistance and the division order, the Soviet regimental commander would specify in his maneuver plan a tempo of the attack, expressed in kilometers per hour. Current Soviet norms for mechanized units usually specify a tempo of between 5 and 20 kilometers per hour. At the slowest tempo, the lead elements of the regiment would expect to reach the rear of the battalion position in thirty minutes, allowing an average of five minutes per barrage. Without getting too involved in mathematical calculations, it is obvious that, from the norms in Table 7.2, there is simply not enough time to fire battalion destruction missions. In fact, there is not enough time to shift fires, to resupply the guns with ammunition, and to redeploy to avoid counterbattery fire.

The Soviet solution to this problem is to use disruption as the criterion for fire planning, rather than destruction, and to divide available artillery into two units, one firing even number barrages and the other firing odd number barrages.[17] As one unit fires, the other displaces and registers for the next barrage. If the attacking Soviet regiment is supported by a regimental artillery group of two or more battalions, each barrage will be a battalion mission. Otherwise, barrages will be battery missions.

The Soviet justification for disruption missions is based upon a number of calculations. For example, they estimate that, upon lifting of the barrage, riflemen will require on the average three quarters of a minute to reoccupy their firing point and prepare to fight. An ATGM such as the TOW will require from one to one and a half minutes to go back into action, and vehicle-mounted weapons will require two to three minutes to reoccupy firing positions. In sum, these Soviet calculations show that, ignoring the effects of collateral damage or casualties, resistance for the first minute following the lifting of a barrage will be limited to scattered small arms fire, and the enemy will need up to three minutes to reconstitute the defense in its entirety.

Looking at Table 7.3, it is apparent that attacking troops can expect to be at or within the defensive position before the defense is fully reconstituted, even allowing for maximum troop safety and the slowest speed of attack. Since the barrage has shifted to the next line, the attack can roll on without any loss of momentum.

Table 7.3
Time for Attacking Forces to Cross the Troop Safety Area (Minutes)

Depth of the Safety Area	Speed of the Attack (km/hr)													
	7	8	9	10	11	12	13	14	15	16	17	18	19	20
200 m	1.71	1.50	1.33	1.20	1.10	1.00	0.90	0.85	0.80	0.75	0.70	0.60	0.63	0.60
300 m	2.58	2.25	2.00	1.80	1.60	1.50	1.38	1.28	1.20	1.12	1.06	1.00	0.94	0.90

Source: *Voennyi Vestnik*, no. 4, 1980, p. 67.

Fire Planning and Fire Control

It has become a standard Soviet practice to reinforce first echelon maneuver battalions and regiments with artillery assets from higher headquarters. A Soviet tank or motorized rifle battalion operating at an extended distance from the regiment would expect to have an artillery battalion attached. Similarly, first echelon maneuver regiments are often reinforced by attachment of one or more artillery battalions from division assets. In this circumstance, artillery battalions are generally organized into a regimental artillery group (RAG) normally commanded by the organic artillery battalion commander in an MRR or by the senior artillery commander for a tank regiment. Similarly, organic and attached artillery at division is usually organized into a division artillery group (DAG) commanded by the commander of the division artillery regiment.

The formation of RAGs and DAGs serves to centralize control of artillery assets at those levels of command. It also fits the Soviet practice of providing commanders with the assets to fight the battle and not expecting to provide them with significant additional support. Soviet commanders generally expect to execute their orders using their "own" (organic and attached) assets, and do not rely upon significant additional support.

In the Soviet Army lexicon, the artillery battalion commander is the "basic shooter," the central figure in artillery fire support. He plans fire support, assigns mission priorities, directs the actions of battery observation posts, and coordinates artillery reconnaissance and displacement. He is physically located with the combined arms commander or, if assigned to an artillery group, at the group command post. Battery commanders, with communications and navigation equipment and optical and night vision devices mounted in their MT-LB, fire their batteries. They accompany the artillery battalion commander on his reconnaissance and direct and adjust fire in their assigned sector according to the battalion commander's fire support plan. Their fire missions are cleared through the battalion commander.

This system departs from the standard practice in U.S. and NATO armies in that battery commanders act as artillery forward observers, and though they may happen to be collocated with maneuver company commanders, they are seldom either subordinate to or responsive to them. Maneuver company commanders must request artillery support through their battalion commander, not through the artillery observer.

Since the artillery battalion commander is normally with the combined arms commander, the battalion chief of staff actually runs the battalion in combat. He controls computations of firing data, reconnaissance and occupation of firing positions, displacements, and resupply. Since he is the man on the ground who makes the battalion shoot, move, and communicate, he must be an experienced and able artilleryman as well as a skilled staff officer.

In the same vein, the senior battery officer runs the battery while the battery commander is at the front firing his battery. His specific functions are similar to those of the battalion chief of staff.

Artillery Tactics

Soviet artillerymen like to be a part of the action, and it is normal for direct support battalions to be within 2 kilometers of the front lines. For this reason, artillery batteries expect to engage targets by direct as well as indirect fire. The M-1973 and M-1974 howitzers are equipped with direct fire optical sights for this purpose, and their basic load includes HEAT rounds for direct fire missions, which are a standard part of battery field training. This is not to say that direct fire missions are a standard artillery role; they are not. It does point out, however, that Soviet artillerymen assume that they will receive direct fire missions, and they are prepared to execute them.

The basic formation for a battery in the field is an inverted triangle, as illustrated in Figure 7.2. The battalion command post is located inside the battalion position, and battery trains are to the rear of the guns. This scheme is a direct result of Soviet World War II experience on the vast open expanses of the North European Plain running through central Russia and Eastern Europe. It facilitates computation of firing data so that artillery strikes fall in the nice orderly straight lines so desired by Soviet maneuver force commanders.

Soviet artillerymen, however, recognize that constraints imposed by man-made or natural terrain features, as in mountains or built-up areas, will force deviations from this ideal, and they understand that such a regular geometric pattern is easily recognizable and very susceptible to ground and air attack. Therefore, they are experimenting with any number of variations, including split batteries, where the two gun sections are separate and staggered, and batteries in column

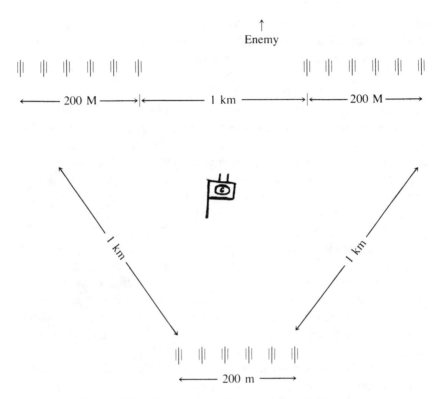

Figure 7.2.   Standard artillery battalion deployment

rather than in triangular formation.[18] In all of these cases, however, they use automated fire control systems and improved survey capabilities so that the fire pattern remains the same, and all formations are still described in terms of the standard triangle formation.

The battalion plans and implements its own local security plan. While Soviet writings have not addressed this problem, a battery equipped with SP howitzers has fewer personnel and vehicles than a towed howitzer battery and may therefore be less able to implement an adequate local security plan.

While Soviet artillerymen recognize a threat from ground attack, they believe that the main threat is counterbattery.[19] As noted earlier, they credit U.S. artillery with being able to initiate a counterbattery mission within three and a half to four minutes, using data from counterbattery radar. For this reason, Soviet artillery batteries prepare two or three alternate positions and change location after every one or two missions. In addition, they construct dummy positions to mislead enemy reconnaissance and conduct false registrations with one or two pieces from dummy positions to confuse enemy sound ranging and counterbattery radar.

Concern with the threat of enemy counterbattery is reflected in the Soviet Army's own counterbattery missions. Soviet military writings stress that a major mission for all reconnaissance is the location of enemy fire support means, especially those with nuclear capabilities.[20] The means of locating enemy artillery includes radar, sound ranging, observation, and ground and air patrolling. It seems that counterbattery is a semi-independent mission assigned to a Soviet artillery battalion that is not part of an artillery group. A battalion with this mission is in direct communication with reconnaissance and artillery location elements and thereby carries on what amounts to an independent hunt for enemy artillery. While Soviet sources are not clear on this point, the implication seems to be that counterbattery missions are under the direct (*neposredstvennyi*) command of the combined arms commander assigning the mission. MRL battalions are considered to be particularly well suited to counterbattery missions.

This discussion makes it obvious that Soviet artillery battalions expect to displace often to avoid counterbattery or to keep up with the maneuver elements. Displacement is preceded by an artillery reconnaissance group (ARG) that selects and marks the battalion march route and selects and organizes the ground in the new position.[21] While the composition of the ARG is not fixed, it normally includes a command element, a representative of each firing battery, a work party, and sapper elements.

The ARG is normally commanded by the battalion chief of staff, and each firing battery is represented by a firing platoon commander. A fire direction element is almost always included. The ARG is usually preceded by sappers with mine detectors and a CBR monitoring team to ensure that the area is clear of mines and free of contamination. The work party usually physically marks out positions and routes on the ground and provides local security. If the route to the new position is long or difficult to follow, road guides may be posted to guide the batteries on the march. Displacement is usually on order and by battery.[22]

Obviously Soviet artillery can hardly be understood simply in terms of hard data as to numbers of tubes, ranges, and density of fire. Its effectiveness lies in how it is used and how it contributes to the success of the maneuver forces. Clearly, Soviet artillery is increasingly better equipped, organized, and trained to execute its mission.

Perfection, however, belongs only to the Gods, especially on the battlefield. The need for high volumes of fire, problems in target acquisition, the fluidity of the modern battlefield, and the "fog of war" must all inevitably result in gaps in fire support when demand outstrips its availability or capability. These gaps are filled by that other key source of fire support for Soviet ground forces, frontal aviation.

Air Support of Ground Forces

The Soviet Army has traditionally viewed tactical air power as a major extension and reinforcement of the fire support capabilities supporting the ground forces. During World War II, Soviet frontal aviation, flying its Il-1 *Sturmovik* fighter-bombers, acted almost as a branch of Soviet artillery.[23] The role of Soviet frontal aviation has expanded far beyond what it was in 1945.

Soviet frontal aviation is the largest of the three branches of the Soviet Air Force. Its mission is to provide close air support, air defense, and tactical airlift for the ground forces. Its current inventory includes more than 9000 modern aircraft, of which 2600 are fighter-bombers specifically designed for the ground attack role, 1700 are fighters for the air defense role, and 3500 are helicopters (which include 1000 of the heavily armed HIND attack helicopters).[24] Most of these are modern aircraft, the bulk of them having come into service within the past ten years.

This modernization of the inventory in frontal aviation has been accompanied by a shift of emphasis from air defense to ground attack. As an example, today's frontal aviation is larger than the entire Soviet Air Force was in 1976. At that time, frontal aviation had only 4500 aircraft, of which 2100 were MiG-21 fighters and the remainder were mostly obsolescent MiG-17s and the FL-28s.[25]

Frontal aviation is employed as an operational tactical asset, at *front* level and below. While it has multiple roles, as earlier noted, the specific role of interest in this discussion is that of ground support. In that role, frontal aviation performs three functions:

- Adds depth to the battlefield by striking targets beyond the range of field artillery

- Increases the tempo of the battle by adding air-delivered ordnance to direct and indirect fires
- Adds flexibility by quick response to fluid tactical situations[26]

Since it is an operational-tactical asset, control of frontal aviation assets is always vested in the ground forces combined arms (*obshchevoiskovoi*) commander.

Since World War II, relatively scarce aircraft assets have been centralized in Tactical Air Armies (TAA), subordinate to what would be, in wartime, Soviet fronts. At this time, there are sixteen TAA, one in each group of forces and in each military district in the USSR. Each TAA is tailored to its mission, so there is no standard organization. As a general rule, however, a TAA can be described as comprising two or more divisions and one or more independent regiments. Divisions and regiments are nearly always mission-specific in that they contain a single class of aircraft (e.g., fighter-bombers), although they may contain a mix of models. An exception to this rule is helicopter regiments, which often contain armed, transport, and reconnaissance helicopter squadrons. The general pattern for organization is based upon a basic element, a flight, normally comprising four aircraft. There are three flights in a squadron, three squadrons in a regiment, and three regiments in a division. Thus, a regiment contains approximately thirty-six aircraft, and a division, more than a hundred.

Command and Control

The system for air-ground control within a Soviet front is depicted in Figure 7.3. Although the diagram appears at first glance to be rather complex, the system is actually quite simple. It shows at each command post, from *front* to regiment and occasionally battalion, a collocated frontal aviation coordinating element that provides communications directly to the aviation coordinating element at higher headquarters and to a corresponding aviation unit. Tasking for aviation units is through the TAA chain, and for ground units, through the *front* chain. When an aviation unit is assigned a mission, it is coordinated directly at the aviation liaison group with the supported ground unit.

The control of aircraft in flight within the area of the front is exercised through one or more control and target identification posts, equipped with communications, radars, and IFF to vector aircraft on

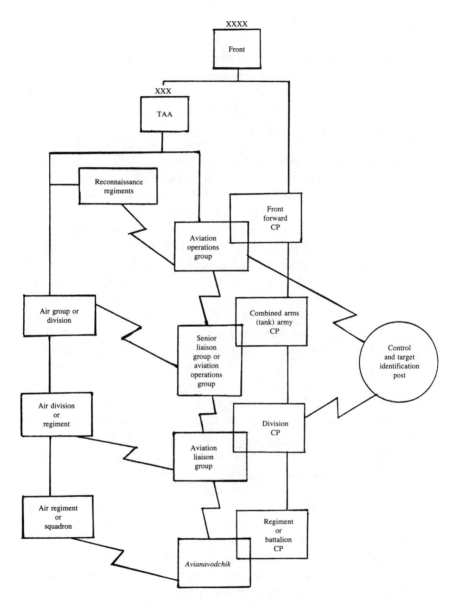

Figure 7.3.   Air-ground control and coordination within the Soviet *Front*

their missions. The control and target identification posts do not have any role in the planning of air operations or in mission assignments. They are, however, crucial to the Soviet system in that they provide the centralized control that makes the system work.

The commander of the TAA, usually an air force colonel general, is subordinate to the general of the *front*. His only link with the air force is through logistics and administrative channels for air force specific support. The TAA commander and his staff are located at the *front* headquarters, and the TAA commander is the *front* commander's deputy for aviation. At the headquarters of each army subordinate to the *front,* there is an aviation operations group of six to eight officers under one of the TAA deputy commanders. The aviation operations groups are the liaison between the TAA and army commanders. At each division headquarters, there is an air liaison group of four to five officers commanded by a deputy commander of an air division in the TAA. The air liaison group is often divided into sections, with one section working under the division chief of staff to ensure coordination of air operations with the ground maneuver plan, while the air liaison group commander accompanies the division commander to provide him with direct access to air assets during the conduct of the battle.

Regiment is the lowest level in the Soviet Army at which there is a dedicated air-ground interface. First echelon tank and motorized rifle regiments normally are assigned a forward air guide (*avianavodchik*) who has vehicle-mounted communications connecting him to aircraft in flight and to the air liaison group at division. The *avianavodchik* is a rated pilot, usually from an aviation regiment.

There are some new variations being introduced into the Soviet system for air support of ground forces. The variations involve decentralization of air assets by attaching them to command levels below *front.* Soviet aviation literature increasingly uses the term *armeiskaia aviatsiia* (army aviation), especially in referring to rotary-wing aircraft. Apparently, front commanders are now attaching regiments or groups of helicopters to first echelon armies so that army commanders control their own air assets. The command relationships for army aviation are a duplication of the model at *front*. The *armeiskaia aviatsiia* commander is operationally subordinate to the army commander and advises him on the employment of his unit.

There are also some indications that decentralization of small aviation units to control of first echelon divisions is in the experimental stage. It is referred to as *aviatsiia po divisii* (aviation at division). It is important to understand, however, that in the Soviet armed services, frontal, army, and division aviation are terms describing the level of ground forces command to which aviation units may be subordinated. Pilots, crews, and equipment are and remain air force assets. In fact, no permanent command relationship exists below *front*. A *front* commander will have a TAA. He may allocate control of some of those assets to army commanders for specific operations. In turn, army commanders may suballocate some assets to divisions. Control of tactical air assets remains, however, firmly in the hands of the *front* commander.

Tactics and Techniques of Employment

Soviet combined arms commanders appear not to be bound by fixed rules or norms in planning the use of their air assets. Rather, they are guided by general principles and concepts related to aircraft capabilities and to general combined arms tactical and operational practices. For instance, frontal aviation seems to concentrate its operations in the area of operation of the supported front commander, an area that may be as wide as 300 kilometers and may extend as far as 500 kilometers to the front and rear of the FLOT. This is because the TAA is an asset of the front commander, and he is not greatly interested in expending his assets beyond his area of responsibility. A contributing factor is the Russian tendency to compartmentalize and concentrate on one's own responsibility and to avoid wider responsibility and entanglement in someone else's trouble.

Another increasingly standard practice is to use fixed-wing aircraft principally against deep targets and rotary-wing aircraft primarily against targets near front line troops. This practice grows out of the Soviet perception of the relative characteristics of these two different types of aircraft and the characteristics of their own command and control system. The Soviet Air Force believes that high-performance aircraft are much less vulnerable in deep penetrations of enemy air space than are helicopters. In addition, the control posts are better able to track and vector high-performance aircraft at medium to high altitudes deep in enemy air space than they are helicopters at very low altitudes. On the other hand, the high density of weapons near the FLOT is a greater threat to fixed-wing aircraft than to helicopters, and a hovering helicopter can more accurately locate and engage targets than can a high-speed aircraft.

This practice of categorizing targets by depth is a tactical rationale for the establishing of army aviation, as earlier discussed. A combined arms or tank army, with its much narrower and shallower area of responsibility and greater concern for the conduct of the battle, would naturally be much more concerned with the employment of helicopters than would a *front* commander.

At all levels, air strikes are a means the ground commander can use to extend the battlefield and to increase the intensity of combat, and they are integrated with other means of accomplishing this goal, as shown in Figure 7.4. As a rule, deep targets, those beyond the range of artillery, have been fixed by intelligence and missions are preceded by some degree of preplanning. Pilots study maps and photographs prior to the mission, and a plan of attack is worked out. Control and target identification posts work out flight paths to and from the target and vector aircraft around known air defenses, or perhaps artillery or supplemental strikes are used to suppress air defense weapons. While the Soviet Army prefers to employ its air assets in

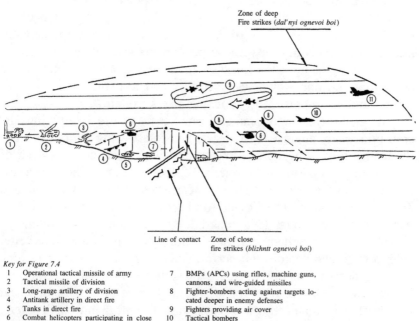

Zone of deep
Fire strikes (*dal'nyi ognevoi boi*)

Line of contact   Zone of close
fire strikes (*blizhntt ognevoi boi*)

Key for Figure 7.4

1	Operational tactical missile of army	7	BMPs (APCs) using rifles, machine guns, cannons, and wire-guided missiles
2	Tactical missile of division		
3	Long-range artillery of division	8	Fighter-bombers acting against targets located deeper in enemy defenses
4	Antitank artillery in direct fire		
5	Tanks in direct fire	9	Fighters providing air cover
6	Combat helicopters participating in close fire strikes	10	Tactical bombers
		11	Designated units from long-range aviation
6A	Combat helicopters in long-range fire strikes		

Figure 7.4.   Schematic of Air Support

preplanned missions, they do occasionally conduct what we call armed reconnaissance missions. The Soviet term is "free hunting." In the Soviet mind, free hunting implies an excess of available air assets compared to target requirements, a situation that is unlikely in most situations.

To reduce exposure to air defenses, the Soviet norm for fixed-wing aircraft is to complete a target pass in ten seconds to reduce the chance of destruction by air defense weapons. This ten-second norm allows three to six seconds to escape the target area.

Soviet tactics for fixed-wing aircraft attacking ground targets are based upon four maneuvers:

- The combat turn or chandell is a relatively flat, low-level approach to the target followed by a climbing 180-degree turn to the left or right after release of the ordnance, to escape anti-aircraft fire. This is the most preferred tactic.
- The half loop entails a high-altitude approach, a diving attack, and exit from the target area after a climbing, vertical 180-degree turn.
- The loop entails overflying the target and executing a vertical loop to engage the target. This maneuver is particularly suited to free hunting flights.
- The pitch-up is similar to the U.S. toss-bombing technique wherein the aircraft executes a climb at a predetermined release point and a computer releases the bomb which is lofted to the target, while the aircraft escapes the area. This maneuver is mostly used for delivery of mass destruction weapons such as chemical or nuclear warheads.

The Soviet Army increasingly prefers to use helicopters rather than fixed-wing aircraft for close air strikes for a number of reasons. The Mi-24 HIND armed helicopter has evolved into a formidable weapons system with great battlefield survivability. It has proven itself in Afghanistan, where it has been much more effective at finding and attacking fleeting battlefield targets than have fixed-wing aircraft. It can carry a wide variety of ordnance, including a 12.7mm machine gun in the nose or a Gatling gun in a turret under the nose, and pods carrying one hundred and twenty-eight 57mm rockets and four ATGMs mounted on wing pylons.

The Soviet Army believes that armed helicopters have great battlefield survivability. It believes that helicopters operating at altitudes under 200 meters above the surrounding terrain are extremely difficult for battlefield radar, IR, optical, or visual means to acquire or track. The effective range of helicopter weapons permits engagement of targets from stand-off ranges of more than 3000 meters. Helicopters' maneuverability and small cross section make them difficult to locate and hit on a battlefield. Specifically, the Soviet Army believes that rugged construction and armor protection give the HIND high battlefield protection (Fig. 7.5). Soviet sources claim that even when major subsystems, such as hydraulics, oil systems, or turbine fans, are damaged, the aircraft may continue to fly for as long as thirty minutes.

Armed helicopters hardly ever operate singly. Normally they are employed in pairs or in flights of four. In Afghanistan, the command ship normally spots the target and hovers out of effective range of the target while the flight commander directs the attack by the remaining ships; which make firing runs from various unexpected directions.

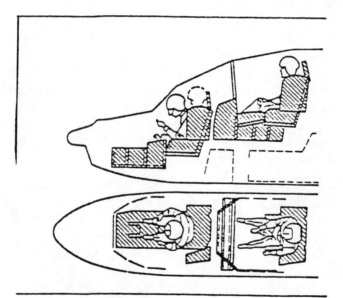

Protection against direct hit by .50 caliber round

Figure 7.5.   Armor protection of the HIND helicopter

Source: *Tekhnika i Vooruzhenie,* no. 8, 1981, p. 8.

The East German Army is experimenting with using a light helicopter as a command and control ship for helicopter fire missions. The light helicopter usually precedes the gunships at a lower altitude and breaks away at the point of engagement. This tactic has been demonstrated to General Kulikov.

Soviet commanders also employ helicopters as part of fire sacks, or ambushes. In this situation, gunships are parked in concealed, defiladed positions until called, whereupon they rise above the masking terrain, deliver their ordnance, and withdraw by contour flying.

Helicopters and fixed-wing aircraft perform many similar roles for the Soviet Army. Both conduct preplanned fire strikes or may be on call either airborne or on strip alert. Both types of aircraft may conduct free hunting flights. Fixed-wing aircraft are better suited for deep strikes and helicopters are better for strikes near the FLOT, although this is a relative, not an absolute, rule. Particularly in periods of limited visibility or in a confused tactical situation, helicopters are preferred due to their flight characteristics. Fixed-wing aircraft seem to be the preferred platform for delivery of mass destruction weapons, and it is unlikely that helicopters have a nuclear weapons delivery role.

While air superiority and air defense are not within the scope of this chapter, it is important to mention that the Soviet Army believes that effective air-ground operations are only possible when ground attack aircraft are defended from attack by hostile aircraft. Helicopters, however, are less vulnerable to air attack than are fixed-wing fighter-bombers, because they are difficult for high-performance aircraft to locate.

Frontal aviation is an air weapon tailored to the needs of Soviet combined arms commanders. In its fire support role it has matured from the World War II mission of extending and reinforcing artillery to its own unique mission of adding flexibility to fire support and extending the battlefield. Frontal aviation is a full partner and aggressive participant in the ground war.

Conclusions

In Russian military history, artillery has had the traditional role of "king of battle" and maintains that role today. Soviet artillery provides close and continuous fire support to the maneuver forces with an impressive array of modern and effective artillery and missiles. Modern Soviet artillery has the technology and the tactics to accompany maneuver forces, to survive on the modern battlefield, and to quickly respond to fire support requirements.

In the pre–World War II era, the Red Army came to perceive air power as an extension and reinforcement of artillery, the traditional means of fire support for ground forces. During World War II, air support functioned virtually as if it were a branch of Soviet field artillery.

In the postwar period, frontal aviation has matured into the largest branch of the Soviet Air Force. It is an operational-tactical asset with a multi-role mission of providing air support, air defense, and tactical airlift for the ground forces. Ground support has become the principal role, and its functions have expanded from those of an adjunct to artillery to those of an independent means of adding to the combat power of Soviet ground forces.

Soviet artillery and frontal aviation provide combined arms commanders with flexible and responsive combat support and unprecedented destructive capacity. They are an essential and integral part of the Reliable Shield of Socialism.

Notes

1. Robert K. Massie, *Peter The Great,* New York: Alfred A. Knopf, 1980, pp. 342–43.

2. *Sovetskaia Voennaia Entsiklopediia,* 8 vols., 1976–1980, Moscow: Voenizdat, vol. 1, p. 277.

3. Marshal of Artillery G. Peredel'skii, "Basic Directions in the Training of Artillery and Missilemen," transl. Cpt. Eugene D. Betit, *Field Artillery Journal,* November/December, p. 11. The comment on SP artillery was by the translator.

4. Col. Engr. In. Burtsev, *"Budshchemu Voinu-o Boevoi Tekhnike, Samokhodnaia Gaubitsa"* ("Military Technology for a Future War, A Self-Propelled Howitzer"), *Znamenosets,* no. 6, 1979, pp. 12–13.

5. Lt. Col. S. Sverdlov, *"Strel'ba Divizionom Po Nabliudaemym Tseliam"* ("Observed Fire by Artillery Battalion"), *Voennyi Vestnik,* no. 5, 1981, p. 73.

6. Ibid.

7. *Soviet Military Power,* Washington, D.C.: Dept. of Defense, 1981, p. 28. See also David C. Isby, "Soviet Self-Propelled Artillery: Capabilities and Concepts," *Jane's Defense Review,* vol. 2, no. 3, 1981, p. 201.

8. DDB-1100-241-80,"Warsaw Pact Forces Equipment Handbook: Armored Fighting Vehicles," Defense Intelligence Report, DIA, April 1980, pp. 3–89.

9. Isby, op. cit. See also *"Divizion-Osnovnaia Ognevaia Edinitsa Artillerii"* ("The Battalion is the Basic Artillery Unit"), *Voennyi Vestnik,* no. 10, 1981, p. 55.

10. USAREUR Pam no. 30-60-1, "Identification Guide, Weapons and Equipment, East European Communist Armies," vol. II, *Artillery,* 15 January 1973, p. 112.

11. *Soldat und Technik,* no. 7, July 1981, p. 372. Transl. in JPRS 79499, 23 November 1981, pp. 11–13.

12. *Soviet Military Power,* op. cit., p. 28.

13. Sverdlov, op. cit.

14. Gen. Lt. of Artillery E. V. Stroganov, *"Ognevoi Udar"* ("Fire Strike"), *Voennyi Vestnik,* no. 11, 1980, p. 67.

15. Ibid.

16. Ibid.

17. Maj. I. B. Mikhailink, *"V Interesakh Vysokikh Tempov Nastupleniia"* ("In the Interest of a High Tempo of Attack"), *Voennyi Vestnik,* no. 4, 1980, pp. 64–67.

18. See, e.g., Sr. Lt. A. Glushakov, *"Batterei na Dvukh Ognevykh"* ("Battery in Two Sections"), *Voennyi Vestnik,* no. 12, 1981, pp. 62–64.

19. Col. Engr. V. Nazarenko, *"Radiolokatsiia Polevoi Artillerii"* ("Radar Location of Field Artillery"), *Znamenosets,* April 1979, pp. 30–31. See also Stroganov, op. cit.

20. R. G. Simonian and S. V. Grishin, *Razvedka v Boyu (Reconnaissance in Battle),* Moscow: Voenizdat, 1980, p. 12.

21. Col. V. Nesterov and Lt. Col. E. Dubrovskii, *"Divizion: Osnobnaia Edinitsa Artillerii"* ("Battalion: The Basic Unit of Artillery"), *Voennyi Vestnik,* no. 10, 1981, p. 61.

22. V. Ia. Lebedev, *Spravochnik Ofitsera Nazemnoi Artillerii (Field Artillery Officer's Handbook),* Moscow: Voenizdat, 1977, pp. 32–38.

23. *Sovetskaia Voennaia Entsiklopediia,* op. cit., vol. 8, pp. 334–35.

24. *The Military Balance 1981–1982,* London: International Institute for Strategic Studies, 1981, p. 14.

25. *The Military Balance 1976–1977,* London: International Institute for Strategic Studies, 1976, p. 10.

26. *Sovetskaia Voennaia Entsiklopediia,* op. cit., vol. 8.

CHAPTER 8

Logistics

The logistician draws the line beyond which
the tactician dares not tread

For a number of years, this was the opening sentence in the bloc of instruction on logistics at a senior U.S. service school. It was delivered in measured, solemn tones by a distinguished professor of formidable reputation and demeanor. It was received by the owl-eyed, attentive, and suitably awestruck students in much the same way as the proverbial hog viewed the wristwatch: with intense interest but no comprehension.

After all, it was their experience that the economic might of the United States fed and fueled the engines of war of its own armies and those of its allies with enough excess capacity to support the civilian economy as well. In Vietnam, the logistic system supplied the guns and still operated a huge consumer outlet providing easy access to cold soft drinks and beer, refrigerators, air conditioners, stereo sets, tailor-made clothes, cosmetics, and a bewildering array of cameras and watches.

Their experience with logistics was with a demand-pull model: operational requirements established usage factors which the logistics system must fill. Further, the principles of war, taught in the Department of Tactics, do not even mention logistics. It seemed to those students that the good professor had got the cart before the horse: operations determines logistics, and not the other way around.

Had a Soviet officer been present in that classroom however, he would have completely understood the professor. Even under the best of conditions, Soviet troops are supplied at a Spartan level, and units in Afghanistan reportedly live a grim life with food shortages and crowded, unsanitary living conditions, lacking even such basic amenities as clean underwear, bedsheets, and baths.[1] In addition, logistics considerations are fundamental to three of the six Soviet laws of war and four of the eleven principles of military art, discussed in Chapter 1, which our hypothetical Soviet officer would have studied.

The Soviet Concept of Logistics

Many analysts have noted that the Soviet Army's logistics system, the *tyl* (rear), must perform the same basic supply, maintenance, and evacuation functions as the logistics services of any other large modern military establishment. However, it is naive to presume that it therefore operates to perform these functions in the same way as they were done in other armies. This is clearly not the case.

It should not be very surprising that the Soviet military logistics structure is very compatible with the Soviet economy as a whole. Simply stated, this means that Soviet military logistics is controlled from the top by

- Rigidly centralized authority
- Detailed top-down planning
- Strict accountability and control

Like the rest of the Soviet economy, the Soviet military is governed by what is reverently called "the plan," a mass of detailed regulations and priorities controlling everything from housing and diet to the distribution of equipment and expendables.

At the same time, as one proceeds down the chain of command, there is increasing reliance upon individual ingenuity and even "sharp practices" bordering on illegality to compensate for deliberate or accidental shortages or delays. As in the Soviet civilian economy, it is this shadow logistics system, laconically referred to among the troops as "self-supply," that really makes Soviet military logistics function.[2]

Rather than demand-pull, the concept governing Soviet military logistics is supply-push. In a supply-push logistics model, logistics is closely controlled at every level, with resources being distributed to subordinate commands in accordance with priorities established in the operational plan. In turn, subordinate commanders use logistics planning factors in selecting feasible courses of action, and in allocation of resources among their subordinates.

Peter Vigor noted that victory in the Soviet style of mobile warfare depends first of all upon providing the combat forces with the necessary material for war in the requisite quantities.[3] In this sense, Soviet logistics does indeed draw the line on Soviet tactics. As a matter of fact, Soviet logistics and tactics are often so inextricably intertwined that it is virtually impossible to separate them. For example, the tactical concept of echeloning forces described in Chapter 3 can be understood as supply-push tactics. Rather than sustaining units in combat by replacing losses, they are used up or expended, to be replaced by elements of the second echelon, which are supplied according to the commander's plan. In this sense, the integration of operations and logistics extends to the supply of entire units, as well as materiel and manpower.

As one might suspect, Soviet logistics operates on a priority basis. The first priority, of course, is ammunition; an army that recognizes artillery as being the God of War would naturally be most concerned with keeping the guns fed. A close second in priority to ammunition is POL, petroleum, oils, and lubricants, to keep mechanized forces moving. The third priority is maintenance and replacement of the technology of modern warfare, which is critical to the Soviet style of mechanized combat. Rations to sustain the troops are the fourth priority, and everything else fits into fifth priority. As is the case with other Soviet priorities, logistics priorities are not exclusive, but are used as planning guides for allocation of resources.

Ammunition Resupply

The Soviet concern with ammunition resupply has historic roots in the experience of the Red Army in World War II. To open the final battle for Berlin, Marshal Zhukov poured 7,140,000 rounds of artillery upon the German positions to "stun and shake" the defenders.[4] Although modern Soviet battlefield tactics no longer foresees massive breakthrough operations on the scale of World War II, the Soviet perception of the modern battlefield, as described in Chapter 4, comprising a number of short, violent battles between maneuvering forces, predicts heavy consumption of ammunition in compressed periods of time that are erratically spaced in both time and distance.

While the problem of ammunition resupply remains familiar, the solution on the modern battlefield is complicated by the high tempo of combat, which makes it impossible to rely on accumulated stocks on the ground. Not only must the ammunition logistics chain deliver large quantities of munitions in gross tonnages by type and caliber, it must be increasingly flexible as to when and where it is delivered as the chain nears the guns. The Soviet Army has instituted ammunition resupply procedures that it thinks will meet these demands.

Essentially, Soviet ammunition resupply procedures mirror the rear-to-front, supply-push concept that underlies all of Soviet logistics. The standard planning factor for consumption and supply is the *boevoy komplekt* (BK), or unit of fire.[5] The generic term BK, unit of fire, refers to the basic load of ammunition for a battalion.[6] The calculation of a BK is on a per gun (per howitzer, tank, aircraft, BMP, etc.) basis determined by the types and quantities of ammunition in magazines and ready racks. These quantities, aggregated at battalion level, are expanded to include reloads in organic supply vehicles.[7] Thus, there are any number of BK, corresponding to motorized rifle (tank, artillery, etc.) battalions.

It is important to understand that a BK, a fire unit, is a quantitative measure of ammunition storage and carrying capacity within a battalion. It is not related to ammunition expenditures to achieve some given mission or level of destruction. Commanders use data such as that in Table 7.2, or nomograms such as Figure 5.6 to calculate quantities of ammunition and rates of expenditure necessary to accomplish an assigned combat mission. The chief of artillery, by using the results of those computations, can calculate the number of BK required by period of time, and this figure is what the chief of the rear uses for timely procuring, packaging, transporting, stocking, and delivering of ammunition.[8]

Petroleum, Oil, and Lubricants

The largest bulk item in the supply chain of a modern, mechanized field army is the liquid petroleum products necessary to keep vehicles running and aircraft flying. Petroleum, oil, and lubricants are the lifeblood supporting the mobility and maneuverability of combat forces on and over the battlefield. The problem is indeed significant. Various Western sources estimate that a Soviet motorized rifle division may require between 190 and 220 metric tons of POL daily to maintain itself in the field, and in the offense it will consume as much as 500 to 600 metric tons of POL per day.[9] With a total of 236 POL trucks and 195 POL trailers in the division inventory, the stockage level in the division is roughly 1200 metric tons of POL.[10] This tonnage, plus what is in vehicle tanks and jerry cans, means that a motorized rifle division can operate approximately three days on the offense, or up to six days under normal conditions, before it runs out of fuel. Of course, no division commander is going to run his command completely out of POL, and it is unlikely that the resupply rate would fall to zero, but these rough figures are useful for understanding the size and complexity of the POL supply problem, as well as the Soviet capacity for dealing with it.

POL Procurement

In the Soviet Armed Forces, the Fuel and Lubricants Supply Directorate under the chief of rear services procures POL for the Soviet Armed Forces and supervises the storage and distribution of the POL stocks of the Ministry of Defense. At the national level, allocations are made according to priorities of the minister of defense and are apparently refined by military district, or theater of military operations (TVD) in wartime. The availability of POL to the military is, of course, bounded by the extraction and refinery capacities of the Soviet petroleum industry, as reduced by requirements for export and for the nonmilitary sectors of the economy. In spite of some insistent predictions to the contrary, the USSR has not become a net importer of petroleum and continues to export a portion of its production to earn hard currency and to support its Warsaw Pact and COMECON allies. Although precise figures on POL consumption by the Soviet Armed Forces are not available, a constant drumbeat of articles urging fuel conservation makes it obvious that the Soviet Army does not receive nearly as much POL as it would like.

POL Distribution

The POL distribution system is outlined in Figure 8.1. POL is shipped from refineries and natural stocks directly to depots at *front* level, where it is stored in fixed or semi-fixed installations. Shipment is mostly by pipeline and railroad tank car, but capacities may be augmented by bulk road shipments, mostly along the Soviet military highway system. It does not appear that TVDs have any POL storage or transportation function; all assets for handling POL in the theater actually belong to the Fuel and Lubricants Supply Directorate of the Ministry of Defense. The TVD commander's function in the POL chain is to suballocate his authorized POL consumption between subordinate *front* commanders, according to the TVD campaign plan.

The bulk POL distribution system terminates in field POL depots at *front* and army levels. *Fronts* operate terminals for commercial pipelines, such as the *Druzhba* pipeline serving Eastern Europe from the USSR, and field POL depots are generally located near railheads with facilities for handling large POL shipments. *Front* facilities are often satellited off of large commercial facilities.

Army depots are usually semi-permanent field fortifications resembling the schematic shown in Figure 8.2. Storage is generally in rubberized fuel bladders set into engineer-constructed field fortifications. Stockage at army depots is delivered primarily by field pipeline, with supplemental bulk delivery by road and rail. Field pipelines are installed and maintained by the pipeline regiment attached to each *front*. These regiments lay PMTP-100 field pipe in 10-meter quick-connect sections at a rate of 2 to 3 kilometers per hour. Once installed, a single pipeline can deliver 75 cubic meters of POL per hour to virtually any distance, as long as sufficient booster pump stations and pipe sections are available. Army is the lowest level maintaining bulk POL stocks. Division POL trucks and trailers are refilled at the army POL supply depots and directly refuel vehicles.

At the tactical level, there are two basic methods for distributing POL: delivering of POL to vehicles, and driving vehicles to the POL distribution points.[11]

Direct delivery to units is the preferred method because it interferes least with operations, but it puts the greatest demand on delivery means. When this system is used, an ATZ-4-131 or ATMZ-4.5-375 POL truck is dispatched forward from the battalion rear to be intercepted by a guide from the company to be refueled, who leads it to each vehicle. When this method of distribution is being used extensively, POL trucks may be supplemented by general purpose trucks carrying cans, or converted to POL tankers by mounting a rubberized bladder in the bed. Another variant is to use a self-contained POL system called the TZA-7.5 mounted in a helicopter. This is a 7500-liter tank and pumping system normally mounted as a unit on a MAZ-500 truck but capable of being ground-mounted or inserted into an

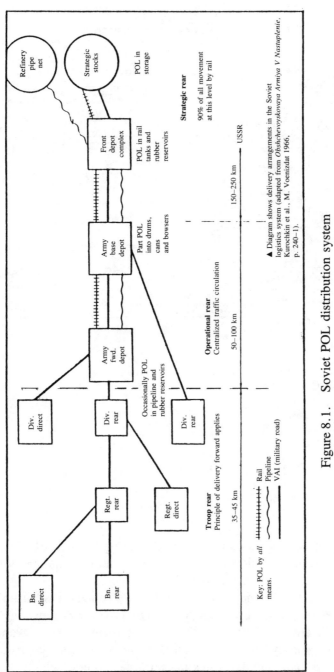

Figure 8.1. Soviet POL distribution system

Source: C. N. Donnelly, "Rear Support for Soviet Ground Forces," *International Defense Review*, no. 3, 1979, p. 347.

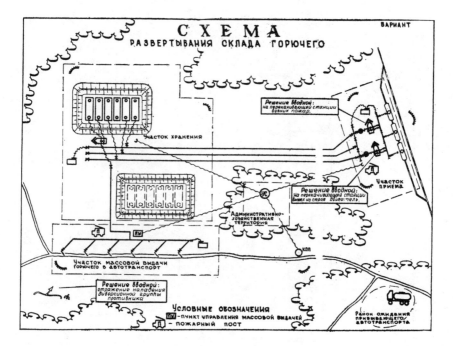

Key
1   Railhead
2   Storage area of rubber fuel bladders behind earthworks
3   POL distribution point
4   Command post
5   Traffic control post
6   Holding area
7   Firefighting post

Figure 8.2.   Soviet army depot

Source: *Tyl i Snabzhenie*, no. 12, 1981, p. 24.

MI6 helicopter or AN-12 cub aircraft. Refueling by aircraft is normally used to supply small reconnaissance or security units operating at extended distances from the main body.

When on the move, the standard method for refueling is for units to refuel at centralized field refueling points (*polevoi zaprovchnyi punkt*, or PZP). PZPs are normally located along the main axes of advance or along main supply routes and function more or less like filling stations. Along main supply routes in rear areas, single vehicles and logistics convoys are the principal consumers. PZPs are organized roughly as shown in Figure 8.3. A POL truck, POL trailer, and a stock of lubricants are positioned in pull-off areas on both sides of the road so that vehicles can drive by and top off.

Along the route of advance for combat forces in the forward areas, a different system is often used. It is based upon a distribution system designated TAPZ-755, which is essentially a pump, filter, and fuel tester mounted on a two-axle trailer equipped with a 100-meter flexible hose that is deployed on the ground parallel to the route of march.[12]

First section

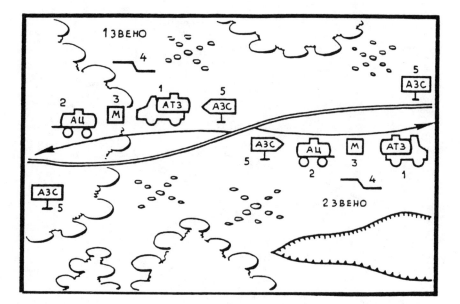

Second section

1 Automatic fuel supply system ATMZ 5-4320
2 POL trailer
3 Lubricant distribution point
4 Personnel shelters (trenches)
5 Control point

Figure 8.3.   Diagram of a field POL distribution point

Source: *Voennye Znaniia*, no. 11, November 1979, p. 25.

At 10-meter intervals there are twin fueling nozzles, as shown in Figure 8.4. The TAPZ-755 is fed by a standard POL truck, and the norm for installing the entire system is five minutes for the three-man crew. Each nozzle decants fuel at a rate of 7.5 liters per minute, and an entire motorized rifle or tank company can refuel in less than ten minutes.

As noted in the discussion of rations, other important but routine activities such as distribution of rations may be accomplished at the PZP during this same time. The disadvantage of the TAPZ-755 is that it requires the unit being refueled to close up, which makes it much more vulnerable to attack, but the Soviet Army apparently feels that

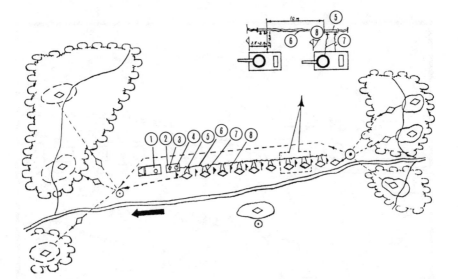

Key
1 POL truck
2 POL trailer
3 Fuel filtration unit
4 Fuel metering device
5 Hose rack
6 Flexible distribution pipe
7 Fuel dispensing hose and nozzle
8 Refueling point marker flag

Figure 8.4.   Field POL distribution point (TAPZ-755)

Source: *Tyl i Snabzhenie*, no. 1, January 1983, p. 61.

the speed of refueling compensates for the problem and justifies the risk.

Tactical aircraft flying from unimproved fields and helicopters dispersed over the battlefield have added a new dimension to the POL problem for the Soviet Army. Instead of refueling a large number of aircraft at a few relatively fixed locations, it is increasingly necessary to service fewer aircraft at a larger number of widely dispersed locations that often change, especially in the case of helicopters. A Soviet approach has been to develop equipment to respond to the problem. The TZA-7.5 system mentioned earlier as being adapted for air transport can be used to refuel aircraft as well as vehicles and can move with aircraft from one field location to another. In addition, a multi-aircraft fueling system, designated GZST-4-1250, has been developed.[13] It can be put into operation in thirty-five minutes by its four-man crew. Its operational configuration is as shown in Figure 8.5. The GZST-4-1250 dispenses fuel at a rate of 1250 liters per minute and can service four aircraft simultaneously. When disassembled into components, it is extremely compact and can be easily carried in any general purpose cargo truck or helicopter. Any fuel supply can be used with the GZST-4-1250, including bladders, POL trucks and trailers, or tank cars.

Exploiting Local POL Stocks

It is unlikely that Soviet commanders would rely entirely upon captured enemy POL stocks or requisitioned local POL stocks to support a military operation. It is well within traditional Soviet military practices and capabilities, however, to exploit any such sources to supplement issued stockage and to cover shortfalls, and it is well within the Soviet "self-supply" tradition for commanders to find their operational capability curtailed if supplemental stocks are not available.

The Soviet Army is equipped and organized to incorporate captured or requisitioned POL stocks into its military supply system. At army level, there are mobile POL laboratories van-mounted on Ural-375 trucks.[14] These systems, designated PLG-3, are served by a five-man crew and in twenty-five minutes or less can test POL samples for contamination and classify them by quality and type. To decant liquid petroleum products from any storage tank, above or below ground, divisions are equipped with MNUM-50M pumping stations.

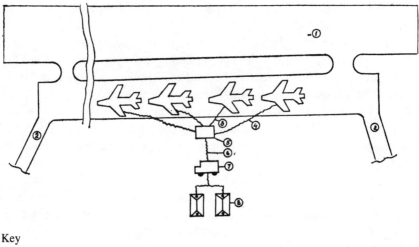

Key
1 Runway
2 Taxiway
3 Refueling hose and nozzle, 20-meter
4 Refueling hose and nozzle, 30-meter
5 Primary fuel storage cell
6 Flexible pressure hose
7 Fuel transfer pumping station
8 Rubber POL bladders

Figure 8.5.   Field POL distribution point for aircraft

Source: *Tyl i Snabzhenie,* no. 1, January 1983, p. 62.

These are small units mounted on single-axle trailers with an integral power unit, the same four-cylinder engine found in the standard UAZ-469 jeep. The MNUM-50M can draw liquid petroleum from two separate sources at a sustained rate of 50 cubic meters per hour and dispenses it by four standard vehicle-fueling nozzles or in a single bulk dispenser. Essentially, the MNUM-50M can turn any bulk supply of POL into a filling station or can use it to fill other bulk carriers.

Maintenance

If one had to select the single most complicated logistics activity in the Soviet Army, it would probably be maintenance. The most important aspects of battle described in Chapters 4 and 5, maneuver and shock, depend upon the mobile firepower of mechanized artillery, motorized rifle, and tank forces. In the Soviet view, effective maintenance is fundamental to combat readiness.

Soviet maintenance practices characterize equipment as combat, base, or support.[15] Combat equipment comprises that which directly participates in battle, including tanks, artillery, and vehicles and equipment directly related to their combat functioning, such as fire direction radars or prime movers. Base equipment includes communications equipment and support equipment for rocket, engineer, chemical, and other branches. Support equipment includes supply, maintenance, transport, medical, and administrative materiel. While all materiel receives equal maintenance, these categories can be used to establish temporary priorities in times of shortage.

Maintenance Responsibility

Of course, maintenance is a command responsibility and an activity of immediate, personal concern to every commander. In the Soviet system, however, staff supervision of maintenance is fragmented among representatives of the various technical services, who operate more or less independently of one another.[16] As described in Chapter 3, several of these technical service special staff officers report to the chief of staff. These include the deputy commander for engineer services, responsible for maintenance of weapons and instruments; the chief of artillery, responsible for maintenance of arms and weapons; the chief of chemical services, responsible for CBR instruments and equipment; and the senior doctor, who supervises medical maintenance. The chief of materiel, who is responsible for maintenance of clothing and shelter, is subordinate to the deputy commander for the rear. The major maintenance problem in tactical units, however, is keeping the tracked and wheeled vehicles rolling. This is the specific responsibility of the deputy commander for technical services, who reports directly to the regimental commander.

It is interesting that in the Soviet Army, the chief of staff exercises maintenance responsibility over a wider spectrum of activities than does the deputy commander for the rear. It is also important to note that responsibility for maintenance of vehicles, the principal maintenance concern, devolves directly upon the commander. Although indications are that this responsibility is often delegated to the chief of staff, the Soviet Army perceives tactical vehicle maintenance as being much closer to an operations concern than a logistics concern.

Organizational Maintenance

Essentially, Soviet organizational maintenance is structured to function in the field in combat. For this reason, garrison and field maintenance procedures do not differ markedly, except in one significant respect: in garrison, the equipment needing service goes to the servicing element, but in combat, the servicing element goes to the machine.[17] In peacetime, centralized facilities are the basis of maintenance, but on the battlefield, mobile maintenance facilities perform service on-site. In general, three principles guide Soviet maintenance procedures:

- Repair at the lowest possible level
- On-site repairs wherever possible
- Evacuation to centralized repair facilities when necessary

In the field, the application of these principles means that the basis of maintenance is services performed by the operator and crew, with limited assistance from the battalion supply and maintenance platoon and the maintenance company at regiment.

Assistance is in the form of mobile repair facilities equipped to remove and replace major subassemblies, such as power plants or transmissions, on-site.[18] The maneuver battalions have an organic repair facility comprising a self-contained workshop mounted on a medium truck chassis. Maneuver regiments have an organic maintenance company comprising sixty-five to seventy personnel organized as shown in Figure 8.6. The wheeled and tracked vehicle repair platoons are mounted in workshop vans that are employed as contact teams. The special repair platoon is equipped to perform electrical maintenance and welding. The recovery platoon operates three armored recovery vehicles to recover damaged or destroyed vehicles. The workshop platoon is organic only to BMP-equipped motorized rifle regiments and is equipped with three workshops mounted in modified armored personnel carriers. Medical maintenance is performed by the supply and service platoon of the regimental medical company, and quartermaster repair is performed by the supply and service platoon at regiment.

In the field, the objective of maintenance is to keep all equipment in continuous service. This places the major responsibility on operators and crews and puts organizational maintenance in a supporting

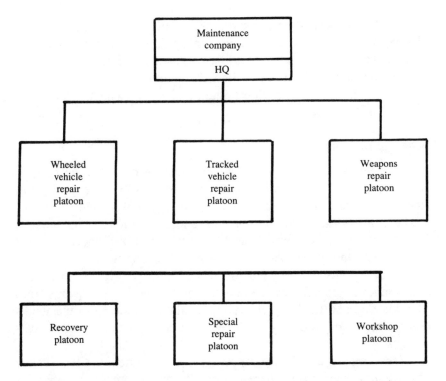

Figure 8.6.   Maintenance company, motorized rifle and tank regiment

Source: DDB-1100-333-82, "Soviet Divisional Organization Guide," DIA, July 1982, p.
25.

and assisting role.[19] The basic maintenance functions are provision of
fuel and lubricants and replacement of assemblies and subassemblies.
Periodic or scheduled maintenance services are viewed as a prophy-
lactic to prevent wear-out (*iznos*).[20] Periodic service is based upon
operating mileage and is performed as the combat situation permits.
The maintenance period and specific services are defined in the technical publications for each piece of equipment, but they all prescribe
two periodic technical services. In addition to these there are prescribed seasonal services to prepare equipment for winter or summer
operations.

The basis of organizational maintenance is that it is performed by
the operator or crew. Soviet drivers are called driver-mechanics (*vod-
itel'-mekhanik*), and their training always includes basic mechanics.

Their principal limitation is a shortage of tools, parts, and equipment. There are no maintenance personnel or facilities in companies, so the only assets that driver-mechanics have are the basic hand tools in the vehicle inventory. Even at battalion, the maintenance capability is so sparse that it can only provide limited assistance, which is mostly in support of the headquarters.

Concept of Maintenance

The Soviet concept of maintenance can be described as centralized control and decentralized execution. Authority is centralized in the commander, and carefully prescribed, detailed maintenance procedures are written out in manuals and regulations. Maintenance equipment and other basic hand tools are centralized and controlled at regiment and above, as are repair parts stockages.

Actual performance of maintenance, however, is decentralized. Most labor is provided by the operator and crew. Contact teams from the wheeled and tracked vehicle repair platoons and from the workshop platoon are normally deployed in support of the maneuver battalions.

Obviously, maintenance capability in the regiment is a lean affair. At battalion and below, there is virtually no maintenance capability other than what the driver-mechanic can perform, and regiment can only supply a maintenance contact team and a shop van to each battalion. The reason for this apparent scarcity of maintenance is that it ensures that tactical combat maneuver units, regiment and below, are unencumbered by an extensive rear. The Soviet perception of the modern battlefield as being characterized by depth and no defined front line, as described in Chapter 4, does not permit extensive stationary rear installations for tactical units. Soviet tactical maneuver elements are organized and equipped to maneuver and fight unencumbered by a maintenance tether.

Direct Support Maintenance

Organizational maintenance in the Soviet system extends from regiment down to the crew. Equipment damaged beyond the capability of repair by crews or contact teams is repaired by the direct support maintenance capability at division or army. It is at this point that the third principle of Soviet maintenance procedures is applied, and the machine goes to the servicing element.

The direct support maintenance element is formed from the maintenance battalion at division. In combat, the maintenance battalion organizes and operates a collection point for damaged vehicles (*sbornyi punkt povrezhdennykh mashin*, or SPPM)[21]. The SPPM is fully mobile in that all its equipment is mounted in vans or trailers or is transported in vehicles organic to the maintenance battalion, but it functions as a stationary site located along a main supply route. Locations are selected to provide cover and concealment, an internal network of trails, and access to water. Engineer support may be provided to improve road networks, construct revetments and fortifications, and erect camouflage.

Figure 8.7 is a schematic showing the organization of a SPPM. Work on evacuated equipment starts at the CBR monitoring post (No. 2), where all personnel and equipment are examined for contamination. Uncontaminated material passes directly into the work area, while contaminated vehicles and personnel are directed to the special work area (No. 21), where heavy decontamination is accomplished in the "dirty" section, and the process is checked and completed in the "clean" section.

The next station, the reception point (No. 18), is the administrative heart of the SPPM. Equipment is inspected by technicians who document necessary repairs. If equipment damage is beyond the salvage capacity, equipment is assigned to the post for disassembly of condemned equipment (No. 17), where it is cannibalized for repair parts. The Soviet practice of sticking to proven designs for systems and subsystems in vehicles and equipment facilitates cannibalization, which is institutionalized in the Soviet maintenance procedure.

Equipment documented for repair is added to the Grand Work Plan, a document that assigns priorities and sequence of work for each end item to be repaired in the SPPM. While awaiting repair, equipment is kept in the park for vehicles awaiting repair (No. 19). The standard priority for repair is normally

1. Command vehicles
2. Rocket launchers
3. Tanks and armored vehicles, with the lightest-damaged vehicles at the top of the list
4. Wheeled vehicles

In general, the SPPM operates by cycling the equipment to be repaired through the various repair posts and sections, according to

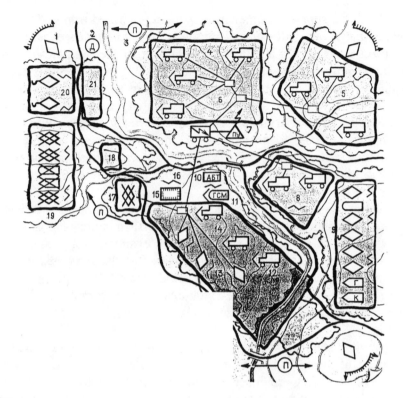

Key

 1 Vehicles from repaired stock selected for defense of the SPPM.
 2 CBR monitoring post
 3 Security patrol routes
 4 Special work section
 5 Wheeled vehicle repair section
 6 Electrical power net
 7 Command post
 8 Weapons repair section
 9 Repaired vehicle park
10 Armored vehicle repair parts supply point
11 Mobile POL distribution point
12 Ordnance machine shop
13 Tracked vehicle repair post
14 Tracked vehicle repair section
15 Ration point
16 Personnel shelter
17 Post for disassembly of condemned equipment
18 Reception point
19 Park for vehicles awaiting repair
20 Recovery vehicle park
21 Special work area

Figure 8.7.   Organization of an assembly point for damaged vehicles (SPPM)

Source: *Tekhnika i Vooruzhenie*, no. 9, 1980.

the specific guidance of the Graphic Work Plan and the repair documents. A centralized repair parts supply point, machine shop, and POL distribution point support the entire SPPM. Armaments are repaired at the weapons repair section, and the special work section repairs optics, navigation instruments, and fire control devices. The SPPM has its own mess section and an organic electric power generator. All communications within the SPPM are by wire.

Once equipment has been repaired, it goes to the repaired vehicle park (No. 9) to await reissue to units according to the priorities of the division commander. In combat, equipment evacuated for repair does not necessarily go back to the unit it came from. This practice gives the division commander some flexibility in reconstituting his forces and is an incentive for organizational maintenance to accomplish as much as possible within its own resources.

Displacement

The SPPM operates from a fixed location, approximately 15 kilometers behind the front lines. As the tactical situation changes, it displaces by infiltrating elements in traffic along the division main route of supply and evacuation. Capability for continuous maintenance support is assured by close adherence to a standardized deployment procedure.

The locations for the SPPM are specified in the division order, and when it is time to displace, the maintenance battalion commander leads a reconnaissance party to the new site. This party includes commanders of the subunits, a CBR monitoring team, and traffic regulators to guide incoming vehicles to their proper locations. The reconnaissance party checks the area for CBR contamination, selects sites for each element of the SPPM, and supervises any engineer efforts at site improvement.

The first operational element to displace to the new site is the CBR decontamination team that operates the special work area. As soon as it is operational, all evacuation is redirected from the old to the new site, and it begins the process of decontaminating incoming materiel and personnel. Then, since no new work is arriving at the old site, the reception point displaces to the new location, where it immediately begins work on the Graphic Work Plan. It spots incoming damaged equipment at the work post sites and directs the overflow to the park for vehicles awaiting repair. The various posts of the SPPM displace by infiltration to the new site as they complete work at the old location. Upon arrival they set up and immediately begin work. Until the central power generator displaces and is operational, individual shop vans depend on their internal power sources. The last element to depart the old location is the deputy commander, who clears the site and ensures that all elements of the SPPM complete the march.

Depot Maintenance

Equipment that cannot be repaired in the field is evacuated from the combat area for rebuilding and repair at centralized facilities, normally at fixed installations. In Chapter 2, it was pointed out that the USSR does not make the sharp distinction between the civilian and military sectors that is so fundamental in the West, and that all property, civil and military, is state property. For this reason, much of the load of depot level repair can be placed upon the existing civilian infrastructure rather than upon dedicated military facilities.

There are, of course, depot maintenance facilities that work on military-unique equipment; however, much of the depot level work devolves on the industrial enterprises that manufactured the materiel in the first place. Not all these installations are within the borders of the USSR; Soviet equipment is manufactured under license in a number of nations around the world, and there is a continuous Soviet effort to integrate industrial output throughout COMECON.[22]

In addition, civil-military integration is an industrial, as well as political, fact of life in the Soviet Union. The most obvious evidence of this fact is in the motor vehicle fleet, in which the same truck models are used in the civilian economy as in the military. In electronics, the same communications equipment is used in public safety organs as is used in the military, and those who have traveled in the USSR have noticed that the radar and ground control equipment at Soviet airports are often the same as those used in the military.

While these factors have obvious advantages for the Soviet Army, the motivation is not entirely, or even primarily, related to national defense. The Soviet economy is a relatively poor and, in many ways, primitive industry that simply cannot afford to produce a wide variety of goods. For example, the per capita gross national product ranks about tenth in the world, behind that of Italy. In another sense, rugged military-style equipment is precisely what the Soviet civil economy needs. The land mass of the USSR is three times that of the United States, but the total paved road network is only equal to that of northeast United States. Cross-country capability is as necessary to the Soviet civilian sector as it is to the military.[23] Whatever the causes, the result accrues to the advantage of the Soviet Army, as there are 450,000 workers engaged in depot repair throughout the USSR, forming a network of facilities and a ready labor supply to perform rear area maintenance.[24]

Rations

Napoleon observed that "an army marches on its stomach," recognizing that feeding the troops has a direct correlation to their combat performance. For this reason, understanding how Soviet soldiers are fed is fundamental to understanding how they fight.

By way of introduction, it must be recognized that gourmet dining is not a Russian achievement. Before the revolution, the first act of a Russian family upon achieving a degree of affluence was to hire a French chef. Since the revolution, as most travelers in the USSR will admit, Soviet cuisine is optimistically described as undistinguished.

A related problem is the chronically dismal state of Soviet agriculture. Bad management and marginal climatic conditions combine to create perpetual shortages of quality food items, such as meat and dairy products and fresh fruits and vegetables, and cause periodic shortages of staple crops such as grain. These shortages force the USSR to be a net agricultural importer of many critical foodstuffs, especially grain.

While problems in Soviet agriculture are not a subject of this book, they influence the structure of Soviet logistics. The responsibility for procurement and distribution of rations in the Soviet Armed Forces belongs to the Central Rations Directorate, subordinate to the chief of the rear and the deputy minister of defense of the USSR.[25] The Central Rations Directorate operates food storage, processing, and shipping facilities and a number of state-owned farms (*sovkhoz*) that raise agricultural products for the armed forces. In addition to the *sovkhoz* under the Central Rations Directorate, military districts and fleets of the Soviet Navy operate *sovkhoz* to feed their own assigned troops.

The requirement to supplement issued rations extends to individual military garrisons and units, where troop labor is used to construct and operate greenhouses, pig sties, and poultry yards to provide rations for assigned personnel and their dependents. Beyond these activities, troop units traditionally participate in the harvest by providing labor and transportation, for which they are paid in kind.

Obviously these activities contribute to the health and welfare of the troops and, at the same time, reduce the military burden on the Soviet economy. However, there is an undeniable military cost in the form of reduced preparedness, which results from time and assets being diverted to agriculture. Marshal V. Tolubko, commander of Soviet Strategic Rocket Forces, stated his opposition to troop participation in agricultural enterprises in a 1983 article in *Tyl i Snabzhenie*, wherein he proposed hiring civilian workers for farming and leaving the military with its primary task of improving combat readiness.[26]

There has not been any direct public response to Tolubko's proposal to put combat readiness ahead of agriculture. A marshal who is head of the primary branch of the Soviet Armed Forces is rather well insulated from public criticism. However, an "All-Army Conference" of food service personnel in February of 1984 examined means of improving the effectiveness of military agricultural enterprises.[27] The official newspaper of the Ministry of Defense, *Red Star*, reported that agricultural enterprises of the Ministry of Defense are to be improved, and a subsequent article in the journal *Communist of the Armed Forces* reported that military "kitchen plots" (for regiments and independent battalions) were to be upgraded to "auxiliary farms" that must annually produce 15 kilograms of meat per ration (a figure that includes not only soldiers, but dependents and civilian workers), in addition to vegetables.[28] Assuming that a motorized rifle regiment comprises approximately 2200 officers and men and about 300 dependents, 15 kilograms of meat per ration converts to 37,500 kilograms or 82,500 pounds of meat per year. Roughly speaking, this converts to 400 hogs or 38,000 chickens. Since animal feed is not part of issued rations, there is an attendant requirement to raise feed grains in addition to vegetables.

All together, this means that each regiment in the Soviet Army must operate a fairly sophisticated agricultural enterprise out of its available personnel and materiel resources. As Marshal Tolubko implied, this requirement must have a significant negative impact on combat readiness. In a less serious vein, one can imagine the mighty

Soviet war machine grinding across the Central European Plain, followed by great herds of cattle and clouds of chickens.

Of course, one can argue that commanders will simply ignore, or greatly underfulfill, the requirement and opt for training instead. This is possible, but such a policy will certainly result in a serious ration shortage in his unit, with attendant morale and health problems. At the very least, it demonstrates the direct impact of Soviet agricultural problems on combat readiness. Since the Soviet economy cannot adequately feed its armed forces in peacetime, it is worth considering what would happen in wartime, when troops would have to cut loose from their auxiliary farms and mobilization would cut into the already inadequate production of the civilian agricultural sector. An implication of the effects on troop morale can be drawn from Soviet experience in Afghanistan, mentioned earlier in this Chapter.

Distribution of Rations

However rations are acquired, divisions operate a ration point that receives perishable and nonperishable items from front/army dumps. The ration point, under command of the chief of the rear, repackages rations into containerized or palletized daily rations (*sutodacha*), the quantity of basic foodstuffs (canned meat or fish, nonperishable vegetables such as carrots, potatoes, and cabbage, and condiments such as brick sugar, salt, tea, and cooking oil) required to feed one battalion for twenty-four hours.[29] Perishable items such as fresh meat, fruit and vegetables, and dairy products are not in the *sutodacha*, but are issued separately, as available.

Bread has long been a traditional staple in the Russian diet, and Soviet divisions have organic field bakeries that make coarse, dark, freshly baked bread around the clock.[30] Bread is not part of the *sutodacha*, but it is always included in every meal and is delivered with the other rations.

The *sutodacha* and supplementary ration items are delivered daily to every regiment and separate battalion in the division on trucks of the division transport battalion.[31] The regiment chief of the rear divides rations into battalion loads on trucks of the regiment's transportation company for delivery to each battalion. While this system is somewhat cumbersome, it reduces the problem of maintaining and storing food stocks in maneuver elements.

Preparation of Rations

Food preparation is accomplished at the battalion rations point (*batal'onyi prodovolstvennyi punkt*, or BPP). Commanded by the battalion chief of the rear, the BPP comprises three trailer-mounted PAK-200 field kitchen units and a PP-40 field range unit.[32] When stationary in the field, the BPP is normally sited in a covered and concealed area approximately 80 by 100 meters in size, close to the battalion rear boundary. A schematic of the deployment is shown in Figure 8.8. The cooking elements, the PAK-200 and the PP-40, are normally dispersed around a central food preparation and washing area, and sanitary facilities are off to one side.

The PP-40 field range is used to prepare the officers' meals. While all ranks get the same rations, the officers have a more sophisticated kitchen and, in most cases, get first selection of the rations. As an aside, this process applies in garrison as well. Rations for families are delivered to the housing area, where wives line up by their husbands' rank to choose food. Wives may not exceed quantities authorized by size of family, but lowest ranking families suffer the poorest quality food and bear the results of any shortages.[33]

The PAK-200 deserves some attention, as it is basic to Soviet nutrition in the field. Essentially, it comprises a pressure cooker with three sections of 100-, 110-, and 150-liter capacity, an integral immersion-type oil-fired heating unit, and water tanks, all mounted on a single-axle trailer. It is charged with raw vegetables, meat or fat, and water, which are boiled under 1.5 atmospheres pressure into a sort of thick soup or thin stew, depending on the ratio of produce to water, that is served as *kasha*—a nutritious, hot, but otherwise undistinguished mush. The water tanks also provide hot water for tea. The entire rig, as the number implies, serves two hundred rations.

The PAK-200 boasts a number of military virtues. It can be charged with virtually any consumables that will submit to heat and pressure, and it will reduce them to a state in which their original form and content are unidentifiable. It is also very mobile. With the 2-meter smoke pipe installed, it can work its culinary magic while on the march behind its prime mover; Soviet units on the march are often characterized by little puffs of black smoke and a faint tail of sparks as field kitchens roll down the road. In recognition of their awkward appearance and strange character, Soviet soldiers have named the PAK-200 "the Potato Cannon."

Feeding the Troops

When troops are not actively engaged in combat and when conditions are stable, as in an assembly area, the BPP is organized as
shown in Figure 8.8, and troops rotate through the mess area on
schedule. The platoon is the basic feeding element, and each PAK-
200 serves at least a company. In a more active combat situation but
where the battalion is in a fixed position, as in the defense, food is
prepared in the BPP, packed in platoon-size insulated containers, and
trucked forward to company supply points. From the company supply
point, containers are man-packed to each platoon position.[34]

When the battalion is on the move, rations packed in insulated
containers are delivered to fighting vehicles at battalion field refueling
points, where platoon commanders distribute them as vehicles are being
refueled.[35] For tactical situations in which it is impossible to issue hot
rations, or for small units isolated from the main body, the chief of

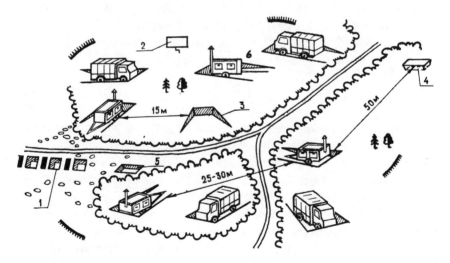

Key
1   Rations receiving area
2   Personnel shelter/dining area
3   Vegetable preparation area
4   Garbage pit
5   Washing location
6   PAK-200 field kitchen in a revetment

Figure 8.8.   Schematic of a battalion rations point (BPP)

Source: *Tyl i Snabzhenie*, no. 12, 1980, p. 46.

the rear issues a dry ration (*sukhoi paek*). It normally comprises canned meat or fish, bread, and any other items available in the supply chain.

Whether a hot or dry ration, every meal in the Soviet Army will certainly contain two items: bread and tea. Every Soviet vehicle crew seems to acquire a samovar, or teapot, and dry Georgian tea, tightly packaged in 5-centimeter-square cubes is always available. For sweetening, raw sugar in cakes is part of the general issue. The sugar is rather stable and has a number of uses, including as a crude delayed arming device. Russian bread is surprisingly weatherpoof, so it is an excellent field ration. Soldiers can carry chunks in a rucksack or pocket, and vehicle crews regularly store a loaf under seats or in any convenient space.

The Soviet military diet, while poor in quality by Western standards, is nutritious, if a little heavy on starch. Most important, it places minimum strain on the supply chain and is readily supplemented by requisitioned or captured stocks. In fact, foraging is apparently an inherent part of the Soviet Army rations program. While living off of the land undeniably reduces demand on the logistics system as a whole, it also diffuses the combat effort to the degree that troops are diverted from combat to scavenging for rations.

Medical Support

Until the twentieth century, military medicine was a rather barbaric affair wherein casualties who were not killed outright were, likely as not, killed by the treatment. Until the U.S. Civil War, anesthesia consisted of placing a stick or rag between the unfortunate patient's teeth to prevent his biting off his tongue in the agony of surgery without benefit of relief from pain. Sanitation was unknown to that hardy band of military surgeons who amputated wounded limbs to preclude gangrene and left those with stomach or chest wounds to a slow and horrible death. As bad as battle losses were, however, it was not until after World War I that military medicine and sanitation progressed to the point where losses due to disease were consistently below battle losses. Today, it is hard to believe that within the past hundred years dysentery, hepatitis, and influenza regularly killed or disabled far more soldiers than enemy bullets.

Modern military medicine has made great progress in managing disease and treating casualties to preserve the fighting strength. In the

NORM FOR DAILY DIET OF A SOVIET SOLDIER IN AFGHANISTAN

Rye bread	500 grams
White bread	400 grams
Butter	30 grams
Sugar	65 grams
Potatoes	550 grams
Oatmeal	40 grams
Meat	200 grams
Fish (canned)	150 grams
Fatback	35 grams
Whole milk	40 grams
Cabbage	120 grams
Eggs	2 each

Figure 8.9.

Source: Soviet soldier's notebook captured in 1984 in Afghanistan.
Furnished compliments of Mr. David Cosby.

Soviet Armed Forces, the Central Military Medicine Directorate is charged with the mission of planning for and providing medical support and of supervising medical training.[36] How well it performs these missions has a direct bearing on the morale, efficiency, and sustainability of Soviet combat forces.

The Soviet style of war, described in preceding chapters, implies a heavy expenditure of human blood, and this is indeed the Soviet experience. Soviet battle losses in World War II included eleven million killed (nine million civilians were also killed). In the last two years of the war, the medical service at the Second Ukranian Front, one of fourteen fronts in the Red Army at that time, treated and returned to duty one million casualties, a figure that does not include those who died of wounds or who were permanently maimed.[37] As a comparison, U.S. wounded for all theaters for the entire war totaled 672,000

As grim as these statistics are, the Soviet Army assumes that the carnage will be considerably higher on the modern battlefield. Official Soviet sources estimate that employment of weapons of mass destruction and modern conventional weapons with enhanced destructive capabilities may increase rates by 25 to 30 percent over those attained in World War II.[38] Soviet military medical research into the specifics of U.S. weaponry has also led to the conclusion that the types of trauma will be much more serious than in the past. For instance, their analysis of the effects of new U.S. munitions used in Vietnam showed 51.2 percent of casualties suffering from two to five wounds, 10 percent suffering from six to ten wounds, and only 15 percent suffering from a single wound; whereas in World War II, more than 70 percent of casualties had but one wound.[39]

The Soviet Army perceives its combat military medical problem in quantitative terms. It must be able to treat large numbers of casualties suffering from extensive trauma. Administratively, this requires categorizing casualties by type and seriousness of their injuries, and medically, it calls for very basic treatment centered around quick, standardized procedures called protocols. The medical system as a whole is geared to moving patients either to the rear for more extensive treatment or back to duty, to avoid clogging installations at any level.

Transportation of Sick and Wounded

Medical transport of masses of casualties is a major problem in the Soviet medical system. Considering the Soviet penchant for deliberate planning and the tendency toward designing specialized equipment, the Soviet inventory of medical evacuation ambulances is remarkably sparse in terms of the expected casualty rates. For instance, there is a total of seventy-four ambulances in a division, a motorized rifle regiment has eighteen ambulances, and a tank regiment has only eight.[40]

This shortfall is created by Soviet field medical practices, which do not foresee use of dedicated transport for medical evacuation. Rather, ambulances are used for the collection of wounded at regiment and battalion. Transportation of casualties between medical treatment facilities in the combat zone is accomplished on empty ammunition and general cargo vehicles deadheading to the rear.[41] It is not hard to imagine how the wounded will fare in a long jarring ride over rough roads, exposed to the elements in the bed of a hard-sprung ammunition truck. While this solution is not particularly desirable from the casualty's point of view, it does reduce congestion on supply routes and is an efficient use of available transport.

Further to the rear, things even out a bit. Empty rail transports may be used to transport wounded. M wagons, freight cars converted to troop transport that are reminiscent of the old 40 and 8s familiar to veterans of World War I, are used to transport troops to the front and can carry casualties on the return trip. Another recent innovation involves the use of freight containers. In this instance, the standarized steel boxes used for containerized freight shipments on roads, rail, and ships are rigged to hold between six and thirty-three stretchers, depending upon the size of the container.[42] Again, this is efficient use of transportation deadheading to the rear.

The Soviet Army does, of course, have helicopters for medevac, and there are medical evacuation aircraft in the air force inventory. The fact is, however, that in a major conflict, very few casualties will benefit from these scarce luxuries. For the vast majority of casualties, the ride to the rear may be as traumatic as their initial injury.

Types of Medical Aid

Soviet medical service provides five types, or levels, of medical aid to the sick and wounded. The types of aid are sequential, becoming progressively more sophisticated as casualties move from front to rear. A schematic of the medical aid system is shown in Figure 8.10.

The first medical treatment a casualty receives is called initial medical assistance (*pervaya meditsinskaya pomoshck'*), or first aid. It comprises immediate treatment rendered at the site where the injury occurred and within the company. It includes self-aid, emergency treatment by comrades, and initial assistance by the company sanitation instructor or aidman. The type of treatment is limited to bandaging, splints, and tourniquets to stop bleeding, as well as administration of painkillers.[43] The next level of treatment occurs at battalion after the casualty has been evacuated from the immediate combat area. This is paramedical treatment (*dovrachnaya pomoshch'*) by the medical specialist at the battalion medical point. It is generally described as continuation of the initial medical assistance and preparation of casualties for transport.

The first time a casualty is seen by a doctor is at the regimental medical point, where he receives primary professional aid (*pervaya vrachebnaya pomoshch'*). Patients are supposed to reach the regimental medical point four to five hours after being wounded. The doctor sorts patients and stabilizes those requiring further evacuation.

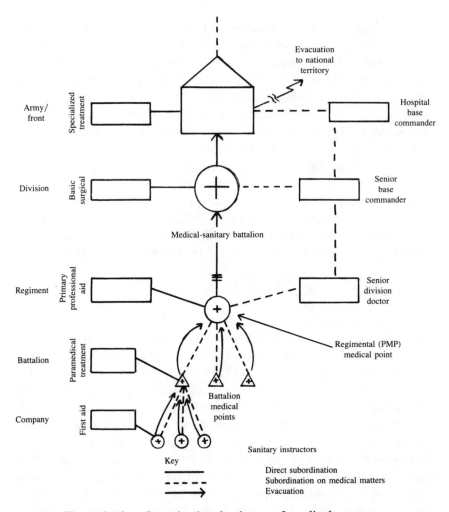

Figure 8.10.   Organizational scheme of medical support

Lightly wounded who can be returned to duty within three days are treated and maintained at the PMP until released.

Casualties needing care beyond that available at the PMP are evacuated to the medical-sanitary battalion (Med-SB) at division, where they receive surgical and therapeutic treatment. Medical norms call for patients to reach the Med-SB eight to twelve hours after being injured, and they may remain at this location if they can return to duty in seven to ten days. More seriously wounded are given emergency treatment and are prepared for the next step in evacuation.

The final stop in field treatment is specialized medical treatment at field hospitals at army or *front*. These hospitals contain specialized sections devoted to specific forms of injury or disease, such as neurology, burns, and the various types of surgery and infectious and noninfectious diseases, and have laboratory and pharmacological capacities. Patients with permanent and long-term disabilities and those who may require extensive rehabilitation are further evacuated to permanent medical facilities in the USSR. Patients remaining at the field hospital level can expect to be returned to duty.

Traditionally, Soviet military personnel on leave either go home or they go to a military recreation institution of one sort or another. Sight-seeing or just traveling are not in the Soviet character. To meet the needs of its military cadre, the Soviet Ministry of Defense operates an extensive network of institutions spread across the USSR. These institutions include sixty-four sanitoria, fourteen rest homes and three children's sanitoria.[44] These are not hospitals in the Western sense of the word, but each sanitorium does specialize in the treatment of ailments of a particular sort, such as pulmonary, circulatory, or dermatological. While the peacetime function of these institutions is recreational, their wartime function is to provide base hospitals for long-term treatment and recovery of casualties.[45] This network of military medical, recreational, and physical recovery institutions provides the mobilization base and the physical installations for rehabilitation and long-term treatment of the seriously wounded.

Obviously, Soviet military medicine is a rather rough affair. A casualty cannot expect to see a doctor for four to five hours after being injured and will not receive surgical aid for eight to twelve hours. In the interim, he is subjected to some pretty rough handling in transit. It does not come close to the U.S. experience in Vietnam, wherein wounded were minutes from a hospital and were transported in specially equipped helicopters manned by skilled paramedics. But then, the United States has never experienced casualties on the scale that the Soviet Army assumes it will have to endure.

Health and Sanitation

Close association with the Soviet Army is certain to breed a quick appreciation for the Soviet concept of sanitation. Regulations require that troops bathe and change underwear at least once a week.[46] As a group, Soviet soldiers are not well trained or disciplined when it comes to field sanitation or personal hygiene, and this is probably especially true of draftees from the more isolated regions of the USSR. This lack of hygiene is apparently causing serious problems in Soviet units, to the extent that outbreaks of infectious diseases are reaching purportedly epidemic proportions.

Red Star reported in early 1984 that "Extraordinary Antiepidemic Commissions" are being formed on ships and in divisions and regiments to enforce hygiene standards and health regulations.[47] In Russian, the first letters for the term "Extraordinary Commission" are *CheKa*, the name of the dreaded predecessor the KGB charged with the draconian enforcement of Soviet authority in the days following the revolution and the early period of Stalin's rule. This symbolism is not likely to be lost among Soviet troops. These commissions, chaired by the deputy commanders, are authorized to enforce stringent control over food preparation and storage facilities, water supplies, latrines, bathhouses, laundries, and barber shops and to punish violators. Since their charter invades the responsibilities of the Central Military Medicine Directorate, the formation of these new *CheKa* clearly implies criticism of the performance of the military medical profession.

The problem of communicable diseases, most notably viral hepatitis and dysentery, in the Soviet Armed Forces, is apparently serious enough to transfer responsibility for enforcement of hygiene and sanitation directly into command channels. The Soviet Army is learning that the problem of disease in modern armies has merely been controlled, not eliminated.

Summary

The Soviet concept of logistics is a Spartan approach that supplies bare necessities and little else. The top-down, supply-push approach permits careful planning and husbanding of scarce supplies at higher levels but places an increasing requirement for "self-supply" at progressively lower levels. As a whole, Soviet logistics emphasizes mechanical requirements at the expense of human requirements. At its best, the system can meet hard needs for ammunition, POL, and maintenance of equipment. Predictably, it is rather less responsive to human needs such as rations and medical care.

Since Soviet logisticians are concerned to a great degree with the management of shortages, tactical units must forage, exploit captured stocks, and cannibalize equipment for repair parts to a degree that is surprising in modern warfare. This thin line between what is logistically necessary and what the rear can supply suggests that a major weakness in the Soviet air-land battle is its logistics tail. Relatively minor interruptions, especially in POL, can have an immediate effect on combat operations. On a longer term, the ration cycle seems particularly vulnerable, especially if the capability to forage is restricted by such measures as contamination of stocks in areas under Soviet control, slowing the advance so that local stocks are consumed or denying local stocks to advancing Soviet forces.

There is certainly a link between health problems in the Soviet Army and the ration chain. Obviously, sanitary food handling practices are one source of trouble, and use of troop labor and resources in care and butchering of livestock may be another source of contaminations. Whatever the causes, sanitation and hygiene are definite weaknesses in the Soviet Army.

A related problem has to do with medical care. The crude nature of Soviet military medicine and the state of medicine in the USSR in general do not appear well suited to the demands of modern warfare, conventional or nuclear. While the Soviet Army appreciates the scope and intensity of its medical problems, it has yet to solve them.

None of the problems in Soviet logistics is easily resolved. They are rooted in the basic weaknesses of the larger Soviet economy from which military logistics support is drawn. Logistics may be the Achille's heel of the Soviet military giant, and at the very least it does draw the line beyond which the Soviet tactician dares not tread.

Notes

1. Radio Liberty Research 205/84, "Interviews with Soviet Deserters in Peshawar," 24 May 1984, p. 2. See also RLR 121/84, "A Soviet Soldier Opts Out of Afghanistan," 19 March 1984, p. 5.
2. RFE 121/84, op. cit.
3. Peter H. Vigor, *Soviet Blitzkrieg Theory*, New York: St. Martin's Press, 1983, pp. 94–96.
4. John Erickson, *The Road to Berlin*, Boulder, Colo.: Westview Press, 1983, p. 558.
5. *Dictionary of Basic Military Terms*, Moscow: Voenizdat, 1965. Published under the auspices of the U.S. Air Force. Translated by the DGIS Multilingual Section, Translation Bureau, Secretary of State Dept., Ottawa, Canada, p. 25.
6. *Sovetskaia Voennaia Entsiklopediia*, 8 Vols., 1976–1980, Voenizdat, Vol. 1, p. 529.
7. *Voennyi Entsiklopedicheskii Slovar*, Moscow: Voenizdat, 1983, p. 88.
8. Col. of Reserves M. Avdeev, *"Obespechenie Artilleriiskikh Podrazdelenii Boyepripasami"* ("Ammunition Supply to Artillery Units"), *Voennyi Vestnik*, no. 4., April 1981, p. 59.
9. See, e.g., C. N. Donnelly, "Rear Support for Soviet Ground Forces," *International Defense Review*, no. 3, 1979, p. 344.
10. DDB-1100-333-82, "Soviet Divisional Organizational Guide," DIA, July 1982, pp. 10–12.
11. Col. Engr. V. Bychkov Kandidat of Technical Science, Col. Engr. A. Petrushin Kandidat of Technical Science, Col. Engr. Reserves A. Rozhkov, *"Zapravka Tekhniki Gorynchim v Polevykh Usloviyakh"* ("POL Distribution in the Field"), *Tyl i Snabzhenie*, no. 1, January 1983, p. 59.
12. Bychkov et al., op. cit., p. 60.
13. Bychkov et al., op. cit., p. 61.
14. *Tyl i Snabzhenie*, no. 4, April 1980, p. 81.
15. V. D. Zelenskii, A. A. Chistov, and G. S. Chalkov *Technicheskoe Obespechenie Tankovykh Podrazdelenii V Sovremennom Boyu* (*Technical Maintenance Support of Tank and Motorized Rifle Units in Modern Combat*), Moscow: Voenizdat, 1982, p. 6.
16. *Obshchevoinskie Ustavy Vooruzhennykh Sil SSSR* (*General Military Regulations of the Soviet Armed Forces*), Moscow: Voenizdat, 1981, chapter 3, pp. 21–77.
17. Zelenskii et al., op. cit., p. 12.
18. DDB-1100-333-82, op. cit., p. 36.
19. Zelenskii et al., op. cit., p. 12.
20. Ibid., p. 11.

21. Col. Engr. V. Mukhin, "Field Deployment of Repair Units," *Tekhnika i Vooruzhenie*, no. 9, September 1980, p. 16.

22. A. I. Titkov, *"Avtomobil'naya Tekhnika XVI Pyatilelki"* ("Automotive Technology in the XVI 5-Year Plan"), *Avtomobil'naya Promyshlennost*, no. 8, 1982, p. 1.

23. Ibid., p. 4.

24. Ibid., p. 5.

25. *Sovetskaia Voennaia Entsiklopediia*, op. cit., vol. 6, p. 563.

26. Chief Marshal of Artillery V. Tolubko, *"Zadacha Gosudarstvennoi Vazhnosti"* ("A Task of Importance to the State"), *Tyl i Snabzhenie*, no. 6, June 1983, p. 15.

27. Col. P. Altunin, *"Vypolnaya Prodovol'stvennyu Programmy"* ("Fulfilling the Agricultural Program"), *Krasnaia Zvezda*, 2 March 1984, p. 3.

28. Col. P. Altunin, *"Voiskovoye Podsobnoe"* ("Military Auxiliary"), *Kommunist Vooruzhennykh Sil*, no. 10, May 1984, pp. 68–69.

29. Col. V. Metlov, *"Sluzhba Pitaniya v Polye"* ("Food Service in the Field"), *Tyl i Snabzhenie*, no. 11, 1983, p. 46.

30. DDB-1100-333-82, op. cit., p. 10.

31. Metlov, op. cit.

32. DDB-1100-333-82, op. cit., p. 18.

33. Col. M. Dracheev and Lt. Col. Engr. B. Tverdokhleb, *"Razvertivanie Batal'onnogo Prodoval'stvennogo Punkta"* ("Deployment of the Battalion Rations Point"), *Tyl i Snabzhenie*, no. 6, June 1980, p. 29.

34. Metlov, op. cit.

35. Ibid.

36. DIA-1150-18-79, "Medical Support of Soviet Ground Forces," DIA, March 1979, p. 2.

37. F. I. Komarov, ed., *Voenno-Meditsinskaya Podgotovka* (*Military-Medical Training*), Moscow: Meditsina, 1983, p. 36.

38. E. V. Genbitskii and F. I. Komarov, *Voenno-Polevaya Terapiya* (*Military Field Therapy*), Moscow: Meditsina, 1983, p. 3.

39. Komarov, op. cit., p. 60.

40. DDB-1100-333-82, op. cit., p. 11.

41. Col. D. Averkiev, *"Tyl Motostrelkogo Batal'ona v Boyu"* ("Rear of a Motorized Rifle Battalion in Combat"), *Tyl i Snabzhenie*, no. 6, June 1980, p. 23.

42. Lt. Col. N. Vololskoy and Cpt. 3d Rank I. L'vov, *"Pogruzka Ranenykh i Bol'nykh na Morskiye Suda"* ("Loading Sick and Wounded onto Ships"), *Tyl i Snabzhenie*, no. 1, January 1984, p. 68.

43. Komarov, op. cit., p. 65.

44. Gen. Lt. I. A. Urov, ed., *Voennye Sanatoni i Doma Otdykha* (*Military Sanatoria and Rest Homes*), Moscow: Voenizdat, 1984, pp. 200–203.

45. Ibid., p. 11.
46. Gen. Col. I Golushko, "Logistical Support in Battle," *Soviet Military Review*, no. 5, May 1984, p. 19.
47. *"V Interesakh Zdrovaya Voinov"* ("In the Interests of Troop Health"), *Krasnaia Zvezda*, 7 January 1984, p. 2.

CHAPTER 9

Prognosis and Predictions

> Know the enemy and know yourself; in a
> hundred battles you will never be in peril.
> When ignorant of the enemy but know
> yourself; your chances of winning and los-
> ing are equal.
>
> Sun Tzu

As is the fate of most sages, the more Sun Tzu is quoted, the less he is understood. To begin with, it is well to remember that Sun Tzu was, in his own right, a great captain who commanded armies in the field and won hundreds of battles. As a combat commander, Sun Tzu certainly was not advocating arcane intelligence studies or dry quantitative analyses. His experience taught him that failure to include an accurate analysis of the enemy's immediate and long-term intentions and capabilities in planning and conducting a campaign meant a high probability of defeat, and that inclusion of these factors in the calculations of the commander will secure victory. Sun Tzu recognized that, while warfare is a supremely physical phenomenon, its course and outcome depend more upon the intelligent application of strength than upon sheer brute force.

Almost a thousand years later, another great captain, Napoleon, made the same point when he wrote in his maxims, "In war, the moral is to the physical as three is to one." Col. Harry Summers, in his book *On Strategy*, made a similar point when he observed that commanders who concern themselves with action and not the goal will rarely attain their objective.[1]

The Theoretical Base

Mankind's understanding of the fundamental relationships governing the physical and mathematical sciences is expressed in laws and principles. Similarly, Marxism-Leninism asserts that there are laws

239

governing historical and social processes. The laws and principles
governing nature and those governing human activity are all neutral
on the battlefield: they operate equally on all sides. The Soviet Army
believes that a fundamental advantage accrues to it for having a superior military theory, superior in that it is based upon a better, deeper,
and therefore more correct understanding of the laws and principles
governing warfare. Note that these laws and principles do not favor
the USSR; they are neutral, or in Soviet jargon, "objective." The
advantage is that through Marxist-Leninist insight, the Soviet Union
better understands their meaning and therefore can apply them to greater
advantage. On the other side, Western military theory is characterized
by "contradictions," distortions or violations, of these objective laws.

Having said all of this, it is often disappointing to analysts that
these laws and principles, described in Chapter 1, are neither especially complicated nor very deep. Others rightly point out that it is
absurd to believe that Soviet military planners argue alternative courses
of action in terms of interpretations of esoteric laws and principles.
Still others question the content of these laws and principles. What
they contain and, conversely, what they omit is a fertile field of debate. For example, why do the Soviet laws and principles concern
themselves with economic and political considerations normally ignored in the West, and why do they ignore economy of force and
simplicity, two concepts of considerable concern in traditional Western military theory?

As interesting as these sorts of debates can be, they are not to be
resolved in this or any other book, and they are not within the scope
of this discussion. It is sufficient to understand that these laws and
principles are not unbending mathematical equations; they are expressions of the Soviet perceptions of the fundamental factors that decide
the course and outcome of war. They are seldom debated or discussed, but they are imbedded in all of the branches of Soviet military
science and in the logic of the Soviet military mind. Understanding
their content and meaning is fundamental to understanding Soviet military theory and practice.

Soviet Military Science—The Mind Applied to War

Soviet military science is extraordinarily sensitive to the intellectual parameter of armed conflict. It hews closely to the Leninist dictum, drawn from Clausewitz, that war is a continuation of politics,

and holds that war is the natural state in the dialectical struggle between social classes and social systems. As Lenin said, "Peace is a temporary, unstable armistice between two wars."[2] Marxism-Leninism is a political theory based upon violent, armed struggle, and much of the writings on communist theory to this day are concerned with armed struggle. For this reason alone it is natural for the Soviet military profession to develop an infrastructure devoted to the serious intellectual investigation of the theory and practice of war and armed combat. In the Western view, war is a temporary, unstable condition that interrupts peace.

The traditional Western perception of warfare stands in sharp contrast to the Marxist-Leninist view. We perceive war as the antithesis of politics resulting from a failure of the political process, as a temporary breakdown in the social order that interrupts the natural stability of the world. Since warfare is irrational and violent, it is treated with contempt in Western, and especially U.S., intellectual circles, and even the military profession is prejudiced against the examination of military theory and prefers to concentrate upon the physical aspects of combat.

No academic institution in the United States or Europe offers an advanced degree in military studies, and few even offer courses on military subjects. Not even the service academies confer baccalaureate degrees in military affairs, preferring instead to confer engineering degrees in some physical science. Within the U.S. military, there are no positions for military academics. The small core of permanent professors at the military academies all head departments teaching traditional academic subjects, and the staff positions in senior service schools and colleges are occupied by line officers who are assigned for every reason other than academic achievement and who are reassigned before they can achieve any academic status.

This results in a curious situation wherein the serious investigation of the problems in military affairs is relegated to the suburbs beyond the boundaries of the military profession; the government and academia to various commercial or quasi-commercial institutions referred to pejoratively as think tanks or beltway bandits. There, quality and integrity are compromised by the gut survival skills of finding sponsors and selling the product. On a wider scale, the entire process is captured by the annual necessity to support the budget for acquisition of new hardware.

Of course, one can argue with some logic that Soviet fascination with "scientific" (in the Soviet sense of applied logic) Marxism-Leninism and its attendant preoccupation with history, laws, principles, rules and norms, and attention to "objective" algorithms and formulae artificially reduce the dynamics of the battlefield to sterile processes more akin to calculus than human struggle. This viewpoint supports a perception that Soviet tactics are templated and that Soviet leaders lack initiative. Indeed, the Soviet preoccupation with the theoretical aspects of warfare could have just these effects, if carried to an extreme.

Soviet Military Scholarship

Soviet military theory, however, must also be given credit for enabling a tenth-rate economic power encumbered with an obsolete political doctrine to become a superpower. In this vein, it is well to remember that Soviet military theory is not the exclusive property of a bunch of mossbacked professors buried in musty, anonymous offices scattered about the outback of the USSR. Soviet military scholars tend to be an elite group of intellectuals in uniform who complement their academic expertise with practical military experience. Their hypotheses, if they withstand rigorous criticism within the community of military scholars, must then survive debate and comment when submitted to the professional military establishment as a whole. Finally, the original theories, bruised, punched, and reshaped by this process, must be proven in exercises in the field before being accepted as an official part of Soviet military lore.

The virtues of this process are visible in Soviet military power. The vice is that change is slow and maddeningly deliberate. It gives the military competition between the United States and the USSR the appearance of the race between a Soviet turtle and a U.S. hare, wherein the turtle deliberately plods along a carefully plotted course, while the hare dashes frantically about on wild goose chases or takes long naps before making serious progress in the competition.

For better or for worse, Soviet military theory describes the Soviet Armed Forces and is the basis of Soviet combined arms tactics. Whether the Soviet system is better than the Western system will be determined only in the crucible of combat. If that dreaded eventuality does come to pass, both sides are likely to discover that, as German Field Marshal Helmuth Von Moltke observed over a century ago, "no plan survives contact with the enemy." In the meantime, knowing the enemy means understanding him as he is and being unencumbered as much as possible by self-imposed prejudices that in themselves may not survive contact with the enemy.

Warfare on a Grand Scale

The Soviet perception of the significance of individuals and small units in combat is well expressed in Tolstoy's epic novel, *War and Peace,* and in Pasternak's great work, *Dr. Zhivago.* In both works, vast space and immutable natural and social forces conspire to overwhelm individuals, who are swept along in the stream of events over which they have no control. On a more prosaic level, Colonel General Biryukov makes the statement that although qualitative factors such as morale and individual bravery and the capabilities of individual weapons can be significant to the outcome of a single battle, in the end, "the law breaks its way through a heap of accidents."[3] He holds that while individuals may defy the odds in single instances, the weight of the laws of war will prevail in the end.

The Soviet perception is that a vast and complex endeavor such as modern war cannot be understood or directed by the entrepreneurial skill of an individual, no matter how talented or brave. The scale of violence demands a managerial approach to armed conflict that is based upon the dispassionate analysis of data and the application of proven and tested procedures.

The Role of Tactics

This actuarial approach to armed combat is diametrically opposed to the British tradition of a "thin red line" standing against superior mass because of bravery and pluck, or the U.S. mythology of a frontiersman or a Sergeant York winning against superior forces because of bravery and skill. The Russian approach is to rely upon Lanchester's equations, which purportedly prove that quantity will dominate quality, other factors remaining equal.[4] The Soviet approach is to evaluate combat equipment in mass rather than as single pieces. In the Soviet view, the whole is greater than the sum of the parts.

The Soviet view of tactics is better typified by the axe than by the rapier. In this analogy, strategy decides when and where to strike, operational art provides the energy and direction to the blow, and tactics, as the blade of the axe, does the damage. This analogy values hardness over flexibility and strength over adroitness, and a chipped or burred blade is not significant if there is sufficient force behind the blow. Soviet tactics is subordinate to operational art and strategy.

In fact, a senior Soviet military academic, Gen. Maj. I. Vorob'ev, made precisely this point in an article in the Soviet military paper *Red Star*.[5] General Vorob'ev told the Soviet Army that Soviet tactics has always occupied, and will continue to occupy, a position in Soviet military science subordinate to the other two levels of armed struggle: operational art and strategy. Simply stated, tactics describes how to use physical force on the battlefield, while operational art explains where and when to use it, and strategy defines the overall purpose or goal. Based upon this viewpoint, General Vorob'ev concludes that weapons of mass destruction and conventional weapons with enhanced destructive capabilities are most effective when employed at higher levels of command.

Soviet tactics, then, accepts a degree of procedural rigidity at division and below so as to complement and provide flexibility to the operations of army and *front* commanders. Companies, battalions, regiments, and even divisions are teeth in the maw of a huge destructive machine. They are there to be used, ground down, broken, discarded, and replaced in a resource-intensive approach to battle.

Conduct of the Battle

The purpose of this resource-intensive, actuarial approach to tactics is to ensure that the enemy war machine will run out of forces before the Soviet Army. In World War II, Soviet losses were twenty million, while German losses were ten million. This ratio was acceptable to Stalin, because he calculated that Germany would run out of people before the USSR, and the Red Army deliberately exploited its numerical superiority to "bleed white" the technically superior *Wehrmacht*. Soviet tactics are designed to take casualties in order to cause casualties.

At some point, this process of wearing down the enemy will result in opportunities to advance into the depth of his position, and at this time, the operational commander, at army or *front*, can launch his second echelon, perhaps formed as an operational maneuver group to complete the destruction of the enemy. In this way, tactics serves operational art. While operational art is specifically outside of the scope of this book, it is well to remember that continuity in the battle and sustainability of the overall effort are concerns of operational commanders. Armies and *fronts* are not used up; they carry on the battle by replacing their destroyed parts.

Since combat is resource-intensive and sustainability of tactical units over time is not critical to the Soviet system, combat equipment, in the Soviet view, should be tough to kill but not necessarily of long service life. The rough finish and mechanical crudeness of Soviet equipment, the disregard of crew comfort, and the extensive use of subassemblies of proven design in a wide range of equipment favor mass manufacture and wide interchangeability of parts in cannibalization—the reconstitution of a few vehicles from the wrecks of many.

The process of reconstitution is also inherent in Soviet units, since regiments habitually plan to reconstitute as battalions, and battalions as companies, as they suffer progressive battle losses. In this light, it is worth reconsidering conventional wisdom about Soviet reduced strength divisions deep within the USSR. It has been assumed traditionally that these units would have to be brought up to full strength by mobilization prior to being committed. While this is an obvious approach from a traditional Western viewpoint, it would be entirely consistent with Soviet practices to move at least some of them to the forward area as understrength divisions, to be brought to full strength with the remnants of the first tactical echelon.

Supporting the Battle

Soviet tactical logistics, being spared the demands of sustaining combat forces with a continuous stream of new equipment and personnel replacements, is streamlined in comparison to Western logistics. Soviet tactical logisticians are free to concentrate their resources on the three major tasks of resupply of ammunition and POL, maintenance, and evacuation.

Since tactical units are "used up" rather than sustained in combat, Soviet logistics is supply-push, rather than demand-pull. Essentially, this means that scarce supplies are allocated by higher headquarters to subordinate commands according to operational priorities and calculated expenditure rates. Soviet commanders who exceed their planned consumption know that the shortfall must be made up from their own resources. Since supplies are nearly always short, this puts a premium upon exploiting captured or local stocks in wartime and upon various shady practices in peacetime. A concomitant characteristic of Soviet military logistics is a high degree of integration with the civilian economy. This is especially noticeable in the procurement and maintenance of noncombat vehicles and equipment, such as general cargo trucks and certain radar and communications equipment, and in some services such as medical support.

An advantage of Soviet logistics is that it provides a favorable tooth-to-tail ratio, less of a logistics structure to support more of a combat structure. It also means that significant civilian assets can be diverted quickly to military use with a minimum of training and reorganization. At the same time, combat troops must spend an inordinate amount of effort in logistics-related functions. Troop maintenance of everything from uniforms—soldiers must even cobble their own boots—to vehicles is at the expense of operational capabilities. Troop labor in supplying rations through farming or foraging is particularly demanding upon combat readiness. While Soviet logistics is effective, it is not necessarily efficient. Rather than being focused upon supplying the needs of the troops, it is structured to manage shortages. This is why two of the six laws of war refer to logistics or logistics-related subjects.

The Psychology of Warfare

The Soviet Army does not intend to "live by bread alone." One of its significant characteristics is a deep and abiding preoccupation with the psychological aspects of warfare, both as they affect their own troops, and as they can be applied to the enemy. Variously referred to as "the moral aspects of combat" or the "psychological steeling" of troops, Soviet respect for the influence of these qualitative aspects of warfare is well grounded in hard battlefield experience. Russian participation in World War I ended when the Imperial Russian Army "voted with its feet" for peace, and in the opening phase of World War II, whole Soviet divisions simply melted away in the face of the German blitzkrieg.

These experiences and appreciation of the unprecedented violence of modern weaponry have combined to sensitize Soviet military leaders to the human factors of battle. The Soviet Army believes that the psychological conditioning of troops and indeed of the whole population is an absolute prerequisite to victory in modern warfare. This is why the correlation of the moral-political strengths of the opposing sides is one of the six laws of war and why military psychology is a component of military science.

On a national scale, premilitary training, civil defense, and the constant warlike drumbeat of Soviet propaganda all serve the goal of psychological preparation of the population as a whole. Within the armed forces, the same ends are served by harsh discipline and by the vast structure of political organs that extend into every company-size unit in the Soviet Armed Forces, and even below that. Western analyses of the effectiveness of Soviet premilitary training, of civil defense, and of the political organs in the Ministry of Defense overlook the psychological aspect of the work, which is probably more important than the stated military missions as far as Moscow is concerned.

Psychology is also applied tactically against enemy troops. In the offense, *udar*, shock, exploits massive violence to degrade the combat effectiveness of the enemy by affecting his psychology as well as physically destroying his combat forces. In the defense, *ustoichivost'*, steadfastness, is applied to exhaust the enemy as well as to steady Soviet troops.

Soviet tactics is very strongly oriented on the enemy's "vital forces" (*zhiviyie sily*) and less strongly upon terrain. This focus upon the enemy does not mean, as some analysts have been led to believe, that Soviet tactics is by and large terrain-independent. Indeed this is not the case. What it does mean is that Soviet tactical commanders focus upon killing enemy troops and using terrain to that end. Identifying and controlling critical terrain are more an operational than a tactical concern.

Command and Control

The fundamental problem for tacticians throughout history has always been to apply the required combat force at the proper time and place. As the confederate general Nathan Bedford Forrest put it, "Git thar fustest with the mostest." The environment of unprecedented violence, the greatly expanded spatial dimension, and the greatly compressed time dimension that characterize the modern battlefield have served to make the tactician's problem even more complex.

The Soviet Army is looking toward a process of automated troop control to resolve the problem. It seeks to reduce the physical pressure on commanders by performing complex space-time analyses and correlation of forces computations electronically in a process described as concept-algorithm-decision.[6] Concept refers to the commander's understanding of his mission and his general plan for executing it. Algorithm is an orderly decision-making process based upon experiential factors and objective input, which produces a range of alternative courses of action to achieve the mission. Decision is the commander's selection from among his alternative courses of action.

The critical part in this process is the algorithm, and Soviet military scholarship has concentrated heavily upon defining its content and structure. This effort has resulted in algorithms that interrelate the diverse factors of friendly forces, mission, enemy forces, topography, and climate in an integrated thought pattern and express their relative influences in mathematical terms. The structure of the algorithms is a form of logic: the reasoned expression of the relationships of various elements to the whole. The mathematical expressions that define the values of the various elements are derived from what the Soviet Army refers to as collective wisdom: a combination of historical experience, professional judgment, and experimental data expressed in tables, graphs, and equations. Many of the calculations are performed by computers, and the ultimate goal appears to be to automate the entire process.

Decision is the commander's selection of a course of action. In reaching a decision, commanders can test various courses of action by varying the input to the algorithm to find which is the most desirable. The decision-making process involves more than merely executing the output of a computer; it requires judgment as to relative value.

In a sense, this system constrains Soviet commanders and is a source of procedural rigidity in Soviet tactics. However, it is a long way from reducing tactics to a rote exercise or from templating standard solutions upon stereotyped problems. It is deterministic in that the solution must lie somewhere along the curves expressed by the mathematical formulae, but the location of the point along a curve can be varied. For example, a commander can vary the number of rounds fired and the period of time in which they are delivered to achieve a desired level of destruction in preparatory fires.

While some feel that this process limits initiative by commanders, the Soviet view is that it helps commanders pressed by time and enveloped in the fog of war to make good tactical decisions consistent with those of other tactical commanders and with the intentions of the operational commander. The practical results of this system are that it likely inhibits the few really brilliant tacticians, reinforces the mediocre and poor tacticians, and supports the average tacticians. This outcome is certainly compatible with the Soviet view of man as a collective animal and with the Soviet perception of war.

This suggests that the efficiency of Soviet military operations is correlated with the scale of warfare. The larger the scale of operations, the more effective Soviet forces will be. Conversely, there is an implication that as the scale of action decreases, the weaknesses in the Soviet Army will be less compensated for by its gross strength. This may be the lesson of Afghanistan, where companies and platoons are more significant than regiments and divisions.

The point to be learned is that, in evaluating the battlefield capabilities of the Soviet Army, going from the microcosm of the individual soldier and the small unit to the macrocosm of the army and *front* will lead to an underevaluation of the Soviet Army, while going the other way, from the macrocosm of the total Soviet defense establishment to the microcosm of its small units will generally lead to an overevaluation of its capabilities.

Nuclear and Conventional

Soviet tactics does not make a sharp distinction between nuclear and conventional warfare. In part, this is because the Soviet Army believes that the enhanced destructive effects of some modern munitions approach those of tactical nuclear weapons, and in part it reflects Soviet pessimism over the likelihood that a conventional war can long remain such. It is also a reflection of the pragmatic fact that at levels below division, terrain and the physical capabilities of weapons and equipment dictate operations more than considerations of the possible use of nuclear weapons. For example, company defensive strong points must be mutually supporting, that is, within the range of one another's principal weapons, regardless of whether nuclear weapons can be employed. It is this point, not possible nuclear effects, that decides distances between units.

On the other side of the coin, Soviet tactics is entirely focused upon war-winning, and if faced with defeat in a conventional war, the Soviet Army would be likely to resort to nuclear weapons regardless of any non–first use doctrine. In this situation, the Soviet Army would not wish to indicate a decision by a change of tactics.

The question of employment of chemical weapons appears less ambiguous. Soviet tactics appears to assume the widespread use of chemical contaminants. While Soviet sources do not make specific reference to employment of their own chemical weapons, training exercises virtually always require negotiation of contaminated areas, presumably caused by employment of their own weapons. The well-documented Soviet superiority over NATO in offensive and defensive chemical capability makes chemical warfare an easy and inexpensive way to quickly alter the correlation of forces in favor of the Soviet Army in any local situation.

The case for biological weapons is less certain. Soviet tactical commanders are apparently concerned that they may suffer the effects of enemy use of biological agents, but there do not appear to be any institutions for Soviet tactical employment of biological agents. The abysmal state of Soviet medicine can provide a clue as to why tactical commanders would prefer to avoid such weapons. However, tactical considerations do not apply to employment of biological agents at the operational or strategic level.

A Soviet Army—A Russian Army

The Soviet Army is above all a Russian Army. Nearly 80 percent of its personnel are draftees drawn from the peoples of the ancient Russian Empire. For this reason, its character is that of the Russian people, and it mirrors the strengths and weaknesses of the society from which it is drawn. Unlike in Czarist times, when a significant portion of the professional military leadership was drawn from foreign sources or was at least educated abroad, the 20 percent of the Soviet Army that is its professional core, the *kadre*, is now all-Russian and is exclusively trained and educated in the Soviet Union. Thus, not only is the character of the Soviet Army uniquely Russian, so are its outlooks and attitudes.

Soviet military theory is a product of Soviet and Russian experience and history. Its greatest crucible was the terrible experience of World War II, which, on the Eastern Front, was fought on a scale and at an intensity unmatched in any other theater. Unlike on the Western Front, where U.S., British, and French forces more or less cooperated in joint operations, Soviet combat commanders had no contact with other national forces. Such non-Soviet manpower as was available was organized into carbon copies of the Red Army and was held strictly under Soviet command. Perhaps no other major military force in this half of the twentieth century is so completely home-grown. Even the PLA of the People's Republic of China had Soviet advisers well into the decade of the 1950s, and most of its equipment is of foreign origin or design.

An outcome of this isolation is that while the Soviet Army must perform many of the functions that other armed forces perform, it does not perform them in the same way. It has its own perception of problems and its own uniquely Russian solutions. Another outcome is that the Soviet Army performs some functions that are not at all similar to those traditional in other armies.

Whereas the West expects armies to be a political servant of the state, the Soviet Army, although subservient to the CPSU and the state, is expected to be politically active. Political training occupies much of every soldier's time and energy, the army is a "school of life," charged with preparing the young men of the USSR to be good citizens of the state.[7] This requirement includes premilitary training, training while on active duty, reserve training, and training in sport and civil defense. Other functions outside of the traditional role of the military in other nations include economic tasks such as support of the harvest and major construction projects such as the building of the new branch of the Trans-Siberian Railroad from Lake Baikal to the Amur River. While these functions detract from the defensive capability of the Soviet Army in the strictest sense of the word, they significantly enhance the prestige and importance of the Soviet Armed Forces to the government and to the population as a whole.

How to Beat Them In the Field

This book is about how the Soviet Army fights; it is not about how to fight the Soviet Army. Still, it is logical at this point to suggest flaws in the Soviet armor that might be exploited. After all, the military is like most things in that every capability is achieved at the cost of compromise. Each capability has inherent to it a corresponding weakness. The great captains of military history have all shared a common trait: the ability to detect or to create a fatal flaw in the enemy and to exploit that flaw. The great campaigns in military history all share a common characteristic: a victorious commander who changed an enemy's strength into weakness. The quote from Sun Tzu at the opening of this chapter is aimed precisely at these points: one must know one's enemy very well indeed to find and exploit his flaws and to change his strength into weakness.

This study suggests that there are three general areas worthy of serious and detailed examination as flaws in the Soviet Army or as strengths with the potential of becoming weaknesses. In general terms, these are Soviet military science, Soviet logistics, and the Soviet emphasis upon large-scale warfare.

The Soviet "scientific" approach to warfare extends from the national to the lowest tactical level. Essentially, it emphasizes calculations of relative correlations of forces and the use of algorithms and mathematical formulae in developing and selecting courses of action. A major input to this decision-making process at all levels is knowledge of the enemy's capabilities, intentions, and deployments, and the massive Soviet intelligence apparatus is precisely targeted upon providing this information.

"Garbage in, garbage out" is a remark computer specialists often make. It is a way of saying that the quality of the output of any analytical process cannot exceed the quality of the input. A well-crafted and properly executed denial and deception campaign can deny key information to Soviet commanders and may introduce spurious data into the Soviet decision-making process which, because of its careful structure and "objective" nature, is particularly vulnerable to this form of manipulation.

At the tactical level, feints, dummy fortifications, and false communications patterns deliberately designed to present a false picture to the Soviet commander are means that should be practiced and employed regularly. Other measures that should be practiced include tactical marches without use of radios, radio silence when in assembly areas, use of messengers rather than electronics for routine communications, and use of relay to offset transmission sites from actual command locations. The requirement is not simply for secure communications; the pattern of communications must also be changed.

Soviet military publications devote a great amount of space to descriptions of standard deployments used by the various NATO armed forces. Replication of these Soviet perceptions in dummy installations is an effective way of confusing Soviet intelligence collection and analysis. The key is to show the Soviet commander something he expects to see in a form that he can recognize; it is not necessary that the depiction be strictly accurate from the Western viewpoint.

Secrecy is a problem that seems virtually insoluble in open Western societies. Still, there are some steps that should be taken to at least make intelligence collection challenging to the Soviet Army. A start would be to eliminate unit identification markings on tactical vehicles and identifying patches on field uniforms. Soviet soldiers are routinely trained in the identification of these markings. Mail to combat units should be addressed by post office numbers rather than unit titles, and it does not seem advisable or necessary to publish assignment orders for key staff and command personnel, let alone for every person in uniform, in the open press. Finally, the mundane but nonetheless necessary arts of camouflage and light and noise discipline must be taught and enforced.

The bare-bones Soviet logistics system is certainly adequate to support combat operations, but it obviously lacks excess capacity. Soviet tactical norms presume consumption of fairly precise quantities of supplies, especially POL and munitions, and any degradation of the available supply rate is certain to be reflected rapidly in combat operations.

The Soviet POL distribution appears to be particularly vulnerable to interdiction. The destruction of one army level POL distribution point would probably halt the equivalent of a division in a matter of days, and interdiction of rail lines and pipelines would have a major impact on rates of advance.

Soviet field POL installations are mobile, but once established, they are not easy to move. Further, pipelines, rail lines, and the field installations where they terminate should be relatively easy to identify and locate because of their unique deployment patterns. These are soft targets that are extremely vulnerable to attack with any number of conventional munitions.

Ammunition resupply is more difficult to interdict than POL resupply, but here too the tonnages and numbers of supply vehicles should be relatively easy to locate and attack. Analysis of vehicular traffic patterns near the front should afford fairly accurate indications of the locations of ammunition storage facilities, as the great majority of supply vehicles are involved in hauling ammunition.

It is worth investigating whether concentrating reconnaissance and deep attack assets on finding and destroying a few relatively soft and stationary logistics targets might prove more effective in disrupting Soviet combat operations than "holding the second echelon at risk." At the very least, a large number of relatively hard, mobile combat units are much more difficult to target effectively and destroy.

Concomitant with attacks on Soviet logistics installations should be a campaign to deny access to local or captured stocks. This effort should be concentrated specifically against rations and petroleum supplies. As the need to forage increases, combat power perforce will be dissipated and rates of advance will slow. It would be instructive, for example, to inventory the number of filling stations and their in-ground storage capacities in an axis 10 kilometers wide along the autobahn from Helmstedt to Amsterdam. A similar inventory of sources of foodstuff also might prove illuminating.

Consideration of strategies to turn the Soviet preference for warfare on a large scale into a disadvantage are also worth investigating. Soviet tactics suggest, and performance of Soviet troops in Afghanistan has demonstrated, that as one goes down the Soviet tactical structure, military operations become less efficient. This suggests that it would be most effective to fight the Soviet Army in situations in which tactical units are isolated and unsupported. Earlier, it was remarked that in the Soviet Army, the whole is greater than the sum of the parts. This is to suggest that the reverse is equally true: the sum of the parts is less than the whole.

Of course, the rub is how to force a Soviet Army bent on concentrating its combat power to do the opposite, to disperse its combat power. In part, the answer to this is included in the preceding two proposals. A well-executed denial and deception plan can cause Soviet commanders to deploy needlessly. An effective attack on logistics, particularly on POL resupply, will slow rates of advance and curtail mobility and maneuverability. Beyond those factors, judicious use of terrain, skillful use of natural and artificial barriers, and thoughtful consideration of when and where to fight can further isolate forces. For example, built-up areas can be turned into extensive obstacles, barriers, and fortifications. It should be iterated that the objective is not to halt a Soviet advance in some form of a forward defense; the goal is to diffuse a Soviet offensive so that it can be absorbed in a large number of small battles.

Having proposed all of this, a few afterthoughts come to mind. Defeating the Russian bear is as much a matter of outthinking as of outmuscling him. An effective strategy that is thoughtfully designed to exploit the Soviet reality is a greater deterrent in peacetime and offers a better opportunity for victory in war than gross inventories of exotic military hardware. It is also a significantly less expensive option and at least partly explains why we feel increasingly less secure even while spending increasingly larger amounts on defense. This soft approach is also heretical in the American engineering and cost-accounting approach to defense.

There are also some ethical considerations implied in these proposals. Denial and deception call for some limitations on freedom of information. A deception plan described in the *Times* is not a deception plan. In Western Europe, an in-depth battlefield as proposed here will place much of the terrain and population of friendly nations in the fighting. Given the existing disparity of forces, this is probably what would happen anyhow in spite of optimistic plans for a forward defense. Finally, the whole concept of attacking logistics and creating barriers has some aspects of a scorched-earth policy and could be seen as advocating attacks on the civilian population, two proposals that are unattractive to Western morality and personally threatening to NATO allies. However, the hard fact is that if resources are available, the Soviet Army is going to take them, so the local population is going to be deprived in any circumstance. It is simply impossible to fight a gentleman's war with a bear. It is far better to have an effective strategy that will discourage his depredations in the first place or that will limit his incursion if war does occur.

Prognosis

At this point, it is worthwhile to consider what changes might occur in Soviet battlefield tactics during the rest of this century. It is necessary to admit at the outset that the business of predicting the future is chancy under the best of conditions, and when dealing with a secretive nation such as the Soviet Union, the problems of foresight are greatly complicated.

For all of that, by now the reader should have realized that the

Soviet Army is remarkable in its logical, deliberate, and conservative approach to change. In the short range, change is slow, and Soviet military operations equipment and organization are surprisingly stable. It is only now fielding the second generation of tanks since the venerable T-34 of World War II, and Soviet tank platoon tactics and organization have not changed very much from the days of the Battle of Berlin.

Still, the Soviet Army of the 1980s bears little resemblance to the Red Army of 1945 or, for that matter, the Soviet Army of the Khrushchev era. It has evolved from a primitive, infantry-heavy mass into an armored, mechanized, sophisticated fighting machine. Even as late as the early 1970s, virtually all Soviet artillery was towed, while today it is virtually all self-propelled and mostly armored. Even the few towed pieces in the inventory are moved by armored, tracked prime movers.

Other changes include increasing use of helicopters for air mobility and fire support and armored vehicles for airborne units. The rear has been supported with an extensive inventory of tactical and LOC bridging and with a vast fleet of general-purpose trucks. Today, the entire Soviet Army and all its equipment and supplies ride.

The lesson is that the Soviet Army does change over time, and these changes are significant. Change is deliberate and follows established patterns, however. It does not occur in a haphazard fashion, but only after careful consideration and debate have set the general pattern and direction. It is upon some of these patterns and directions that this prognosis will focus.

Tactics, being much more concerned with action on the battlefield than with operational art or strategy, is much more sensitive to change, and responds more rapidly to the leaps of technology that the Soviet Army refers to as the revolution in military affairs. Tactics, in this sense, addresses how to fight, while operational art and strategy are concerned with when, where, and for what purpose to fight. According to Gen. Col. V. A. Merimskiy, Deputy Chief of Combat Training for the Soviet Ground Forces, in "combined arms battle, tactics remain basic form of action and, it follows, the basis upon which operational and strategic success is achieved."[8] Thus, while tactics remains clearly subordinate to operational art and strategy, it governs operational and strategic planning by establishing what is and is not possible to achieve on the battlefield.

General Colonel Merimskiy and General Major Vorob'ev, who was quoted earlier, agree that the fundamental aspects of Soviet tactics on the combined arms battlefield, maneuver and shock, are unlikely to change in the foreseeable future. The application of these two aspects, together with the integrated action of all branches in the combined arms concept, describes how to fight on either a conventional or a nuclear battlefield by defining how to achieve an advantageous correlation of forces in space and time. However, new technologies will offer radically new ways to apply these fundamentals.

A current topic of considerable interest to Soviet tacticians is the problem of locating and striking deep targets, especially nuclear delivery systems, on a fluid battlefield.[9] The Soviet approach to this problem is to develop the organization and technology to integrate intelligence and reconnaissance with strike means, either artillery or missile or air, by means of automated command and control to create a near real-time capability to engage critical targets. Variously referred to as a reconnaissance strike complex or a reconnaissance fire complex (RUK or ROK), the Soviet system is likened to the U.S. SOTAS or COPPERHEAD system, complete with "smart" munitions. This suggests a degree of decentralization in fire control and fire planning and the introduction of some sophisticated data processing and data links. It also suggests the introduction of precision guided munitions and enhanced conventional warheads into the Soviet arsenal.

There is also a trend toward increasing firepower in Soviet units. New artillery and multiple rocket launcher systems and larger-bore tank guns have already appeared in the inventory, and other systems are certainly on the way. The new BMP variant, for example, replaces the low-velocity 72mm gun with a 30mm high-velocity automatic cannon and the SPANDREL ATGM.[10] In motorized rifle battalions, a 40mm automatic grenade launcher has been added to the inventory as a crew-served weapon. The sum of these changes points to increasing firepower per unit in volume of fire, effective range, and accuracy without a corresponding increase in total numbers of troops or combat vehicles. This is a qualitative approach to increasing combat power by increasing the ratio of firepower to troops.

There seems to be a corresponding trend toward reducing gross manpower in combat units. The newest family of tanks, the T-64/T-72, has replaced the loader with an automatic device, and the new

BMP has sacrificed crew space for at least one rifleman to accommodate a larger turret for the new gun system. At the same time, there is a new trend toward making Soviet equipment more user-friendly. Automatic transmissions, laser rangefinders, and better optics all serve to make equipment easier to operate from the perspective of the crew, and the whole science of human engineering, adapting designs to human needs, is just starting to receive serious attention in the Soviet Army.

Perhaps these developments relate to Soviet demographic problems wherein future draft cohorts will be smaller, with an increasing proportion of less well-educated Asian minorities. As anyone who has had to deal with Soviet equipment knows, the general characteristics have been that they are simple to manufacture and maintain, but difficult to operate. Now this situation may be reversing. If this is a correct trend, it means that it will be simpler to train combat troops but that the cost of equipment will be much greater and the maintenance structure must become much more extensive and sophisticated.

In sum, the future of Soviet tactics seems to be in qualitative rather than quantitative improvements in combat power. Combat equipment will become harder to kill and more maneuverable. Weapons will be more lethal, have longer range, and possess greater accuracy and higher rates of fire. Data links and data processing will speed up decision making and simplify command and control. On the negative side, the costs of defense will climb for the development and acquisition of more sophisticated weapons and equipment. An associated cost will be for the logistics requirements to supply and maintain combat forces. Over time, the traditional Soviet high tooth-to-tail ratio will probably decline.

In Conclusion

It is, of course, eminently human to view the world from one's own steeple and to assume that to the degree that anyone else's description of the world differs, it is inferior. While the self-satisfied preen their feathers and engage in paeans of self-praise over the superiority of the view from their own steeple, the true professional soldier behaves otherwise. He accepts the validity of his potential enemy's viewpoint and uses it to locate his opponent's steeple—so that he may blow him out of it if need arises.

It is not possible to learn how to "think like a Russian" or, for that matter, like any other nationality, unless one has had to exist for a very long time in that peculiar environment. However, study and experience can reveal how the Soviet military profession thinks about its affairs. This is what is meant by "know the enemy," and it is toward this end that this book has been written.

The center of gravity of this book is Soviet tactics. Tactics, however, cannot be looked at without attention to the higher levels of the military art. Certainly, Soviet tactics is sufficiently important to deserve serious investigation in its own right, but it would be incorrect to believe that one need only understand tactics to know the Soviet Army; that is to be concerned with the action and to ignore the goal, as Colonel Summers put it. The goal of Soviet tactics is destruction of the enemy on the battlefield, but this goal serves the wider purpose of operational art and tactics. The serious military student, having mastered this part of the discipline, will seek to master the rest.

Notes

1. Harry A. Summers, *On Strategy*, Novato, Calif.: Presidio Press, 1982.
2. Peter H. Vigor, *Soviet Blitzkrieg Theory*, New York: St. Martin's Press, 1983, p. 34.
3. G. B. Biryukov and G. Melnikov, *Antitank Warfare*, Moscow: Progress Publishers, 1973, pp. 94–95.
4. Ibid., pp. 98, 99.
5. Gen. Maj. I. Vorob'ev, "*Sovremennoe Oruzhie i Taktika*" ("Modern Weapons and Tactics"), *Krasnaia Zvezda*, 15 September 1984, p. 2.
6. V. V. Druzhinin and D. S. Kontorov, *Concept, Algorithm, Decision*, Moscow: Voenizdat, 1972. Translated and published under the auspices of the U.S. Air Force, pp. 1–5.
7. Col. M. I. Dem'yanenko, ed., *Shkola Zhizni (School of Life)*, Moscow: Lenizdat, 1978, p. 5.
8. Gen. Col. V. A. Merimskiy, *Takticheskaya Podgotovka Motostrelkovykh i Tankovykh Podrazdelenii (Tactical Training of Motorized Rifle and Tank Units)*, Moscow: Voenizdat, 1984, p. 8.
9. MSU. D. F. Ustmov, "*Borot'sya Za Mi, Ukreplyat' Oboronospoanost'*" ("Struggle for Peace, Strengthen Defenses"), *Pravda*, 19 November 1983, p. 4. See also Gen. Col. Ultukhov, ed., *Osnovy Teorii Upravleniya Vorskami*, Moscow: Voenizdat, 1984, pp. 77–85.
10. *Jane's Defense Weekly*, 17 November 1984, p. 887.

Index